Step Forward

Language for Everyday Life

SERIES DIRECTOR
Jayme Adelson-Goldstein

Includes
Student Audio CD

3 Jane Spigarelli

OXFORD
UNIVERSITY PRESS

OXFORD
UNIVERSITY PRESS

198 Madison Avenue
New York, NY 10016 USA

Great Clarendon Street, Oxford OX2 6DP UK

Oxford University Press is a department of the University of Oxford.
It furthers the University's objective of excellence in research, scholarship,
and education by publishing worldwide in

Oxford New York

Auckland Cape Town Dar es Salaam Hong Kong Karachi
Kuala Lumpur Madrid Melbourne Mexico City Nairobi
New Delhi Shanghai Taipei Toronto

With offices in

Argentina Austria Brazil Chile Czech Republic France Greece
Guatemala Hungary Italy Japan Poland Portugal Singapore
South Korea Switzerland Thailand Turkey Ukraine Vietnam

OXFORD and OXFORD ENGLISH are registered trademarks of
Oxford University Press

© Oxford University Press 2008

Database right Oxford University Press (maker)

Library of Congress Cataloging-in-Publication Data
Step Forward : English for everyday life.
    p. cm.
Step Forward 3 by Jane Spigarelli; Step Forward 4 by Barbara R. Denman.
ISBN: 978-0-19-439226-6 (3 : pbk.)
ISBN: 978-0-19-439227-3 (4 : pbk.)
1. English language–Textbooks for foreign students. 2. English language–
Problems, exercises, etc. III. Spigarelli, Jane. IV. Denman, Barbara R.
PE1128.S2143 2006
428.2'4—dc22
                    2006040090

Executive Publisher: Janet Aitchison
Editorial Manager: Stephanie Karras
Editor: Glenn Mathes II
Associate Editor: Olga Christopoulos
Art Director: Maj-Britt Hagsted
Senior Designer: Claudia Carlson
Senior Art Editor: Judi DeSouter
Art Editor: Robin Fadool
Manufacturing Manager: Shanta Persaud
Manufacturing Controller: Eve Wong

Student Book ISBN: 978 0 19 439226 6
Student Book with CD-ROM ISBN: 978 0 19 439655 4
Student Book as pack component ISBN: 978 0 19 439660 8
Audio CD-ROM as pack component ISBN: 978 0 19 439665 3

Printed in China
10

This book is printed on paper from certified and well-managed sources.

The publishers would also like to thank the following for their permission to
adapt copyrighted material:

p. 28 "Parks and Recreation: The Benefits are Endless…" used with permission
of the National Recreation and Park Association

p. 56-57 "Job Outlook 2005: Good News for College Graduates" used with
permission of Job Outlook and the National Association of Colleges and
Employers

p. 70 "History of Earth Day" used with permission of www.earthday.net

p. 112 "'Attitudes and Beliefs about the Use of Over-the-Counter Medicines: A Dose
of Reality' A National Survey of Consumers and Health Professionals" used with
permission of National Council on Patient Information and Education © 2002-2006

p. 126-127 "State Lemon Law Criteria" used with permission of the Center for Auto
Safety

p. 139 "Loveland Police Department Public Safety Survey 2003" used with
permission of Loveland, Colorado Police Department

ACKNOWLEDGMENTS

Cover photograph: Corbis/Punchstock
Back cover photograph: Brian Rose
Illustrations: Laurie Conley, p.2, p.6, p.18, p.32, p.45, p.73, p.118, p.143, p.157;
Geo Parkin, p.4, p.19, p.25, p.78, p.83, p.94, p.106, p.123, p.150, p.158; Claudia
Carlson, p.5; Gary Ciccarelli, p.10, p.13 (two illustrations top right), p.59, p.120;
Jane Spencer, p.11, p.22, p.41, p. 101, p.151; Annie Bissett, p.13, p.27, p.50, p.69,
p.148, p.162; Jay Montgomery, p.17, p.31 (four illustrations); Arlene Boehm, p.20,
p.167; Barb Bastian, p.31 (poster), p. 36 (two ads), p.37 (ad), p.47, p.51, p.61, p.103,
p.112, p.139, p.146, p.147, p.159; John Batten, p.33, p.34, p.39, p.48, p.67, p.87,
p.104, p.111; p.115, p.137, p.160, p.163; Terry Paczko, p.36 (two laptops), p.60,
p.75, p.84, p.88 (document call-outs), p.117, p.132; Guy Holt, p.37 (three cameras);
Karen Prichett, p.88; Mark Hannon, p.38, p.64, p.79, p.90, p.95, p.125, p.139; Mark
Collins, p.45; Tom Newscom, p.46, p.74, p.130, p.131; Bill Dickson, p.81, p.92,
p.98, p.122, p.126, p.135; Karen Minot, p.89, p.145; Matt Zang, p.102; Uldis Klavins,
p.116; Angelo Tillery, p.144.

Photographs: Grant Heilman: p.5 (elementary school); Superstock: p.5 (middle
school); Photo Edit Inc.: David Young-Wolff, p.5 (high school); Photo Edit Inc.:
David Young-Wolff, p.5 (university); The Image Works: p.5 (community college);
Photo Edit Inc.: Davis Barber, p.5 (adult school); Superstock: p.14; Masterfile: p.24;
The Image Works: p.28; Robertstock: Jack Hollingsworth, p. 38 (business woman);
Punch Stock: p.47; Photo Edit Inc.: Jeff Greenberg, p.52 (shipping clerk); The Image
Works: p.61 (community clinic); The Image Works: p.61 (senior center); Punch
Stock: p.61 (pet adoption); The Image Works: p.61 (city hall); The Image Works:
p.66; Masterfile: p.69 (recycling symbol); Photo Edit Inc.: Tony Freeman, p.70;
Painet Photos: Cheryl & Leo Meyer, p.108; Grant Heilman: p.129; Age Fotostock:
p.134; Photographers Direct: Vincent Abbey, p.139 (woman reporting a crime);
Photo Edit Inc.: Michael Newman, p.139 (policeman); Photo Edit Inc.: Eric Fowke,
p.140; Stockbyte/Superstock: p.145; Photo Edit Inc.: Dana White, p.154; Punch
Stock: p.159 (tax form); Susan and Neil Silverman: p.159 (no littering sign);
Superstock: p.159 (group); Getty Images: p.159 (jury); Photo Edit Inc.: David Young-
Wolff, p.150 (woman reading); Corbis: p.168; Index Stock/Grantpix: p.171.

It has been our privilege to work with the gifted *Step Forward
Book 3* editorial and design team: Stephanie Karras,
Meg Brooks, Glenn Mathes, Carla Mavrodin, Maj-Britt Hagsted,
Claudia Carlson, and Robin Fadool. We also want to thank
our students and fellow teachers who have inspired us
throughout this project.
Jane Spigarelli
Jayme Adelson-Goldstein

My deep thanks and admiration go to Jayme Adelson-Goldstein
for her grace and joie de vivre. I dedicate this book to Jimmy,
for his constant presence and many kick-starts while I wrote.
–Jane

I am indebted to Jane, an outstanding author and teacher, for
her unwavering commitment to the intermediate learner. I
dedicate this book to Glenn, with thanks for his wisdom and
indefatigable spirit.
–Jayme

ACKNOWLEDGMENTS

The Publisher and Series Director would like to acknowledge the following individuals for their invaluable input during the development of this series:

Vittoria Abbatte-Maghsoudi Mount Diablo Unified School District, Loma Vista Adult Center, Concord, CA

Karen Abell Durham Technical Community College, Durham, NC

Millicent Alexander Los Angeles Unified School District, Huntington Park-Bell Community Adult School, Los Angeles, CA

Diana Allen Oakton Community College, Skokie, IL

Bethany Bandera Arlington Education and Employment Program, Arlington, VA

Sandra Bergman New York City Department of Education, New York, NY

Chan Bostwick Los Angeles Technology Center, Los Angeles, CA

Diana Brady-Herndon Napa Valley Adult School, Napa, CA

Susen Broellos Baldwin Park Unified School District, Baldwin Park, CA

Carmen Carbajal Mitchell Community College, Statesville, NC

Jose Carmona Daytona Beach Community College, Daytona Beach, FL

Ingrid Caswell Los Angeles Technology Center, Los Angeles, CA

Joyce Clapp Hayward Adult School, Hayward, CA

Beverly deNicola Capistrano Unified School District, San Juan Capistrano, CA

Edward Ende Miami Springs Adult Center, Miami Springs, FL

Gayle Fagan Harris County Department of Education, Houston, TX

Richard Firsten Lindsey Hopkins Technical Education Center, Miami, FL

Elizabeth Fitzgerald Hialeah Adult Center, Hialeah, FL

Mary Ann Florez Arlington Education and Employment Program, Arlington, VA

Leslie Foster Davidson Mitchell Community College, Statesville, NC

Beverly Gandall Santa Ana College School of Continuing Education, Santa Ana, CA

Rodriguez Garner Westchester Community College, Valhalla, NY

Sally Gearhart Santa Rosa Junior College, Santa Rosa, CA

Norma Guzman Baldwin Park Unified School District, Baldwin Park, CA

Lori Howard UC Berkeley, Education Extension, Berkeley, CA

Phillip L. Johnson Santa Ana College Centennial Education Center, Santa Ana, CA

Kelley Keith Mount Diablo Unified School District, Loma Vista Adult Center, Concord, CA

Blanche Kellawon Bronx Community College, Bronx, NY

Keiko Kimura Triton College, River Grove, IL

Jody Kirkwood ABC Adult School, Cerritos, CA

Matthew Kogan Evans Community Adult School, Los Angeles, CA

Laurel Leonard Napa Valley Adult School, Napa, CA

Barbara Linek Illinois Migrant Education Council, Plainfield, IL

Alice Macondray Neighborhood Centers Adult School, Oakland, CA

Ronna Magy Los Angeles Unified School District Central Office, Los Angeles, CA

Jose Marlasca South Area Adult Education, Melbourne, FL

Laura Martin Adult Learning Resource Center, Des Plaines, IL

Judith Martin-Hall Indian River Community College, Fort Pierce, FL

Michael Mason Mount Diablo Unified School District, Loma Vista Adult Center, Concord, CA

Katherine McCaffery Brewster Technical Center, Tampa, FL

Cathleen McCargo Arlington Education and Employment Program, Arlington, VA

Todd McDonald Hillsborough County Public Schools, Tampa, FL

Rita McSorley Northeast Independent School District, San Antonio, TX

Gloria Melendrez Evans Community Adult School, Los Angeles, CA

Vicki Moore El Monte-Rosemead Adult School, El Monte, CA

Meg Morris Mountain View Los Altos Adult Education District, Los Altos, CA

Nieves Novoa LaGuardia Community College, Long Island City, NY

Jo Pamment Haslett Public Schools, East Lansing, MI

Liliana Quijada-Black Irvington Learning Center, Houston, TX

Ellen Quish LaGuardia Community College, Long Island City, NY

Mary Ray Fairfax County Public Schools, Springfield, VA

Tatiana Roganova Hayward Adult School, Hayward, CA

Nancy Rogenscky-Roda Hialeah-Miami Lakes Adult Education and Community Center, Hialeah, FL

Lorraine Romero Houston Community College, Houston, TX

Edilyn Samways The English Center, Miami, FL

Kathleen Santopietro Weddel Northern Colorado Professional Development Center, Longmont, CO

Dr. G. Santos The English Center, Miami, FL

Fran Schnall City College of New York Literacy Program, New York, NY

Mary Segovia El Monte-Rosemead Adult School, El Monte, CA

Edith Smith City College of San Francisco, San Francisco, CA

Alisa Takeuchi Chapman Education Center, Garden Grove, CA

Leslie Weaver Fairfax County Public Schools, Falls Church, VA

David Wexler Napa Valley Adult School, Napa, CA

Bartley P. Wilson Northeast Independent School District, San Antonio, TX

Emily Wonson Hunter College, New York, NY

TABLE OF CONTENTS

Unit	Life Skills & Civics Competencies	Vocabulary	Grammar	Critical Thinking & Math Concepts	Reading & Writing
Pre-unit **The First Step** page 2	• Greet others • Say and spell names of classmates • Alphabetize a list	• Parts of speech	• Review parts of speech • Review prepositions of location	• Alphabetize names • Recognize parts of speech	• Read and write names • Write abbreviations of parts of speech
Unit 1 **Learning Together** page 4	• Identify study skills and habits • Identify study techniques • Identify the educational system of the U.S. • Write a journal entry • Interpret library services • Express indecision	• Study skills and habits • Educational terms • Library service terms **In other words:** • Saying you're not sure	• Review present and past verb forms • Review present and past question forms • Review *Yes/No* questions and answers • Distinguish between adjectives and adverbs • The prefix *dis-*	• Reflect on personal study styles • Compare study habits and personal studying styles • Recognize library services **Real-life math:** • Determine percentages **Problem solving:** • Find ways to make new friends	• Write about personal study styles • Read and write a journal entry • Read an advice column
Unit 2 **Ready for Fun** page 18	• Identify recreational activities • Make predictions • Interpret a flyer • Read and write an email invitation • Make plans with friends • Identify the health benefits of parks	• Places in the community • Recreational activities • Meeting friends **In other words:** • Giving someone a choice **Idiom note:** • *play it by ear*	• Review *be going to* and *will* • Future predictions with *will* • Expressing preferences with *would rather* + verb • The suffix *-ful*	• Reflect on favorite recreational activities • Analyze a list of scheduled events • Compare predictions of future • Recognize the health benefits of parks **Real-life math:** • Calculate ticket costs **Problem solving:** • Resolve disagreements in preferences	• Read and write an email invitation • Write questions about future predictions • Read an article about the health benefits of parks **Writer's note:** • Use commas in letters and emails after the greeting and the closing
Unit 3 **A Job to Do** page 32	• Describe workplace and school policies • Interpret memos • Interpret computer ads • Make comparisons • Give and respond to job feedback • Identify the benefits of and sources for job training	• Computer vocabulary • Office vocabulary • Job training **In other words:** • Responding to negative feedback	• Comparisons with adjectives • Review superlatives • Answering questions with superlatives • Review superlative forms • The suffix *-tion*	• Resolve business-related conflicts • Compare features of products • Reflect on store preferences • Reflect on appropriate workplace behaviors **Real-life math:** • Calculate averages **Problem solving:** • Analyze and compare job benefits	• Read and write a memo • Read computer ads • Read an article about workplace training **Writer's note:** • Sign and print your name at the end of a formal business letter

Listening & Speaking	CASAS Life Skills Competencies	Standardized Student Syllabi/ LCPs	SCANS Competencies	EFF Content Standards
• Listen for and give personal information • Talk about the location of objects	0.1.2, 0.1.4, 0.1.5, 0.2.1	39.01, 50.03, 50.06	• Listening • Speaking • Sociability	• Listening actively • Speaking so others can understand
• Talk about personal study styles • Discuss the first day of English class • Listen for career information • Talk about career plans • Talk about reading habits **Grammar listening** • Listen for present or past verb tenses **Pronunciation:** • Differentiate between "sh", "ch", and "j" sounds	L1: 0.1.2, 0.1.5, 4.8.1, 7.4.1, 7.4.5 L2: 0.1.2, 0.1.5 L3: 0.1.2 L4: 0.1.2, 0.1.3, 0.1.5, 6.0.3, 6.0.4, 6.2.6, 7.2.5 L5: 0.1.2, 2.5.6 RE: 0.1.2, 0.1.5, 7.2.6, 7.3.1, 7.3.2, 7.4.1	L1: 49.02, 49.09 L2: 39.01, 49.03, 49.16 L3: 49.16, 50.02 L4: 49.02, 50.04, 50.05 L5: 39.04, 46.01, 49.02, 49.04, 49.16 RE: 49.01, 50.02, 50.04, 50.05, 50.08	Most SCANS are incorporated into this unit, with an emphasis on: • Knowing how to learn • Participating as a member of a team • Seeing in the mind's eye	Most EFFs are incorporated into this unit, with an emphasis on: • Conveying ideas in writing • Reading with understanding • Reflecting and evaluating
• Talk about recreational activities • Ask and answer questions about future predictions • Listen for and talk about preferences • Listen to a recorded message of community events • Discuss community parks **Grammar listening:** • Listen for predictions, plans, or promises **Pronunciation:** • "j" and "ch" sounds	L1: 0.1.2, 0.1.5, 2.6.1, 4.8.1, 7.5.1 L2: 0.1.2, 0.1.5, 0.2.3, 2.6.1 L3: 0.1.2, 7.2.5 L4: 0.1.2, 6.0.3, 6.0.4, 6.1.1, 6.1.2 L5: 0.1.2, 2.6.1, 2.6.3 RE: 0.1.2, 0.1.3, 0.1.5, 2.6.1, 7.2.6, 7.3.1, 7.3.2, 7.3.3, 7.3.4	L1: 39.01, 0.1.5, 2.6.1, 4.8.1 L2: 39.04, 49.16, 49.02, 49.03 L3: 49.16, 49.03, 50.02 L4: 49.02, 49.03, 49.16 L5: 39.01, 49.03, 49.04, 49.16, 49.17 RE: 39.01, 49.16, 50.02	Most SCANS are incorporated into this unit, with and emphasis on: • Applying technology to task • Participating as member of a team • Seeing things in the mind's eye	Most EFFs are incorporated into this unit, with an emphasis on: • Cooperating with others • Learning through research • Speaking so others can understand
• Talk about computers • Discuss problems in school • Ask and answer questions about shopping in different stores • Listen to evaluations of employees • Discuss job training **Grammar listening:** • Listen for comparatives **Pronunciation:** • "v", "b", and "f" sounds	L1: 0.1.2, 0.1.5, 4.1.6, 4.8.1, 7.2.3 L2: 0.1.2, 0.1.5, 4.4.1, 4.6.2, 7.2.5, 7.4.7 L3: 0.1.2, 0.2.1, 4.2.2, 7.4.7 L4: 0.1.2, 0.1.5, 4.4.4, 4.6.1, 6.1.1, 6.1.4, 7.2.5, 7.4.7 L5: 0.1.2, 2.5.5, 4.4.2 RE: 0.1.2, 0.1.5, 1.2.1, 7.2.5, 7.2.6, 7.2.7, 7.3.1, 7.3.2	L1: 35.02, 49.02 L2: 49.02, 49.16, 49.17 L3: 45.01, 49.02, 49.03, 49.16, 50.04 L4: 49.02, 49.03, 50.04 L5: 37.02, 49.02, 49.03, 49.04 RE: 49.01, 49.02, 49.03, 50.04	Most SCANS are incorporated into this unit, with and emphasis on: • Arithmetic/mathematics • Decision making • Interpreting and communicating information	Most EFFs are incorporated into this unit, with an emphasis on: • Cooperating with others • Observing critically • Taking responsibility for learning

Unit	Life Skills & Civics Competencies	Vocabulary	Grammar	Critical Thinking & Math Concepts	Reading & Writing
Unit 4 **Good Work** **page 46**	• Identify appropriate job interview behavior • Describe personal strengths • Identify appropriate post-job interview behavior • Respond to questions during an interview for a promotion • Identify ways to get a promotion • Recognize postive job skills	• Job interview vocabulary • Personal strengths • Ways to persuade • Job skills **In other words:** • Ways to ask	• The present perfect with *for* and *since* • Information questions with the present perfect • Contractions with the present perfect	• Analyze job interview behavior • Reflect on personal strengths • Speculate about possible jobs • Analyze a personal timeline • Determine appropriate qualities for work or school **Real-life math:** • Calculate gross pay **Problem solving:** • Prioritize preparatory steps for job interview	• Read about strengths of different types of workers • Read and write an interview thank-you letter • Read a job application • Read an article about getting a promotion **Writer's note:** • Use a colon after the greeting in a formal business letter
Unit 5 **Community Resources** **page 60**	• Identify community resources • Interpret a community website • Identify problems in the community • Write a letter asking for assistance • Give an opinion on a community or local issue • Identify ways to reduce trash and protect the environment	• Community resources • Community service terms • Environmental protection terms **In other words:** • Apologizing	• *Yes/No* questions with the present perfect • The present perfect with *ever, already,* and *yet* • Review the simple past and the present perfect • The prefix *un-*	• Analyze a community website • Formulate solutions to community problems • Speculate on ways to improve the community • Examine statistics about the environment **Real-life math:** • Analyze a line graph **Problem solving:** • Find ways to get involved in the community	• Read about community action • Write a letter to a school board member • Read an article about Earth Day
Unit 6 **What's Cooking?** **page 74**	• Identify kitchen items and actions • Describe the procedure for making a recipe • Express food preferences • Take and give restaurant orders • Request nutritional information about menu items • Identify methods of safe food preparation	• Kitchen • Cooking actions • Safe food preparation terms **Idiom note:** • *try to cut down on*	• Separable phrasal verbs • Inseparable phrasal verbs • Possessive pronouns and possessive adjectives	• Compare and contrast usefulness of kitchen tools • Reflect on favorite meals • Analyze food preparation guidelines • Speculate about food safety procedures **Real-life math:** • Calculate the tip on a restaurant bill **Problem solving:** • Resolve restaurant tipping difficulties	• Read about a family recipe • Write about a family recipe • Read about a cooking experience • Read an article about food poisoning **Writer's note:** • Indent the first word of a paragraph

Listening & Speaking	CASAS Life Skills Competencies	Standardized Student Syllabi/ LCPs	SCANS Competencies	EFF Content Standards
• Talk about job interview behavior • Discuss personal strengths • Talk about life events • Listen for and talk about job information **Grammar listening:** • Listen for the present perfect **Pronunciation:** • "th"	**L1:** 0.1.2, 0.1.3, 0.1.4, 0.1.5, 4.1.5, 4.1.7, 4.4.1, 4.8.1, 7.4.5, 7.5.6 **L2:** 0.1.2, 0.1.5, 4.1.7, 4.6.2, 7.4.7 **L3:** 0.1.2, 0.1.5, 0.2.1, 7.4.7 **L4:** 0.1.5, 4.1.2, 4.1.5, 4.4.2, 6.2.1, 6.2.3 **L5:** 0.1.2, 4.1.6, 4.4.1, 4.4.2, 7.4.7, 7.5.1, 8.3.1 **RE:** 0.1.2, 0.1.5, 0.2.1, 7.3.1, 7.3.2, 7.3.3, 7.3.4	**L1:** 35.02, 35.06, 39.01, 49.02, 49.09, 49.10 **L2:** 49.02, 49.12, 49.16, 49.17 **L3:** 39.01, 49.03, 49.09, 49.16, 49.17, 50.02 **L4:** 37.01, 37.02, 37.03, 39.01, 49.02, 49.09, 50.02 **L5:** 37.01, 37.02, 38.01, 39.01, 49.01, 49.02, 49.16, 49.17 **RE:** 39.01, 49.01, 49.02, 49.16, 50.02	Most SCANS are incorporated into this unit, with an emphasis on: • Acquiring and evaluating information • Organizing and maintaining information • Problem solving	Most EFFs are incorporated into this unit, with an emphasis on: • Advocating and influencing • Conveying ideas in writing • Reading with understanding
• Talk about community resources • Discuss safety problems at school • Talk about recycling issues • Listen to a news interview • Discuss ways to reduce trash **Grammar listening:** • Listen for information using the present perfect **Pronunciation:** • "y", "w", and "j" sounds	**L1:** 0.1.2, 0.1.5, 4.1.6, 4.8.1, 7.4.5 **L2:** 0.1.2, 0.1.5, 4.9.4, 7.2.5, 7.3.1, 7.3.2 **L3:** 0.1.2, 0.2.1 **L4:** 0.1.2, 0.1.5, 2.6.2, 5.6.1 **L5:** 0.1.2, 0.1.3, 5.7.1, 7.2.5, 7.3.1, 7.3.2, 7.4.7 **RE:** 0.1.2, 0.1.5, 0.2.1, 4.8.1, 5.6.1, 7.3.1, 7.3.2	**L1:** 0.1.2, 0.1.5, 4.1.6, 4.8.1, 7.4.5 **L2:** 0.1.2, 0.1.5, 4.9.4, 7.2.5, 7.3.1, 7.3.2 **L3:** 0.1.2, 0.2.1 **L4:** 0.1.2, 0.1.5, 2.6.2, 5.6.1 **L5:** 0.1.2, 0.1.3, 5.7.1, 7.2.5, 7.3.1, 7.3.2, 7.4.7 **RE:** 0.1.2, 0.1.5, 0.2.1, 4.8.1, 5.6.1, 7.3.1, 7.3.2	Most SCANS are incorporated into this unit, with an emphasis on: • Creative thinking • Interpreting and communicating information • Reasoning	Most EFFs are incorporated into this unit, with an emphasis on: • Conveying ideas in writing • Reading with understanding • Solving problems and making decisions
• Talk about cooking and restaurants • Discuss meal preparation and favorite foods • Order a meal • Talk about restaurant bills • Discuss safe food preparation **Grammar listening:** • Listen for information using phrasal verbs **Pronunciation:** • Linking of phrasal verbs	**L1:** 0.1.2, 0.1.5, 0.2.1, 4.8.1, 7.4.5, 8.2.1 **L2:** 0.1.2, 0.2.1, 2.7.2, 8.2.1 **L3:** 0.1.2, 1.1.1 **L4:** 0.1.2, 1.6.4, 2.6.4, 6.0.3, 6.0.4, 6.2.3 **L5:** 0.1.2, 1.6.1, 3.1.1, 3.4.1, 3.4.2, 3.5.1, 3.5.3, 3.5.5, 8.2.1 **RE:** 0.1.2, 0.1.5, 0.2.1, 1.1.1, 4.8.1, 7.2.6, 7.3.1, 7.3.2	**L1:** 39.01, 49.02, 49.03, 49.10, 50.02, 50.08 **L2:** 39.01, 49.02, 49.03, 49.14, 49.16 **L3:** 49.01, 49.02, 49.09, 49.16, 49.17, 50.02 **L4:** 39.01, 45.03, 49.02, 49.09, 49.16, 49.17, 50.04 **L5:** 39.01, 49.02, 49.03, 49.16 **RE:** 39.01, 49.02, 49.03, 49.16, 49.17, 50.01, 50.02	Most SCANS are incorporated into this unit, with an emphasis on: • Acquiring and evaluating information • Interpreting and communicating information • Writing	• Most EFFs are incorporated into this unit, with an emphasis on: • Conveying ideas in writing • Cooperating with others • Solving problems and making decisions

Unit	Life Skills & Civics Competencies	Vocabulary	Grammar	Critical Thinking & Math Concepts	Reading & Writing
Unit 7 **Money Wise** **page 88**	• Identify banking services • Describe a personal financial plan • Report a billing or banking error • Fill-in checking account information • Interpret savings account benefits • Identify ways to avoid becoming a victim of identity theft	• Banking • Financial planning • Identity theft terms **In other words:** • Asking about problems	• Real conditionals • Questions with real conditionals • Future time clauses • -al to form adjectives	• Analyze bank webpage • Describe importance of bank services • Speculate about ways to save money • Predict future cause-and-effect scenarios **Real-life math:** • Analyze online bank savings account comparison chart **Problem solving:** • Analyze credit card offers	• Read about financial planning and goals • Write about a financial plan • Write about future plans using the future conditional • Read an article about identify theft **Writer's note:** • In a title, use capital letters for all words except articles and prepositions
Unit 8 **Living Well** **page 102**	• Identify parts of the body and medical departments • Outline a personal health plan • Respond to health advice • Identify healthy choices for diet and exercise • Interpret a medicine label • Ask a health care provider about medicine	• Parts of the body • Medical departments • Medication • Accepting suggestions **In other words:** • Making and accepting suggestions **Idiom Note:** • *run in the family*	• Affirmative and negative statements with *used to* • Questions and answers with *used to* • The present perfect continuous • The prefix *re-*	• Interpret a hospital directory • Speculate about ways to take care of personal health • Compare and contrast lifestyles • Analyze medication statistics **Real-life math:** • Calculate calories burned per hour **Problem solving:** • Resolve difficulties caused by injury	• Read and write an outline about staying healthy • Read an article about using medication safely • Read a medicine label
Unit 9 **Hit the Road** **page 116**	• Identify interior and exterior parts of automobiles • Describe a vacation • Identify features and defects in a product • Negotiate for a lower car price • Interpret information about automobile lemon laws • Read an automobile repair and maintenance log	• Parts of automobiles • Road trip terms • Terms for purchasing a car **In other words:** • Making a deal	• Describing present, past, and future events with time clauses • *and...too, and...not, either, but*	• Analyze the owner's manual of an automobile • Reflect on a past trip • Speculate about expenses after buying a new car • Interpret a car's repair and maintenance log **Real-life math:** • Calculate cost of oil changes for one year **Problem solving:** • Find solutions to car problems	• Read and write about a trip • Read about a car problem • Read an article about lemon laws

Listening & Speaking	CASAS Life Skills Competencies	Standardized Student Syllabi/ LCPs	SCANS Competencies	EFF Content Standards
• Talk about banking services • Discuss bank jobs and duties of employees • Discuss financial planning • Listen for automated account information **Grammar listening:** • Listen for information using real conditional sentences **Pronunciation:** • Silent "h" sounds in linked words	**L1:** 0.1.2, 0.1.5, 1.8.2, 4.8.1, 7.4.5 **L2:** 0.1.2, 0.2.1, 1.8.5, 7.4.7 **L3:** 0.1.2, 0.2.1 **L4:** 0.1.2, 1.5.3, 6.0.3, 6.0.4, 6.2.3 **L5:** 0.1.2, 5.3.7, 7.3.1, 7.4.7 **RE:** 0.1.2, 0.1.5, 0.2.1, 1.8.5, 4.8.1, 7.2.6, 7.3.1, 7.3.2, 7.3.4, 8.3.2	**L1:** 39.01, 42.04, 49.01, 49.02, 49.09, 49.10 **L2:** 39.01, 49.01, 49.02, 49.03, 49.16, 49.17 **L3:** 49.02, 49.03, 49.09, 49.16, 49.17 **L4:** 49.02, 49.03, 49.09, 49.16, 49.17 **L5:** 49.01, 49.03, 49.04, 49.16, 49.17 **RE:** 39.01, 49.01, 49.02, 49.03, 49.16, 49.17, 50.08	Most SCANS are incorporated into this unit, with an emphasis on: • Arithmetic/mathematics • Creative thinking • Seeing things in the mind's eye	Most EFFs are incorporated into this unit, with an emphasis on: • Conveying ideas in writing • Reflecting and evaluating • Solving problems and making decisions
• Talk about doctors' knowledge of the human body • Discuss ways to stay healthy • Listen for a doctor's advice • Listen to a radio program **Grammar listening:** • Listen for information using *used to* **Pronunciation:** • "v" vs "s" sounds in use	**L1:** 0.1.2, 0.1.5, 0.2.1, 2.5.1, 3.1.1, 3.1.3, 3.5.9, 4.8.1, 7.4.5 **L2:** 0.1.2, 0.2.1, 0.2.4, 3.5.2, 3.5.8, 7.1.2, 7.1.3, 7.2.7, 7.4.2 **L3:** 0.1.2, 0.1.5, 0.2.1, 7.4.7 **L4:** 0.1.2, 0.1.5, 3.5.8, 6.0.3, 6.0.4, 6.2.3 **L5:** 0.1.2, 0.1.5, 3.1.3, 3.3.1, 3.3.2, 3.3.3, 3.4.1, 3.4.2, 7.2.3, 7.4.7 **RE:** 0.1.2, 0.1.5, 0.2.1, 3.5.8, 7.2.6, 7.3.1, 7.3.2	**L1:** 39.01, 49.02, 49.09, 49.10 **L2:** 39.01, 41.06, 49.02, 49.16, 49.17 **L3:** 39.01, 41.06, 49.02, 49.09, 49.13, 49.16, 49.17 **L4:** 41.03, 41.06, 49.02, 49.09, 49.16, 50.02, 51.03 **L5:** 41.04, 49.04, 49.09, 49.16, 49.17 **RE:** 41.06, 49.02, 49.16, 50.02	Most SCANS are incorporated into this unit, with an emphasis on: • Interpreting and communicating information • Listening • Organizing and maintaining information	Most EFFs are incorporated into this unit, with an emphasis on: • Observing critically • Reading with understanding • Using math to solve problems and communicate
• Talk about car parts • Discuss trips and vacations • Listen for car terms in conversations **Grammar listening:** • Listen for the event that happened first **Pronunciation:** • The schwa sound	**L1:** 0.1.2, 0.1.5, 1.9.6, 4.8.1 **L2:** 0.1.2, 0.1.5, 0.2.1 **L3:** 0.1.2, 0.2.1, 7.4.2 **L4:** 0.1.2, 1.2.2, 17.71, 1.9.5, 1.9.6, 1.9.8, 6.0.3, 6.0.4, 6.2.3 **L5:** 0.1.2, 1.6.3, 7.4.4 **R E:** 0.1.2, 0.1.5, 2.2.3, 4.8.1, 7.2.6, 7.3.1, 7.3.2, 7.3.4	**L1:** 39.01, 49.02, 49.10 **L2:** 39.01, 49.02, 49.03, 49.13, 49.16, 49.17 **L3:** 49.02, 49.09, 49.13, 49.16, 49.17 **L4:** 45.01, 49.02, 49.09, 49.16, 51.01 **L5:** 38.01, 49.09, 49.16, 49.17 **RE:** 49.16, 49.17	Most SCANS are incorporated into this unit, with and emphasis on: • Creative thinking • Interpreting and communicating • Using computers to process information	Most EFFs are incorporated into this unit, with an emphasis on: • Conveying ideas in writing • Learning through research • Taking responsibility for learning

Unit	Life Skills & Civics Competencies	Vocabulary	Grammar	Critical Thinking & Math Concepts	Reading & Writing
Unit 10 **Crime Doesn't Pay** **page 130**	• Identify safe habits • Identify elements of the criminal justice system • Describe home and neighborhood security • Report a crime to police • Identify careers in public safety • Read a chart about careers in public safety	• Safety • Criminal justice system • Home security features **In other words:** • Sequencing events	• Gerunds as subjects • Compare gerunds and the present continuous • Gerunds and infinitives	• Speculate on ways to stay safe • Determine whether actions are safe or dangerous • Speculate reasons for not reporting crimes • Interpret a chart about careers in public safety **Real-life math:** • Interpret a survey about crime **Problem solving:** • Respond appropriately to an unsafe situation	• Read and write about home security • Read an article about careers in public safety **Writer's note:** • Use quotation marks (" ") to show a person's exact words. Use a comma before you begin the quotation.
Unit 11 **That's Life** **page 144**	• Identify life events • Identify special occasions • Read newspaper announcements • Respond to invitations • Respond to good and bad news appropriately • Interpret information about renting or buying a home	• Life events • Special occasions • Terms used for renting or buying a house **In other words:** • Responding to good news **Idiom note:** • *make it*	• The present passive • The present passive with *by* • *be able to* + verb for ability in the future and past	• Interpret announcements in a newspaper • Speculate about appropriate ways to respond to invitations • Analyze a flyer from a retirement community • Interpret statistic about income spent on rent **Real-life math:** • Calculate wedding expenses **Problem solving:** • Determine how to respond late to a wedding invitation	• Read and write responses to an invitation • Read a retirement community flyer • Write sentences in a chart about different types of parties • Read an article about moving to a new home
Unit 12 **Doing the Right Thing** **page 158**	• Identify civic rights, freedoms, and responsibilities • Describe civic involvement • Read a community volunteer form • Describe a legal problem • Interpret information about protecting civil rights • Recognize the Civil Rights contributions of Rosa Parks	• Civic terms • Community participation **In other words:** • Describing possible reasons **Idiom note:** • *stand up for*	• Verb + infinitive • Verb + gerund or infinitive • Report requests • Word stress in nouns and verbs	• Analyze a pamphlet about civic responsibilities • Draw conclusions on the importance of civic involvement • Reflect on likes and dislikes regarding community involvement • Interpret a webpage from a legal clinic **Real-life math:** • Analyze a voter poll **Problem solving:** • Determine appropriate action in a car accident	• Read and write a letter to the newspaper • Read a form for volunteers • Read an article about the Civil Rights Movement • Write a summary of the article **Writer's note:** • Using examples to help make your ideas clear

Listening scripts	Grammar charts	Vocabulary list	Index
pages 172–182	pages 183–190	pages 191–194	pages 195–198

Listening & Speaking	CASAS Life Skills Competencies	Standardized Student Syllabi/ LCPs	SCANS Competencies	EFF Content Standards
• Discuss ways of staying safe • Talk about home security • Listen to someone report a crime to the police • Discuss issues connected with reporting crimes • Listen to a telephone conversation about a crime • Discuss careers in public safety **Grammar listening:** • Listen for gerunds vs. the present continuous **Pronunciation:** • Stressed words in sentences	**L1:** 0.1.2, 0.1.5, 0.2.1, 3.5.9, 5.5.3 **L2:** 0.1.2, 0.2.1, 8.1.4 **L3:** 0.1.2, 0.2.1, 8.1.4 **L4:** 0.1.2, 5.3.8, 6.7.2 **L5:** 0.1.2, 5.5.6, 7.4.4 **RE:** 0.1.2, 0.1.5, 4.8.1, 5.3.8, 5.6.1, 7.2.6, 7.3.1, 7.3.2, 7.3.4	**L1:** 39.01, 44.02, 49.02, 49.10 **L2:** 39.01, 44.02, 49.01, 49.02, 49.13, 49.16 **L3:** 44.01, 49.16 **L4:** 39.01, 44.01, 49.02, 49.09, 49.16, 51.05 **L5:** 38.01, 49.09, 49.16, 49.17 **RE:** 39.01, 44.01, 49.02, 49.17, 50.02	Most SCANS are incorporated into this unit, with an emphasis on: • Acquiring and evaluating information • Applying technology to the task • Listening	Most EFFs are incorporated into this unit, with an emphasis on: • Conveying ideas in writing • Reading with understanding • Solving problems and making decisions
• Talk about personal experiences with life events • Discuss ways to respond to invitations • Listen to a conversation about a life event • Discuss wedding traditions • Listen to a story about wedding traditions **Grammar listening:** • Listen for the same meaning of two sentences **Pronunciation:** • Show excitement through intonation	**L1:** 0.1.2, 0.1.5, 0.2.1, 1.2.5, 4.8.1 **L2:** 0.1.2, 0.2.1, 0.2.3 **L3:** 0.1.2, 0.1.5, 0.2.1, 1.4.2, 4.8.1 **L4:** 0.1.2, 0.2.1, 2.7.2, 2.7.3, 6.0.3, 6.0.4, 6.1.1, 6.1.3, 6.1.4 **L5:** 0.1.2, 0.2.1, 1.4.3 **RE:** 0.1.2, 0.1.5, 0.2.1, 2.7.1, 2.7.2, 2.7.3, 4.8.1, 7.2.6, 7.3.1, 7.3.2, 7.3.4, 7.4.7	**L1:** 49.02, 49.10 **L2:** 39.01, 39.04, 49.02, 49.03, 49.13 **L3:** 39.01, 49.02, 49.09, 49.13, 49.17 **L4:** 39.01, 49.02, 49.03, 49.09, 49.16 **L5:** 45.07, 49.01, 49.02 **RE:** 39.01, 49.02, 49.16	Most SCANS are incorporated into this unit, with an emphasis on: • Acquiring and evaluating information • Listening • Reading	Most EFFs are incorporated into this unit, with an emphasis on: • Conveying ideas in writing • Reading with understanding • Solving problems and making decisions
• Talk about rights of U.S. residents and citizens • Discuss civic activities and involvement • Listen to a conversation about a legal problem • Talk about community concerns • Listen to a town meeting • Discuss protests and boycotts • Word stress in nouns and verbs **Grammar listening:** • Listen and complete sentences with gerunds or infinitives **Pronunciation:** • Homophones	**L1:** 0.1.2, 0.1.5, 0.2.1, 5.1.1, 5.1.6, 4.8.1 **L2:** 0.1.2, 0.2.1, 0.2.3, 5.6.2, 5.6.3 **L3:** 0.1.2, 0.1.5, 0.2.1, 0.2.4, 4.8.1, 5.6.2 **L4:** 0.1.2, 0.2.1, 5.6.1 **L5:** 0.1.2, 0.2.1, 5.2.1, 5.6.3 **RE:** 0.1.2, 0.1.5, 0.2.1, 4.8.1, 5.6.3, 7.2.6, 7.3.1, 7.3.2, 7.3.3, 7.3.4	**L1:** 39.01, 49.02, 49.10 **L2:** 39.01, 49.02, 49.13, 49.16, 49.17 **L3:** 39.01, 49.02, 49.03, 49.09, 49.17 **L4:** 39.01, 49.02, 49.16, 49.17 **L5:** 39.01, 49.02, 49.03, 49.13, 49.16 **RE:** 49.02, 49.16	Most SCANS are incorporated into this unit, with an emphasis on: • Creative thinking • Interpreting and communicating information • Listening	Most EFFs are incorporated into this unit, with an emphasis on: • Advocating and influencing • Cooperating with others • Reflecting and evaluating

A Word or Two About Reading Introductions to Textbooks

Teaching professionals rarely read a book's introduction. Instead, we flip through the book's pages, using the pictures, topics, and exercises to determine whether the book matches our learners' needs and our teaching style. We scan the reading passages, conversations, writing tasks, and grammar charts to judge the authenticity and accuracy of the text. At a glance, we assess how easy it would be to manage the pair work, group activities, evaluations, and application tasks.

This Introduction, however, also offers valuable information for the teacher. Because you've read this far, I encourage you to read a little further to learn how *Step Forward's* key concepts, components, and multilevel applications will help you help your learners.

Step Forward's Key Concepts

Step Forward is...

- the instructional backbone for single-level and multilevel classrooms.
- a standards-based, performance-based, and topic-based series for low-beginning through high-intermediate learners.
- a source for ready-made, four-skill lesson plans that address the skills our learners need in their workplace, civic, personal, and academic lives.
- a collection of learner-centered, communicative English-language practice activities.

The classroom is a remarkable place. *Step Forward* respects the depth of experience and knowledge that learners bring to the learning process. At the same time, *Step Forward* recognizes that learners' varied proficiencies, goals, interests, and educational backgrounds create instructional challenges for teachers.

To ensure that our learners leave each class having made progress toward their language and life goals, *Step Forward* works from these key concepts:

- **The wide spectrum of learners' needs makes using materials that support multilevel instruction essential.** *Step Forward* works with single-level and multilevel classes.
- **Learners' prior knowledge is a valuable teaching tool.** Prior knowledge questions appear in every *Step Forward* lesson.

- **Learning objectives are the cornerstone of instruction.** Each *Step Forward* lesson focuses on an objective that derives from identified learner needs, correlates to state and federal standards, and connects to a meaningful communication task. Progress toward the objective is evaluated at the end of the lesson.
- **Vocabulary, grammar, and pronunciation skills play an essential role in language learning. They provide learners with the tools needed to achieve life skill, civics, workplace, and academic competencies.** *Step Forward* includes strong vocabulary and grammar strands and features pronunciation and math lesson extensions in each unit.
- **Effective instruction requires a variety of instructional techniques and strategies to engage learners.** Techniques such as Early Production Questioning, Focused Listening, Total Physical Response (TPR), Cooperative Learning, and Problem Solving are embedded in the *Step Forward* series, along with grouping and classroom management strategies.

The *Step Forward* Program

The *Step Forward* program has five levels:

- Intro: pre-beginning
- Book 1: low-beginning
- Book 2: high-beginning
- Book 3: low-intermediate
- Book 4: intermediate to high-intermediate

Each level of *Step Forward* correlates to *The Oxford Picture Dictionary*. For pre-literacy learners, *The Basic Oxford Picture Dictionary Literacy Program* provides a flexible, needs-based approach to literacy instruction. Once learners develop strong literacy skills, they will be able to transition seamlessly into *Step Forward Student Introductory Level*.

Each *Step Forward* level includes the following components:

Step Forward Student Book

A collection of clear, engaging, four-skill lessons based on meaningful learning objectives.

Step Forward Audio Program

The recorded vocabulary, focused listening, conversations, pronunciation, and reading materials from the *Step Forward Student Book*.

Step Forward Step-By-Step Lesson Plans with Multilevel Grammar Exercises CD-ROM

An instructional planning resource with interleaved *Step Forward Student Book* pages, detailed lesson plans featuring multilevel teaching strategies and teaching tips, and a CD-ROM of printable multilevel grammar practice for the structures presented in the *Step Forward Student Book*.

Step Forward Workbook

Practice exercises for independent work in the classroom or as homework.

Step Forward Multilevel Activity Book

More than 100 photocopiable communicative practice activities and 24 high-interest Jigsaw Readings; lesson materials that work equally well in single-level or multilevel settings.

Step Forward Test Generator CD-ROM with ExamView® Assessment Suite

Hundreds of multiple-choice and life-skill oriented test items for each *Step Forward Student Book*.

Multilevel Applications of *Step Forward*

All the *Step Forward* program components support multilevel instruction.

Step Forward is so named because it helps learners "step forward" toward their language and life goals, no matter where they start. Our learners often start from very different language abilities within the same class.

Regardless of level, all learners need materials that bolster comprehension while providing an appropriate amount of challenge. This makes multilevel materials an instructional necessity in most classrooms.

Each *Step Forward* lesson provides the following multilevel elements:

- **a general topic or competency area** that works across levels. This supports the concept that members of the class community need to feel connected, despite their differing abilities.
- **clear, colorful visuals and realia** that provide pre-level and on-level support during introduction, presentation and practice exercises, as well as prompts for higher-level questions and exercises.

In addition, *Step Forward* correlates to *The Oxford Picture Dictionary* so that teachers can use the visuals and vocabulary from *The Oxford Picture Dictionary* to support and expand upon each lesson.

- **learner-centered practice exercises** that can be used with same-level or mixed-level pairs or small groups. *Step Forward* exercises are broken down to their simplest steps. Once the exercise has been modeled, learners can usually conduct the exercises themselves.
- **pre-level, on-level, and higher-level objectives for each lesson and the multilevel strategies** necessary to carry out the lesson. These objectives are featured in the *Step-By-Step Lesson Plans*.
- **Grammar Boost pages in the Step Forward Workbook that provide excellent "wait time" activities** for learners who complete an exercise early, thus solving a real issue in the multilevel class.
- **a variety of pair, whole class, and small group activities** in the *Step Forward Multilevel Activity Book*. These activities are perfect for same-level and mixed-level grouping.
- **customizable grammar and evaluation exercises** in the *Step Forward Test Generator CD-ROM with ExamView® Assessment Suite*. These exercises make it possible to create evaluations specific to each level in the class.

Professional Development

As instructors, we need to reflect on second language acquisition in order to build a repertoire of effective instructional strategies. The *Step Forward Professional Development Program* provides research-based teaching strategies, tasks, and activities for single- and multilevel classes.

About Writing an ESL Series

It's collaborative! *Step Forward* is the product of dialogs with hundreds of teachers and learners. The dynamic quality of language instruction makes it important to keep this dialog alive. As you use this book in your classes, I invite you to contact me or any member of the *Step Forward* authorial team with your questions or comments.

Jayme Adelson-Goldstein

Jayme Adelson-Goldstein, Series Director
Stepforwardteam.us@oup.com

Step Forward: All you need to ensure your learners' success.
All the *Step Forward Student Books* follow this format.

LESSON 1: **VOCABULARY** teaches key words and phrases relevant to the unit topic, and provides conversation practice using the target vocabulary.

New vocabulary is introduced through vibrant art and high-interest listening texts.

Standards-based objectives are identified at the beginning of every lesson.

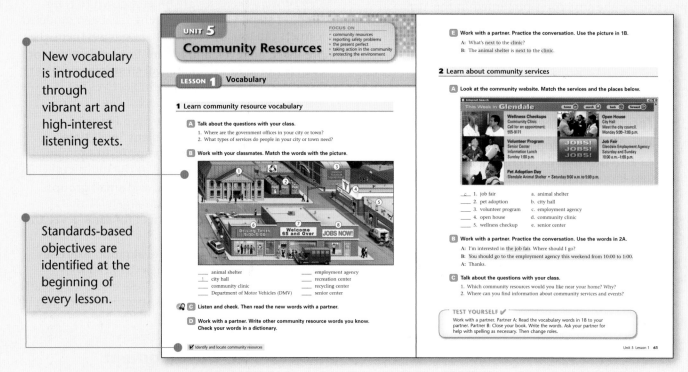

LESSON 2: **REAL-LIFE WRITING** expands on vocabulary learned in Lesson 1 and furthers learners' understanding through reading and writing about a life skills topic.

Learners write about their personal experiences using the vocabulary.

Life skills readings help learners practice the vocabulary in natural contexts.

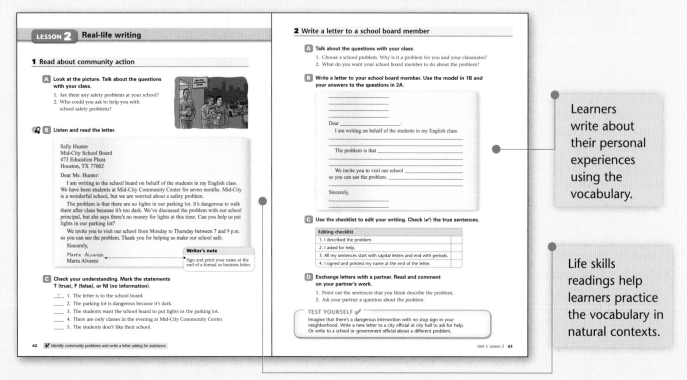

LESSON 3: **GRAMMAR** provides clear, simple presentation of the target structure followed by thorough, meaningful practice of it.

Clear grammar charts make learning grammar easy.

LESSON 3 Grammar

1 Learn *Yes/No* questions with the present perfect

A Read the conversation and the project report. When will the electrician arrive?

A: Have you painted the cafeteria?
B: Yes, I have.
A: Has the electrician fixed the air-conditioning?
B: No, he hasn't.
A: When will he fix it?
B: He'll be here tomorrow.

Senior Center Project Report:

	yes	no
1. paint cafeteria	✔	
2. fix air-conditioning		✔
3. buy lunch tables	✔	
4. repair stove		✔
5. advertise programs	✔	
6. start lunch program		✔

B Study the chart. Underline the 2 present perfect questions in the conversation above.

YES/NO QUESTIONS WITH THE PRESENT PERFECT

Yes/No Questions			Answers					
Have	I you we they	repaired the stove?	Yes,	I you we they	have.	No,	I you we they	haven't.
Has	he she			he she	has.		he she	hasn't.

C Complete the questions and answers. Use the project report in 1A.

1. ___Have___ the workers ___painted___ the cafeteria? ___Yes, they have.___
2. _____ the office manager _____ new lunch tables? _____
3. _____ the electrician _____ the air conditioning? _____
4. _____ the office manager _____ the _____ lunch program? _____
5. _____ the office manager _____ the center programs? _____
6. _____ they _____ the stove? _____

64 ☑ Use *Yes/No* questions in the present perfect to ask about personal, work, and academic experiences

---

D Work with a partner. Talk about class activities.

A: Have you completed exercise C?
B: Yes, I have.
A: Has Maria written the answers on the board?
B: No, she hasn't.

Need help?

Class activities
done the homework
read ___
talked to ___
learned ___

2 Learn the present perfect with *ever*, *already*, and *yet*

A Study the chart. Circle the correct word in the sentences below.

Present perfect with *ever*, *already*, and *yet*	Notes
A: Have you **ever** volunteered at an animal shelter? B: No, I haven't. *or* No, I've never volunteered before.	*ever* = at any time (not ever = never) Use *ever* in *Yes/No* and information questions and in negative statements.
A: Have you **already** served lunch to the seniors? B: Yes, I have. They've **already** eaten.	*already* = some time before now Use *already* in questions when you expect a *yes* answer and in affirmative statements.
A: Have you called the clinic **yet**? B: No, I haven't. I haven't found the number **yet**. I'll call tomorrow.	*yet* = at any time until now Use *yet* in *Yes/No* questions and in negative statements.

1. We haven't (already / ever) used that new copy machine.
2. Have you (yet / ever) visited city hall?
3. I haven't signed the paper (yet / ever).
4. Has Sam (already / yet) painted the kitchen?

B Match the questions and the answers. Then practice them with a partner

___d___ 1. Has Maria been to New York yet?
_____ 2. Has George already been to Miami?
_____ 3. Have they ever gone to Russia?
_____ 4. Have you ever been to Mexico?

a. No, I haven't ever been there.
b. Yes, he went twice last year.
c. No, they plan to go next year.
d. No, she's going next week.

C Get the form. Work with your class. Correct the sentences.

1. Marisol hasn't never volunteered. ___Marisol hasn't ever volunteered.___
2. I haven't done my homework already. I'll do it tonight. _____
3. Natasha went to the DMV yet. She got her license last week. _____
4. Michael has ever been to a job fair. Maybe he'll go next week. _____

Unit 5 Lesson 3 65

Learners work together to increase fluency and accuracy, using the grammar point to talk about themselves.

---

3 Grammar listening

🔊 Listen and circle the correct answer.

1. a. Mark has been to Los Angeles.
   b. Mark has never been to Los Angeles.
2. a. He's been to the recreation center three times.
   b. He's taken three classes at the recreation center.
3. a. She has gotten a new dog.
   b. She's planning to get a new dog.
4. a. Toshi has already started working.
   b. Roberto has already started working.
5. a. She's never written a letter to the school board.
   b. She wrote three letters to the school board.
6. a. He hasn't been to the job fair.
   b. He's been to the job fair twice.

Grammar listening exercises help learners identify the grammar point in spoken English.

4 Practice the present perfect

A Work with a partner. Complete the questions.

1. Have you ever been to _____? (place in your state)
2. Have you ever read _____? (name of a book)
3. Have you ever visited _____? (name of a community resource)
4. Have you eaten _____ yet today? (a meal you eat every day)
5. Have you spoken* to _____ yet today? (name of a person in your class)

*speak-spoke-spoken

B Work with another pair. Ask and answer the questions in 4A. Give as much information as possible.

A: Have you ever been to Miami?
B: No, I haven't. I'd like to go there some day.
A: Have you ever read "Romeo and Juliet"?
B: Yes, I have. But, I haven't read it in English yet.

Miami

TEST YOURSELF ✔
Close your book. Write 6 sentences using the information you learned about your classmates. Use the present perfect, *ever*, *already*, and *yet*.
Yana hasn't ever visited city hall.

66 Unit 5 Lesson 3

Test Yourself, at the end of every lesson, provides learners with ongoing self-assessment.

LESSON 4: **EVERYDAY CONVERSATION** provides learners with fluent, authentic conversations to increase familiarity with natural English.

Model dialogs feature authentic examples of everyday conversation.

Pronunciation activities focus on common areas of difficulty.

Listening activities build listening skills.

Real-life math exercises help learners practice language and math skills.

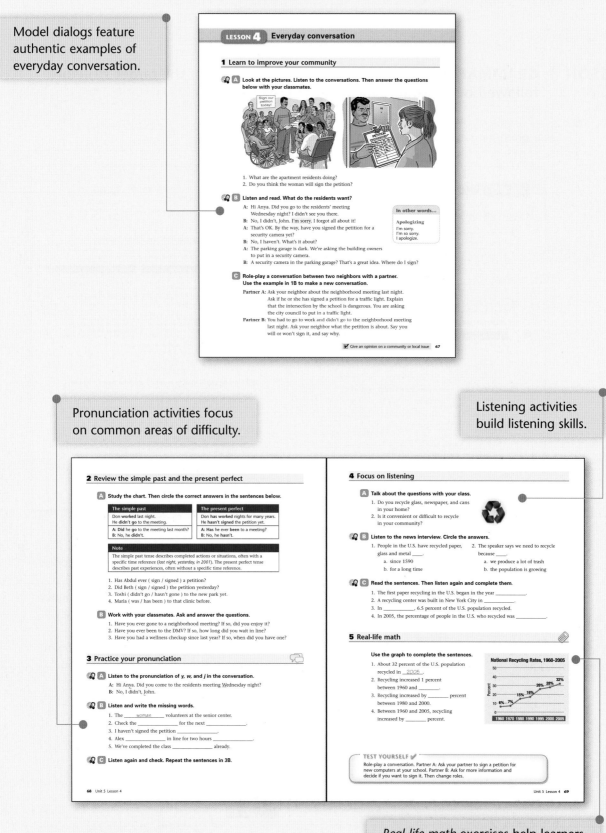

LESSON 5: **REAL-LIFE READING** develops essential reading skills and offers both life skill and pre-academic reading materials.

High-interest readings recycle vocabulary and grammar.

LESSON 5 Real-life reading

1 Get ready to read

A How do you help keep your neighborhood clean?

B Read the definitions.

environment: [noun] the world around you
natural resources: [noun] things produced by the earth that people use
pollution: [noun] things that make the environment dirty or dangerous
litter: [noun] paper, cans, or other trash that is left in a public place

C Look at the definitions in 1B and the picture in 2A. What do you think Earth Day is about? Circle the answer.

a. celebrating the earth's birthday
b. taking care of the earth
c. studying how the earth began

2 Read and respond

A Read the article.

Happy Earth Day!

Every year on April 22nd, people around the world celebrate Earth Day. On that day, people volunteer to pick up litter, clean up the environment, and plan ways to take care of the earth's natural resources.

Earth Day began in 1970 when a group of Americans became upset about pollution in the air and water. They worried that too much of the earth's water and air was unclean, unsafe, and unhealthy. So, they started an event to help people think about creating a cleaner, healthier, and safer earth. Now, over 174 countries around the world and hundreds of millions of people celebrate Earth Day each year.

Here are a few Earth Day success stories from communities around the world.

• Amelia, Ohio, USA: 300 volunteers collect more than 700 bags of litter, 46 tires, 1 refrigerator, and over 100 other items from the Ohio River.

China's 2005 Earth Day stamp made people think about protecting the environment.

• Toronto, Canada: hundreds of volunteers plant thousands of trees and bushes¹ in Rouge Park. Volunteers have planted more than 100,000 trees and bushes in the area since 1989.

• Vera Cruz, Brazil: a special bus visits 1,500 school students to teach students what they can do today to make the environment healthier for the future.

¹bush: a plant, smaller than a tree, usually 3–5 feet tall.

Source: www.earthday.net

70 ✓ Identify ways to reduce trash and protect the environment

---

B Listen and read the article again.

C Mark the statement T (true), F (false), or NI (no information).

___T__ 1. On Earth Day, people try to make a healthier, cleaner earth.
_____ 2. Five thousand people participated in the first Earth Day.
_____ 3. Over 174 countries celebrate Earth Day.
_____ 4. Volunteers in Canada have planted many trees since 1989.
_____ 5. In Brazil, students learn how to improve the environment for the future.

D Study the chart. Complete the sentences below.

> **Word Study: The prefix un-**
>
> The prefix *un-* means *not*. Add *un-* to the beginning of some adjectives to make its meaning negative.
> clean–unclean   People want a clean environment.
>   **Unclean** air and water can be dangerous.
>
> | healthy | unhealthy | happy | unhappy |
> | safe | unsafe | important | unimportant |

1. Many volunteers work on Earth Day to create a ___clean___ environment.
2. Some people worry that the earth's water is _____ and _____.
3. Earth Day began because people were _____ about pollution.
4. On Earth Day, it's _____ to work together to take care of the earth.

3 Talk it over

A Read the statistics. Think about the questions. Make notes about your answers.

1. Where does all that trash go?
2. What are some ways people can produce less trash?

> **Trash Statistics**
> The average American throws away 4.4 pounds of trash every day. That means a family of four throws away 6,424 pounds of trash every year.

B Talk about your answers with your classmates.

> **BRING IT TO LIFE**
> Look around your neighborhood. Write an idea for an environmental improvement you and your neighbors could make. Talk about your idea with your classmates.

Unit 5 Lesson 5 71

Word Study exercises help learners identify and use grammatical elements found in words in the readings.

REVIEW AND EXPAND includes additional grammar practice and communicative group tasks to ensure your learners' progress.

UNIT 5 Review and expand

1 Grammar

A Complete the sentences. Use the present perfect.

1. I ___haven't been___ to the new clinic yet. (be)
2. Tom _____ at the DMV for ten years. (work)
3. The students _____ their homework yet. (do)
4. We _____ already _____ a letter to the school board. (write)

B Complete the questions and answers. Use the verb in parentheses.

1. _Have_ they _planted_ the trees? (plant)   Yes, _they have_ .
2. _____ the mayor _____ his speech? (finish)   No, _____ .
3. _____ the celebration _____? (start)   Yes, _____ .
4. _____ you _____ Ramon? (see)   No, _____ .
5. _____ you _____ to city hall? (go)   No, _____ .

C Complete the sentences with *ever, already,* or *yet.*

1. Victor hasn't ___ever___ been to the new movie theater, but he plans to go there this weekend.
2. I haven't seen the new movie _____. I'm going to see it with Victor this weekend.
3. We've _____ bought the tickets. We bought them yesterday.
4. Min hasn't _____ gone with us before, but she's going with us tomorrow.
5. She hasn't bought tickets _____. She will do it in the morning.

D Complete the sentences with the past or present perfect. Use the verbs in parentheses.

1. I _____ have worked _____ here for two months. Last year, I _____ worked _____ in a clinic. (work)
2. Tom _____ home from work again yesterday. He _____ home for three weeks now. (stay)
3. We _____ many times about Tom's health. We _____ about it yesterday, too. (talk)
4. He _____ to the clinic several times. Last month I went with him. (go)

72 Review and expand

---

2 Group work

A Work with 2–3 classmates. Write a paragraph about the picture. Share your paragraph with the class.

Every year in April, the people in my neighborhood celebrate Community Clean-Up Day...

B Interview 3 classmates. Write their answers.

1. Have you ever helped with a neighborhood project? What?
2. Have you ever seen a problem in your neighborhood? What?
3. Have you ever gone to a town or neighborhood meeting? Why or why not?

C Talk about the answers with your class.

> **PROBLEM SOLVING**
>
> **A** Listen and read about Paulina.
>
> Paulina has lived in Lake City for two weeks. She wants to get involved in the community. She hasn't met many people yet. She hasn't had time to learn much about the city yet. She hasn't ever volunteered for community work before, but she thinks it might be a good opportunity to meet some nice people. Unfortunately, Paulina doesn't know where to begin. She doesn't know how or where to volunteer.
>
> **B** Work with your classmates. Answer the questions.
>
> 1. What is Paulina's problem?
> 2. What can Paulina do? Make a list of places she can go or call to get involved.

Unit 5 Review and expand 73

Grammar exercises provide a review for additional practice.

Problem solving tasks encourage learners to use critical thinking skills and meaningful discussion to find solutions to common problems.

Step Forward offers many different components.

Step-By-Step Lesson Plans

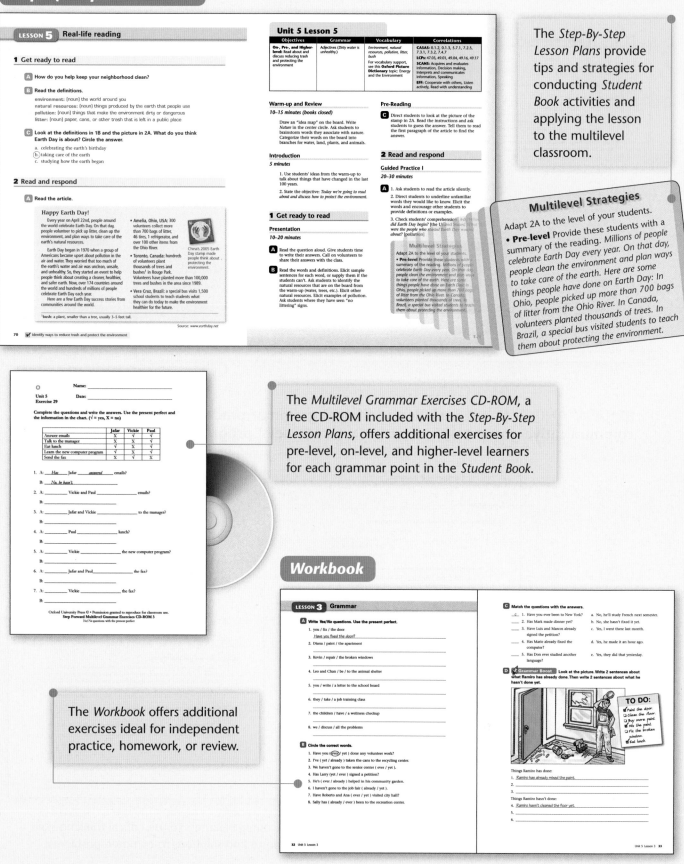

The *Step-By-Step Lesson Plans* provide tips and strategies for conducting *Student Book* activities and applying the lesson to the multilevel classroom.

Multilevel Strategies

Adapt 2A to the level of your students.

• **Pre-level** Provide these students with a summary of the reading. *Millions of people celebrate Earth Day every year. On that day, people clean the environment and plan ways to take care of the earth. Here are some things people have done on Earth Day: In Ohio, people picked up more than 700 bags of litter from the Ohio River. In Canada, volunteers planted thousands of trees. In Brazil, a special bus visited students to teach them about protecting the environment.*

The *Multilevel Grammar Exercises CD-ROM*, a free CD-ROM included with the *Step-By-Step Lesson Plans*, offers additional exercises for pre-level, on-level, and higher-level learners for each grammar point in the *Student Book*.

Workbook

The *Workbook* offers additional exercises ideal for independent practice, homework, or review.

Multilevel Activity Book

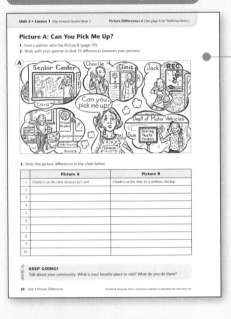

The *Multilevel Activity Book* features over 80 reproducible activities to complement the multilevel classroom through a variety of pair, small group, and whole-class activities.

Audio Program

Audio CDs and Cassettes feature the listening exercises from the *Student Book* as well as conversations, pronunciation, and readings.

Test Generator

ExamView®
Assessment Suite

The *Test Generator CD-ROM with ExamView® Assessment Suite* offers hundreds of test items for each *Student Book*. Teachers can print out ready-made tests or create their own tests.

Professional Development

Professional Development Task 8

Imagine you want your learners to practice listening carefully during a group task. One behavior you could demonstrate would be leaning forward. Make a list of at least three other behaviors or expressions that careful listeners use.

The *Professional Development Program* offers instructors research-based teaching strategies and activities for single- and multilevel classes, plus Professional Development Tasks like this one.

The First Step

Let's get started

1 Get to know your classmates

STUDENT AUDIO

A **Listen and repeat. Underline 1 example of the present, past, and future in the conversation.**

A: Hello. I'm Chen.

B: Hi, Chen. I'm Maria. It's great to meet you. Is this your first English class?

A: No. I studied with Mr. Hopkins last year. How about you?

B: This is my first class, and I'm going to study hard. I really want to improve my pronunciation.

B **Practice the conversation with 5 classmates. Use your own information.**

C **Write the first names of the classmates you met.**

2 Alphabetize a list

A **Read the names of Chen's classmates. Mark the sentences T (true) or F (false).**

_____ 1. All the names end with a capital letter.

_____ 2. These students are all in the same class.

_____ 3. The students' names are in alphabetical order.

B **Work with your classmates. Make a list of all the students in your class. Put the list in alphabetical order.**

Chen's Classmates

Ali	Nami
Diana	Paulina
Maki	Ramiro
Maria	Wen
Miguel	

3 Review parts of speech

A **Read the chart. Then write the part of speech next to the words below. Use the abbreviations from the chart.**

Four Important Parts of Speech		
Parts of speech	Answer the questions	Examples
A **noun** (n.) names a person, place, thing, or idea. Specific names of people, places, or things begin with a capital letter.	Who? What? Where?	<u>Alma</u> and <u>Tom</u> are classmates. They study <u>English</u> at <u>Rose Adult School</u>.
An **adjective** (adj.) describes a noun. Adjectives often come before a noun.	Which one? What kind?	This is Alma's <u>first</u> class. It's an <u>English</u> class.
A **verb** (v.) shows an action or a state of being. The form of the verb changes to show the time (tense) of the action.	What's happening? What happened? What will happen?	Tom <u>is studying</u>. She <u>studied</u> last year. They <u>will study</u> later.
An **adverb** (adv.) describes a verb, adjective, or other adverb. Many adverbs end in -ly.	How? How often?	Alma learns <u>quickly</u>. She <u>always</u> does her homework.

1. instructor <u>n.</u>   4. carefully ____   7. excellent ____

2. learn ____   5. begin ____   8. usually ____

3. new ____   6. New York ____   9. improve ____

B **Work with a partner. Use the prepositions below to talk about the picture in 1A.**

on   in   next to   above   below   in front of   behind

A: *The clock is above the board.*
B: *The board is below the clock.*

C **Work with your classmates. Write as many sentences as you can about your classroom.**

The teacher writes quickly.
A large dictionary is next to the computer.

FOCUS ON
- study skills and habits
- writing a journal entry
- present and past verb forms
- career plans
- identifying library services

LESSON 1   Vocabulary

1 Learn study skills and habits vocabulary

A   **Talk about the questions with your class.**

1. What do you do to study English?
2. Are good study skills and habits more important for children or for adults?

B   **Work with your classmates. Match the words with the pictures.**

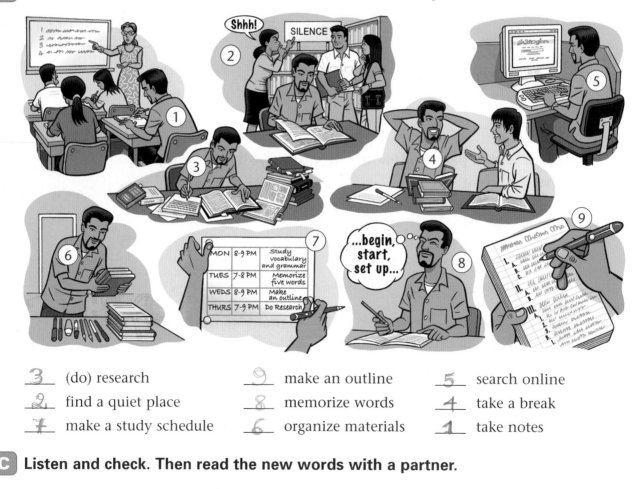

_3_ (do) research	_9_ make an outline	_5_ search online
_2_ find a quiet place	_8_ memorize words	_4_ take a break
_7_ make a study schedule	_6_ organize materials	_1_ take notes

C   **Listen and check. Then read the new words with a partner.**

D   **Work with a partner. Write other study words you know. Check your words in a dictionary.**

E Work with a partner. Practice the conversation. Use the pictures in 1B.

A: What do you do when you study at home?

B: Sometimes I make an outline. Sometimes I memorize words.

2 Learn about the educational system

A Look at the pictures. Then complete the brochure with the schools.

Schools in the U.S.

elementary school

adult school

middle school

community college

high school

university

In the United States, most children begin kindergarten at age five. They usually attend _elementary school_ 1 from kindergarten to fifth grade. From grades six to eight, kids often go to _____. From there, they 2 go on to _____, which is 3 usually grades nine to twelve, and receive their diploma.

Adults can attend an _____ 4 with or without a high-school diploma. Adults who attend a _____ 5 or a _____ must have a 6 high-school diploma or a GED (general educational development certificate).

B Work with a partner. Practice the conversation. Use the words in 2A.

A: Who can attend elementary school?

B: Children in kindergarten to fifth grade.

C Talk about the questions with your class.

1. Is it easier for adults or for children to memorize things? Why?
2. Which study skills are most difficult for adult students?

TEST YOURSELF ✔

Close your book. Work with a partner. Make a list of as many new words from the lesson as you can. Alphabetize your list.

1 Read a journal entry

A **Look at the picture. Talk about the questions with your class.**

1. What are the students doing?
2. How do they feel?

 B **Listen and read the journal entry.**

Monday, September 10
The first day of English class was very interesting. Our teacher asked us to practice speaking English in groups. I was nervous at first. I usually like to work alone. I didn't want to make a mistake and feel embarrassed, but everything was fine in the end.
Our first assignment was to tell the group why we were studying English. I had a lot to say, but I was worried about my pronunciation. My group had four students. Before we began, Kim whispered to me that she was nervous. I said, "Me too." I guess Maria heard us because she said, "Me three." Then Ali said, "Me four." We all laughed a lot. After that, we practiced a lot of English. I want to work in groups again tomorrow.

C **Check your understanding. Circle _a_ or _b_.**

1. The teacher wanted the students to ____.
   a. work alone
   b. work in groups

2. The students were nervous because ____.
   a. it was fun and they laughed
   b. they didn't want to make a mistake

3. The students talked about ____.
   a. their reasons for studying English
   b. their first day of English class

4. In the end, the students ____.
   a. practiced a lot of English
   b. were very quiet

✔ Write a journal entry about a class experience

2 Write a journal entry

A **Talk about the questions with your class.**

1. Do you like to study alone or with other people?
2. What are some reasons people get nervous in class?

B **Write a journal entry in your notebook. Use the model in 1B and the questions below to help you.**

Paragraph 1:
What did you think about your first day of English class?
What assignments did your teacher give you?
How did you feel about that?

Paragraph 2:
What was the first assignment?
How did you feel about it?
Would you like to do this assignment again in the future?

> **Need help?**
>
> **Assignments**
> introduce ourselves
> meet our classmates
> give a presentation
> write about ourselves
> talk about our goals

(Day), (Date)

The first day of English class was very exciting.

Our teacher asked us to introduce ourselves.

C **Use the checklist to edit your writing. Check (✔) the true sentences.**

Editing checklist	
1. I wrote about my first day of English class.	
2. I wrote about one class activity.	
3. I used capital letters for the first letters of the day and date.	
4. I wrote my story in the past tense.	

D **Exchange journal entries with a partner. Read and comment on your partner's work.**

1. Point out one sentence that you think is very interesting.
2. Ask your partner a question about his or her first day of class.

TEST YOURSELF ✔

Write a new journal entry in your notebook about another day of class.
What did you do? How did you feel about the activity?

1 Review present and past verb forms

A Read the paragraph and the notebook page. What classes does this student take?

I write my assignments in a notebook. In my English class we learn five new words every day. I always write and memorize them. On Monday night I wrote my journal entry. On Tuesday night I answered the questions for my computer class. Today is Wednesday. I'm studying at the library now. I'm memorizing my new words for the day.

Homework Assignments:

Date: Mon. 9/26   Class: English

1. Learn 5 new words

2. Write journal entry – due Wed.

Date: Tue. 9/27   Class: Computers

Chapter 2: questions p. 24 – due Thurs.

Date: Wed. 9/28   Class: English

Learn 5 new words

B Study the charts. Underline 1 example of each verb form in the paragraph above.

Simple present			
I learn	new words every day.	I don't learn	new words every day.
He learns		He doesn't learn	

Present continuous			
I'm learning	new words now.	I'm not learning	new words now.
He's learning		He isn't learning	

Simple past			
I learned	new words yesterday.	I didn't learn	new words yesterday.
He learned		He didn't learn	

C Complete the sentences. Use the verbs in parentheses.

1. Blanca _____is not taking_____ notes in her English class now. (not take)

2. Estelle _____ a journal entry yesterday. (write)

3. Jerry always _____ the questions in class. (answer)

4. They _____ a test now. (take)

5. Yesterday, we _____ about different kinds of schools. (learn)

6. We _____ in groups yesterday. (not work)

D **Get the form. Work with your class. Correct the sentences.**

1. Paulo doesn't taking notes now.   _Paulo isn't taking notes now._
2. Yan memorize words every day.   _____
3. We is taking a break now.   _____
4. Mia search online yesterday.   _____
5. I don't take notes yesterday.   _____
6. They do research now.   _____

2 Review present and past *Yes/No* question forms

A **Study the charts. Then circle the correct words below.**

YES/NO QUESTIONS AND ANSWERS

Simple present	Present continuous	Simple past

A: Do you study every day?
 B: Yes, I do. OR
    No, I don't.
	A: Are you studying now?
	 B: Yes, I am. OR
	    No, I'm not.
		A: Did you study yesterday?
		 B: Yes, I did. OR
		    No, I didn't.

A: Does she study every day?
 B: Yes, she does. OR
    No, she doesn't.
	A: Is she studying now?
	 B: Yes, she is. OR
	    No, she isn't.
		A: Did she study yesterday?
		 B: Yes, she did. OR
		    No, she didn't.

1. **A:** (Does / Did) the students do their homework?

   B: Yes, they (do / did).

2. **A:** (Are / Is) they helping each other?

   B: Yes, they (are / do).

3. **A:** (Do / Does) you like to work in a group?

   B: Yes, I (am / do).

4. **A:** (Does / Is) Kim like to work alone?

   B: No, she (doesn't / isn't).

B **Write your answers to the questions. Then ask and answer the questions with a partner.**

1. Did you go to the library yesterday?   _____
2. Are you listening to music now?   _____
3. Do you always speak English in class?   _____
4. Did you learn any new words today?   _____
5. Are you studying in the library now?   _____
6. Do you make a study schedule?   _____

3 Grammar listening

🎧 **Listen to the sentences. Check (✔) *Simple present*, *Present continuous*, or *Simple past*.**

	Simple present	Present continuous	Simple past
1.		✔	
2.			
3.			
4.			
5.			
6.			

4 Practice present and past verb forms

A **Think about your answers to these questions.**

1. What is something you did for fun ten years ago?
2. What is something you do for fun on the weekends?
3. Are you having fun right now?

B **Work with a partner. Ask and answer the questions in 4A.**

A: *What is something you did for fun ten years ago?*
B: *I took dance lessons.*
A: *What is something you do for fun on the weekends?*
B: *I go to the movies.*
A: *Are you having fun right now?*
B: *Yes, I am.*

C **Talk about your answers with the class.**

Rita took dance lessons ten years ago.
She goes to the movies on the weekends.
She's having fun in class right now.

TEST YOURSELF ✔

Close your book. Write 3 complete sentences about yourself. Use the simple past, the simple present, and the present continuous.
   I played baseball ten years ago.

1 Learn to talk about careers

STUDENT AUDIO **A** **Look at the pictures. Listen to the conversations. Then answer the questions below with your classmates.**

1. What did Tara do last year?
2. Where does Carlos work now?

STUDENT AUDIO **B** **Listen and read. What career does the counselor suggest?**

Counselor:	What kind of career are you thinking about?
Student:	I'm just not sure. There are so many choices.
Counselor:	What kinds of things do you like to do?
Student:	Well, I volunteered at a hospital last year and I enjoyed that. I'm studying biology now. I like my class and I'm doing well.
Counselor:	You should think about a career in health care. It's a good field and it's growing quickly.

> **In other words...**
>
> **Saying you're not sure**
> I'm just not sure.
> I really don't know.
> It's hard to say.

C **Role-play a career conversation with a partner. Use the example in 1B to make a new conversation.**

Partner A: You're the school counselor. Ask the student about career plans and things he or she likes to do. Listen. Then suggest a career in computer arts.

Partner B: You're a student. You are talking to your school counselor. You don't know which career is right for you. You drew some pictures for the school paper last year and you are taking a computer class now.

☑ Respond to questions about career choices and interests   **11**

2 Learn about adjectives and adverbs

A Study the charts. Then circle the correct words below.

Adjectives	
quick	We took a **quick** break.
careful	He's a **careful** worker.
hard	It's **hard** work.
good	She got **good** grades in math.

Adverbs	
quickly	We finished the lesson **quickly**.
carefully	He works **carefully**.
hard	They work **hard**.
well	She did **well** in math.

Notes
• Adjectives describe nouns. We took a **quick** break.
• Adverbs often give more information about the verb in a sentence. We finished the lesson **quickly**.
• Most adverbs end in *-ly*, but some adjectives and adverbs have the same form (*hard-hard*).
• Some adjectives and adverbs are irregular (*good-well*).

1. The counselor spoke (clear / (clearly)) about careers.

2. There are so many kinds of careers. It isn't an (easy / easily) choice.

3. Some people know what they want and can decide (quick / quickly).

4. People who do research on careers usually find (good / well) jobs.

B Complete the sentences with an adjective or adverb.

1. I memorize words _____quickly_____.

2. I am a _____ worker.

3. I read the assignment _____.

4. I take notes _____ in class.

5. I usually get _____ grades on my tests.

3 Practice your pronunciation

A Listen to the pronunciation of the *sh, ch,* and *j* sounds in these sentences.

1. I'm just not <u>sure</u>.

2. There are so many <u>ch</u>oices.

3. I en<u>j</u>oyed that.

4. You <u>sh</u>ould think about it.

B Listen to the words in the chart. Underline the letter(s) in each word that make the *sh, ch,* or *j* sounds.

"sh"		"ch"		"j"	
1. <u>sh</u>ow	3. sugar	5. change	7. choose	9. Joe	11. jar
2. cash	4. sure	6. catch	8. much	10. object	12. enjoy

C Work with a partner. Partner A: Say a word from the chart. Partner B: Point to the word you hear. Then change roles.

4 Focus on listening

A **Talk about the questions with your class.**

1. Why is education important for a career?
2. In addition to education, what else is important for a career?

B **Listen to the story. Mark the sentences T (true) or F (false).**

_____ 1. At Freemont, students study and prepare for their careers at the same time.

_____ 2. Freemont students do not study the usual subjects like math and science.

_____ 3. Both Marie and Malik found careers they love.

C **Listen again. Check (✔) _Marie_ or _Malik_.**

	Marie	Malik
1. Who studied banking?	✔	
2. Who likes making things?		✓
3. Who came to the U.S. from Jamaica?	✓	
4. Who was offered a job at a bank?	✓	
5. Who helped build an apartment building?		✓
6. Who is taking classes in the evening?		✓

Marie

Malik

5 Real-life math

Read the information and do the math problems. Label the chart with the correct percentages. Then compare your answers with the class.

A survey asked 8,000 people about their careers. Here's what they said:

1,680 people: "I have the career I started in."

_1,680 ÷ 8,000 = .21 or 21%_

2,400 people: "I changed careers once."

_____ ÷ _____ = _____ or _____%

3,920 people: "I changed careers two or more times."

_____ ÷ _____ = _____ or _____%

How many times have you changed your career?

21% have the career they started in

_____ changed careers two or more times

_____ changed careers once

- - - TEST YOURSELF ✔ - - -

Role-play a conversation about career choices. Partner A: You are a school counselor. Ask your partner about his or her interests. Suggest a career. Partner B: Respond. Then change roles.

1 Get ready to read

 A **Is there a library in your neighborhood? How often do you go there?**

B **Read the definitions.**

check out: (verb) to take, or borrow, for a period of time and then return
librarian: (noun) a person who works in or is in charge of a library

C **Look at the title and the picture in the newspaper advice column in 2A. Answer the questions.**

1. Who is the person in the picture?
2. What does she do?

2 Read and respond

 A **Read the advice column.**

ASK ALLISON

Dear Allison,
    I usually listen to English on the radio in my car. Unfortunately, my car isn't running. I'm driving my brother's car. The radio is broken, so it only has a cassette player. I'm so bored in the car now! What should I do?
—Sad Student

Dear Sad Student,
    Audio books are books recorded on cassettes or CDs. They're a great way to listen to English. You can check them out from the library for free.

Dear Allison,
    I need to research career choices. I want to search for jobs online, but I don't have a computer. What should I do?
—Looking in Laredo

Dear Laredo,
    Don't worry. Most libraries have computers. Get a library card— it's free— and you can be online in no time. Many libraries even let you sign up for the computer in advance so you don't wait in line.

Dear Allison,
    My son is in high school. His homework is very difficult. I try to help him, but sometimes it's over my head.[1] Please help.
—Frustrated Father
P.S. I dislike computers. Please don't tell me to use one!

Dear Frustrated,
    Don't worry! Your library can help. Many libraries have free homework help centers. Go to the library with your son and ask a librarian for advice.

---

[1]over (my) head: too difficult to understand

 ✔ Identify and match library services with needs

B Listen and read the advice column again.

C Mark the sentences T (true), F (false), or NI (no information).

    <u>T</u> 1. You can listen to audio books with a cassette player.

    <u>   </u> 2. Sometimes you can sign up for a computer at the library.

    <u>   </u> 3. Library cards don't cost any money.

    <u>   </u> 4. You can go online at the library.

    <u>   </u> 5. You can pay for help with homework at the library.

    <u>   </u> 6. A librarian can help you do homework.

D Study the chart. Circle the correct words below.

Word Study: The prefix -dis

The prefix *dis-* means "not". Add *dis-* to the beginning of some verbs and adjectives to change their meaning.

dis + like = dislike   Sam **likes** books but he **dislikes** computers.

organized	disorganized	obey	disobey
agree	disagree	honest	dishonest

---

1. A person who lies, or doesn't tell the truth is ((dishonest) / disorganized).

2. Jack and I have different opinions. We (agree / disagree).

3. The librarian keeps the books in order. She's very (organized / disorganized).

4. Mark and Bill talk loudly in the library. They (obey / disobey) the rules.

5. Ben said that he broke the window. He's a very (honest / dishonest) boy.

6. Mel (likes / dislikes) tests because he gets very nervous.

3 Talk it over

A Think about the questions. Make notes about your answers.

1. What kinds of things do people read every day? Name at least five.

2. What was the last thing you read outside of class? What do you like to read?

3. Should libraries buy more computers or more books? Why?

B Talk about the answers with your classmates.

BRING IT TO LIFE

Visit a local library. Check out a book or an audio book and bring it to class.
If you don't have a library card, get an application form and bring it to class.

---

1 Grammar

A Complete the sentences with the correct forms of the verbs in parentheses.

1. (work) Sometimes in class, we _____work_____ in pairs. Right now,
   I'm working_____ alone. Last week, we _____ in groups.
2. (listen) Sam _____ to the radio right now. He usually
   _____ to music in the car,
   but yesterday he _____ to the news.
3. (memorize) Ivan always _____ new words in English. Last night,
   Ivan _____ five new words. Now, he _____
   three more words.

B Unscramble the questions. Write short answers with your own information.

1. do / Did / night / you / research / last
   A: Did you do research last night?
   B: Yes, I did. (or No, I didn't.)

2. computers / you / studying / Are
   A: _____
   B: _____

3. take / you / notes / in / Do / class
   A: _____
   B: _____

4. make / a study schedule / you / Do
   A: _____
   B: _____

C Complete the sentences. Use the correct adjective or adverb.

1. We answered the questions <u>easily</u>. The answers were _____easy_____.
2. Mike is <u>careful</u>. He works _____.
3. It's a <u>good</u> picture. You draw _____.
4. Your answer was _____. You speak <u>clearly</u>.

D Complete the paragraph with the correct form of the verbs in parentheses.

Right now, I _'m listening_____ (listen) to the radio and
I _____ (write) in my journal. Today was my second class.
We _____ (not work) in groups today. We _____ (work)
in pairs. I _____ (practice) with Maria today and we
_____ (have) a lot of fun. Maria always _____ (speak)
slowly and clearly. It's easy to understand her. We _____ (learn) a lot
together today.

2 Group work

A Work with 2–3 classmates. Write a paragraph about the picture. Share your paragraph with the class.

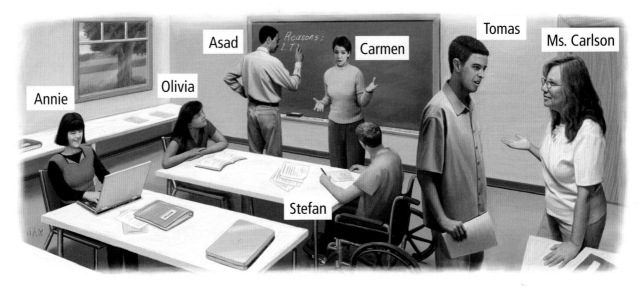

Annie is searching online. Tomas is talking to Ms. Carlson...

B Interview 3 classmates. Write their answers.

1. Where do you like to study? Why?
2. Are you taking other classes in school?
3. Where did you learn English before?

Mei
1. the library—likes quiet places
2. yes—a computer class
3. In China

C Talk about the answers with your class.

PROBLEM SOLVING

A Listen and read about Teresa.

    Teresa is a new student in an English class at Mid-City School. The class started three weeks ago, but today is Teresa's first day. She likes the class and the teacher very much, but she's a little worried about making friends. The students in the class already know each other very well. Some even studied together last year. Teresa doesn't like being the only new student in the class. All the other students are having fun together. Teresa feels alone.

B Work with your classmates. Answer the questions.

1. What is Teresa's problem?
2. What should Teresa do? Think of 2 or 3 solutions to her problem.

UNIT 2

Ready for Fun

FOCUS ON
- recreation
- email invitations
- the future
- making plans with friends
- health benefits of parks

LESSON 1 Vocabulary

1 Learn recreation vocabulary

A Talk about the questions with your class.

1. Where do you go to have fun?
2. What are some of your favorite recreational activities?

B Work with your classmates. Match the words with the picture.

_3_	amusement park	_5_	gym	_9_	swimming pool
_7_	bowling alley	_4_	nightclub	_2_	theater
_1_	farmers' market	_8_	playground	_6_	zoo

C Listen and check. Then read the new words with a partner.

D Work with a partner. Write other recreation words you know. Check your words in a dictionary.

E **Work with a partner. Practice the conversation. Use the picture in 1B.**

A: Do you go to the farmers' market?

B: Yes, I go there once a month.

A: Do you go to the zoo?

B: No, I never go there.

2 Learn to describe places and events

A **Look at the pictures. Match the places and the adjectives below.**

It's **exciting**!

It's **loud**!

It's **entertaining**.

It's **crowded**.

It's **relaxing**.

It's **boring**.

__e__ 1. bowling at the bowling alley   a. exciting

____ 2. exercising at the gym   b. relaxing

____ 3. riding a roller coaster   c. entertaining

____ 4. seeing a play   d. crowded

____ 5. dancing in a nightclub   e. loud

____ 6. people watching at the park   f. boring

B **Work with a partner. Practice the conversation. Use the words in 2A.**

A: *What are they doing?*

B: *They're riding a roller coaster.*

A: *Is it fun?*

B: *Yes. It's exciting.*

C **Talk about the questions with your class.**

1. Do you prefer relaxing or exciting activities? Why?
2. Which activities do you think are entertaining? Which are boring?

TEST YOURSELF ✔

Close your book. Work with a partner. Make a list of as many new words from the lesson as you can. Alphabetize your list.

1 Read an email invitation

A Look at the flyer. Talk about the questions with your class.

1. What are some fun and inexpensive places to visit in your community?
2. Do you like to go places with a group of friends, just one friend, or alone?

STUDENT
AUDIO

B Listen and read the email.

> **Writer's note**
>
> In a letter or email, use a comma (,) after the greeting and the closing.

> ✉ **Email - Message (Plain Text)**
>
> | Reply | Reply to All | Forward | Print | Save | Delete | Previous | Next |
>
> From: Tanya Sokolov
> To: Meera Varma
> Subject: Weekend Plans
>
> Hi Meera,
>
> How are you? How was your English class this week? My class was fine, but I'm glad it's Friday. I'm ready to have some fun.
>
> Would you like to get together this weekend? How about tomorrow? I'm going to go to Recreation Park around noon to go swimming. We could go together. If you are busy, we could do something on Sunday. On Sunday, I'm going to go out to dinner with my sister. Then we're going to go bowling. Would you like to come with us? Think about it. I'll call you tonight.
>
> Talk to you soon,
> Tanya

C Check your understanding. Mark the statements T (true), F (false), or NI (no information).

_F_ 1. Tanya and Meera are in the same English class.

____ 2. Tanya had a test in class today.

____ 3. Tanya wants to go swimming at 12:00 on Saturday.

____ 4. She also wants to go bowling on Saturday.

2 Write an email invitation

A **Talk about the questions with your class.**

1. Where would you like to go this weekend?
2. Who could you invite to go with you?

B **Write an email. Invite someone to go out with you. Use the model in 1B and the questions in 2A to help you.**

✉ **Email - Message (Plain Text)**

Reply | Reply to All | Forward | Print | Save | Delete | Previous | Next

From: _____
To: _____
Subject: _____

Hi _____

    How are you? How was _____ this week? My _____ was fine, but I'm glad it's Friday. I'm ready to _____.

    Would you like to _____ this weekend? How about _____?

I'm going to go to _____

_____ Think about it. I'll call

you _____.

_____

Need Help?

Would you like to...
get together?
go out?
do something?
hang out?

C **Use the checklist to edit your writing. Check (✔) the true sentences.**

Editing checklist	
1. I wrote a subject line to tell the person what the email is about.	
2. I wrote the name of the place that I'm going to and the time.	
3. I invited someone to go out with me this weekend.	
4. I used a comma after the greeting and closing in my email.	

D **Exchange emails with a partner. Read and comment on your partner's work.**

1. Point out one sentence that you think is very interesting.
2. Ask your partner a question about his or her weekend plans.

TEST YOURSELF ✔

Write a new email. Use a computer if possible. Invite a classmate to go out with you this weekend. Give information about the time, the day, and the place you want to go.

1 Review *be going to* and *will*

A Read the conversation. Where are they going to go?

> **Sam:** What are you going to do tomorrow?
> **Ken:** I'm going to study all day.
> **Sam:** Let's go to the pool. We'll be home by 3:00. We won't stay late. I promise!
> **Ken:** Well, I guess I can study tomorrow night. OK, I'll go.
> **Sam:** Great! I'll see you tomorrow.

B Study the chart. Underline the 4 examples of *will* and circle the 2 examples of *be going to* in the conversation above.

The future with *be going to* and *will*	Notes
I'm **going to** study all day. I'm **not going to** go out.	• Use *be going to* to talk about future plans. • Use *will* for promises.
We'**ll** be home by 3:00. We **won't** stay late.	

C Complete the conversations with the correct forms of *be going to* or *will*. Use the words in parentheses to help you.

1. **A:** When _____*are*_____ we _____*going to*_____ go shopping this weekend? (plan)

   B: I don't know. I _'ll_____ call you when I get up. (promise)

   A: What time _____ you _____ get up? (plan)

   B: I _____ get up early tomorrow. (plan)

   I _____ call you at 9:15. (promise)

2. **A:** When _____ you _____ clean the garage? (plan)

   B: I _____ clean it soon. (plan)

   A: When?

   B: I _____ clean it before I go out tonight. (promise)

   A: Are you sure?

   B: Yes, I won't forget. I _____ clean it before I go out. (promise)

3. **A:** _____ you _____ go to work tomorrow? (plan)

   B: No, I'm not. I _____ go to an amusement park. (plan)

   A: Have fun. I _____ talk to you next week. (promise)

D **Get the form. Work with your class. Correct the sentences.**

1. I will to call you later today.   _I will call you later today._
2. We going to go to class next week.   _____
3. She are going to work tomorrow.   _____
4. They're study tonight.   _____

2 Learn about future predictions

A **Study the chart. Then complete the predictions below with _will_. Use the verbs in parentheses.**

Predictions with _will_
Ten years from now, our city **will have** better parks and community centers. There **will be** more playgrounds and swimming pools in the future.

Note
Use _think_ or _probably_ with _will_ to make predictions about the future. I **think** they'**ll build** a new baseball stadium next to the park. They'**ll probably start** next year.

1. There _____will be_____ many positive changes in our city next year. (be)
2. The city _____ a new park in our neighborhood. (build)
3. The new park _____ probably _____ nice. (be)
4. I think my neighbors and I _____ the new park very much. (enjoy)
5. The city _____ new buses. (buy)
6. The new buses _____ less pollution. (cause)

B **Answer the questions. Use your own information. Then ask and answer the questions with a partner.**

1. What will you do for fun next weekend?

   _____

2. What do you think the weather will be like next week?

   _____

3. Will you take a vacation next year?

   _____

4. Where do you think you will work five years from now?

   _____

5. Where will you live ten years from now?

   _____

3 Grammar listening

🎧 **Listen to the sentences. Check (✔)** *Plan, Promise,* **or** *Prediction.*

	Plan	Promise	Prediction
1.	✔		
2.			
3.			
4.			
5.			
6.			

4 Practice future predictions

A **Think about the year 2075. Think about your answers to these questions.**

1. Do you think the president of the United States will be a man or a woman?
2. What kind of recreation do you think will be popular?
3. Do you think people will stay home more or go out more?
4. Do you think most people will live in houses or apartments?

B **Work with a partner. Ask and answer the questions in 4A.**

A: *Do you think the president will be a man or a woman in 2075?*
B: *I think the president will be a woman.*

C **Write 3 more questions about the future with your partner. Ask and answer the questions with another pair of students.**

A: *What do you think will be the biggest city in the world in 50 years?*
B: *I think the biggest city will be Beijing.*

TEST YOURSELF ✔

Close your book. Write about your future. Write 2 sentences about your plans, 2 prediction sentences, and 2 promises. Use *will* or *be going to.*

---

1 Learn to talk about preferences

STUDENT AUDIO 🎧 **A** **Look at the pictures. Listen to the conversations. Then answer the questions below with your classmates.**

1. What are the man and woman going to do on Wednesday night?
2. When will they decide what to do on Friday night?

STUDENT AUDIO 🎧 **B** **Listen and read. What are the people going to do on Saturday?**

A: Would you like to get together this Saturday?

B: Sure. What would you like to do?

A: Well, on Saturday night there's a soccer match at the stadium or there's a free concert in the park. Take your pick.

B: I think I'd rather go to the concert. Should I pick you up at 7:00?

A: Let's play it by ear*. I'll call you on Friday night.

B: Sounds good.

*Idiom note: play it by ear = to wait and decide later

> **In other words...**
>
> **Giving someone a choice**
> Take your pick.
> It's up to you.
> Your choice.

C **Role-play a conversation about preferences with a partner. Use the example in 1B to make a new conversation.**

Partner A: Ask your friend to get together on Saturday. There's a new movie opening on Saturday or a party at the community center.

Partner B: Your friend asks you to get together on Saturday. Listen to your friend's ideas. You'd rather go to the party. You can pick your friend up at 2:00.

2 Learn to ask about and express preferences

A Study the chart. Complete the sentences below with *would rather*.

Expressing preferences with *would rather* + verb	Note
A: Would you **rather see** a movie or a play? **B: I would rather see** a movie. **A: Would** they **rather stay home** or **go out**? **B:** I think they**'d rather go out**.	Use *would rather* + verb to talk about preferences, or what you want to do.

1. **A:** _____ you _____ buy a car or a motorcycle?

   B: I _____ buy a car.

2. **A:** _____ Sara _____ study or go dancing?

   B: She _____ study because she has a big test tomorrow.

B Work with a partner. Ask and answer the questions in the chart. Write your partner's preferences.

Would you rather...	My partner's preference
watch a movie or a sports event?	
stay home or go dancing?	
read a book or watch TV?	
eat Chinese food or Italian food?	

C Take a class poll. Talk about the answers with the class.

Twenty-five students would rather watch a movie. Four would rather watch a sports event.

3 Practice your pronunciation

A Listen to the pronunciation of the *j* and *ch* sounds in these sentences.

"j"
1. Would ^ you like to get together?

"ch"
2. I'll meet ^ you in the park.

B Listen to the sentences. Underline the letters that combine to make the *j* or *ch* sounds.

1. Could you call me tomorrow?
2. I'll get you two tickets for the game.
3. Would you like to go out?
4. What did you do last Saturday night?
5. What should you do when you're sick?
6. I bought you a present.

C Read the sentences with a partner. Then listen again and check.

4 Focus on listening

A Talk about the questions with your class.

1. Is there a park or stadium in your community where large public events take place?
2. Would you rather go to a large public event or have a quiet evening at home?

B Read the questions. Listen to the recorded message. Then write the answers.

1. What holiday will Greenville celebrate this weekend? _____Independant day_
2. How many events are happening this weekend? _____
3. Are there more events in the evening or during the day? _____

C Listen again and complete the flyer.

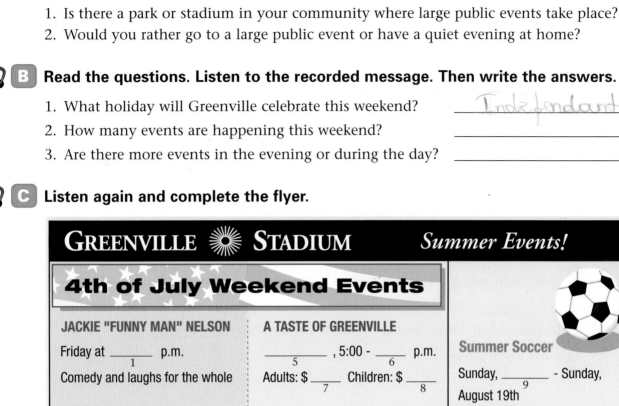

GREENVILLE ✷ STADIUM *Summer Events!*

4th of July Weekend Events

JACKIE "FUNNY MAN" NELSON

Friday at ___1___ p.m.

Comedy and laughs for the whole

___2___ .

Adults: $___3___ Children: $___4___

A TASTE OF GREENVILLE

___5___ , 5:00 - ___6___ p.m.

Adults: $___7___ Children: $___8___

Summer Soccer

Sunday, ___9___ - Sunday, August 19th

8 weeks of soccer

$___10___ per ___11___

5 Real-life math

Read about the Adams family and answer the question.

The Adams family is going to the *Taste of Greenville* festival at the stadium. Mr. and Mrs. Adams have a teenage daughter, a seven-year-old son, and a four-year-old daughter. Mrs. Adams gives the woman at the ticket counter $40.00 for tickets for all the family members. How much change will she receive? _____

TASTE OF GREENVILLE WELCOMES YOU

Adults: $9.00
Children 6 – 12: $5.00
Children under 5: free

TEST YOURSELF ✔

Role-play a conversation about an event. Look at the flyer in 4C. Partner A: Invite a friend to their choice of two events at Greenville Stadium this week.
Partner B: Say which event you'd rather go to. Then change roles.

1 Get ready to read

A **Why are neighborhood parks important?**

B **Read the definitions.**

immune system: (noun) the parts of the body that fight or prevent illness
outdoors: (noun) outside, for example, a park or a beach
strengthen: (verb) to make something stronger
stress: (noun) worry caused by difficulties in life

C **Scan* the article in 2A for numbers. Complete the sentences.**

1. Every mile you walk or run can add _____ minutes to your life.

2. _____ % of Americans often have a high stress level.

3. In Cincinnati, Ohio, teenage crime went down by _____%.

*scan = to look at something quickly to find specific information

2 Read and respond

A **Read the article.**

The Good Life: A Walk in the Park

Studies show that people are happier and healthier when they spend time outdoors. For example, if you're getting a cold, take a walk in the park. It can help strengthen your immune system for 48 hours. Some studies show that when you exercise, you add 21 minutes to your life for every mile you walk or run. Parks are an excellent place to get healthy and stay healthy for free.

Parks are important for more than just physical health. They can also lower stress. Jobs, money, and other things cause stress. 89% of Americans say their lives are too stressful. Spending time outdoors lowers stress and makes people feel good.

Parks are also great places for kids. After-school programs[1] help kids and working parents. These programs teach kids to share and work in teams. Parks also have helpful programs that keep teenagers out of trouble. For example, when the parks in Cincinnati, Ohio started a basketball program late at night on Friday and Saturday, teenage crime went down by 24%.

So if you're ready for better health, less stress, happier kids, and a safer neighborhood, take a walk in the park. The good life is waiting for you!

[1]after-school programs: sports, arts and crafts, or other classes after school

Source: *National Recreation and Park Association*

☑ Identify the health benefits of parks

B Listen and read the article again.

C Complete the sentences. Use the words in the box.

immune system	programs	park	stress	~~outdoors~~	crime

1. People who spend time _____outdoors_____ are usually happier and healthier.
2. A walk in the park can strengthen your _____.
3. You can get healthy and stay healthy for free at the _____.
4. Sports and arts and crafts classes are examples of after-school _____.
5. Some park programs at night help stop teenage _____.
6. Many people say they have too much _____ in their lives.

D Study the chart. Then write the adjectives.
Use the nouns in parentheses.

> **Word Study: The suffix -ful**
>
> Add -ful to the end of some nouns to make an adjective.
> stress + ful = stressful   Too much **stress** is not good for you. My job is **stressful**.
>
> | stress | stressful | beauty | beautiful | help | helpful |
> |---|---|---|---|---|---|
> | care | careful | color | colorful | thank | thankful |

1. Our new neighborhood park is _____beautiful_____. (beauty)
2. The park's trees are very _____ right now. (color)
3. A walk in the park makes life less _____. (stress)
4. The park is very _____ for bringing families together. (help)

3 Talk it over

A Think about the questions. Make notes about your answers.

1. What programs do the parks in your community offer?
2. At the park, would you rather spend time alone, or in a class or program? Why?

B Talk about your answers with your classmates.

> **BRING IT TO LIFE**
>
> Look in the newspaper, look online, or stop by a local park or community center. Find a flyer or other information about programs in your neighborhood. Bring the information to class.

1 Grammar

A Complete the answers. Use the correct forms of *be going to* or *will*.

1. A: What are you going to do tomorrow?

    B: I __'m going to__ go to the park.

2. A: What do you think the park will be like in five years?

    B: It _____ be bigger and cleaner.

3. A: What are you going to do next summer?

    B: I _____ work at the recreation center.

4. A: Will you help me get a job at the recreation center?

    B: Sure, I _____ talk to the boss for you.

B Complete the sentences. Use *will, think,* or *probably*.

1. It ____will____ ____probably____ be hot tomorrow.

2. The park _____ not be open on Sunday.

3. Do you _____ the kids _____ like the rides at the park?

4. I _____ the play _____ start in five minutes.

5. Paul _____ _____ go to Montreal next weekend.

6. How long do you _____ the art show _____ be in town?

C Write the answers to the questions. Use your own information.

1. Would you rather play soccer or watch a soccer game on the weekend?

    _____

2. Would you rather watch TV or watch a movie?

    _____

3. Would you rather go bowling or go dancing?

    _____

4. Would you rather go to an amusement park or go to the theater?

    _____

5. Would you rather go to a nightclub or go to the theater?

    _____

2 Group work

 A Work with 2–3 classmates. Write 6 questions about the recreation center. Share your questions with the class.

POND STREET RECREATION CENTER

Sign up now for summer programs and classes! There's something for everyone!
Programs start June 24th. All classes and trips are at the Pond Street Rec center. See you there!

ART WORKSHOP
Tuesdays and Thursdays
Kids: 3:30–5:00 p.m.
Adults: 6:00–8:30 p.m.
Fee: $20/session

YOGA CLASS
Exercise and relax at the
same time.
Bring a blanket or a mat.
Wednesdays, 7:00–8:00 p.m.
Fee: $10/class

MOUNTAIN BIKE TRIPS
6 Saturdays starting June 24th
8:30–4:30
Fee: $30/trip

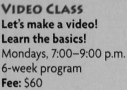

VIDEO CLASS
Let's make a video!
Learn the basics!
Mondays, 7:00–9:00 p.m.
6-week program
Fee: $60

What time will the video class begin?

B Interview 3 classmates. Write their answers.

1. What are you going to do this weekend?
2. Would you rather go to a concert or go to the library?
3. How do you think this neighborhood will change in ten years?

C Talk about the answers with your class.

PROBLEM SOLVING

A Listen and read about Juanita and Anna.

Juanita and Anna are friends. They want to go out together this weekend. Juanita wants to go to an amusement park. Tickets are expensive, but they can have fun there all day. Anna doesn't have much money. She would rather stay home and watch TV during the day and go dancing in the evening. They want to spend the day together, but they can't agree about what to do.

B Work with your classmates. Answer the questions.

1. What is the problem?
2. What should Juanita and Anna do? Think of 2 or 3 solutions to their problem.

A Job to Do

FOCUS ON
- computers and jobs
- writing memos
- making comparisons
- job feedback
- job skills

LESSON 1 **Vocabulary**

1 Learn computer and office vocabulary

A **Talk about the questions with your class.**

1. What computer equipment is in your school's office?
2. What are some ways people use computers at work?

B **Work with your classmates. Match the words with the picture.**

_9_ computer technician	_1_ graphic designer	_7_ monitor
_8_ CPU	_6_ headset	_3_ office manager
_4_ digital camera	_2_ keyboard	_5_ photographer

C **Listen and check. Then read the new words with a partner.**

D **Work with a partner. Write other computer and office words you know. Check your words in a dictionary.**

A: *Is the keyboard on the desk?*
B: *Yes, it is. It's in front of the monitor.*

2 Learn more computer vocabulary

A Look at the pictures. Check (✔) the words you know.

Everyday Definitions

☐ virus   ☐ mouse   ☐ crash   ☐ window   ☐ desktop

Computer Definitions

☐ virus   ☐ mouse   ☐ crash   ☐ window   ☐ desktop

B Complete the sentences. Use the words in 2A.

1. When computers ____crash____ , files and documents are often lost.
2. When you move the _____ with your hand, things on the screen move.
3. When you turn on the computer, the first thing you see is the _____.
4. A _____ is a "secret" computer program that causes computer problems.
5. You might need to close a _____ to see the files on your desktop.

C Talk about the questions with your class.

1. Which computer words are easy to remember? Why?
2. What are two or more computer problems?
3. What are three or more jobs that use computer equipment?

TEST YOURSELF ✔

Close your book. Categorize the new words in 3 lists: *Computer Parts and Equipment*, *Computer Problems*, and *Jobs*. Check your spelling in a dictionary. Compare your lists with a partner.

1 Read a memo

A Look at the pictures. Talk about the questions with your class.

1. What kinds of problems does the company have?
2. What should the company do about these problems?

B Listen and read the memo.

> ### MEMO
>
> **TO:** All Employees
> **FROM:** Miles Baine, President
> **RE:** EMPLOYEES MUST PAY MORE ATTENTION TO COMPANY POLICIES
>
> Many office managers are noticing the following problems:
> 1. Employees are not coming to work on time.
> 2. Some employees are taking longer and longer breaks.
> 3. Coffee and water spills are hurting computer keyboards.
>
> Please follow these company policies:
> • All employees must be at work by 9:00 a.m.
> • Break times are from 10:00–10:15 and 3:00–3:15 daily.
> • Employees may not eat or drink near computers.
>
> If you have questions or comments, please see your office manager.

C Check your understanding. Mark the statements T (true), F (false), or NI (no information).

___T___ 1. The memo is from the company president.

_____ 2. The subject of the memo is company managers.

_____ 3. Office managers are noticing some problems.

_____ 4. Some employees are taking 30-minute breaks.

_____ 5. Employees have two breaks every day.

_____ 6. Employees should only drink water near the computers.

2 Write a memo

A Talk about the questions with your class.

1. What kind of problems do you notice at your school?
2. Which school or classroom policies focus on these problems?
3. Who should students see when they want to talk about problems at school?

B Write a memo to your classmates about school policies. Use the model in 1B and your answers to the questions in 2A to help you.

TO: _____

FROM: _____

RE: _____

Many students and teachers are noticing the following problems:

1. _____
2. _____
3. _____

Please follow these school policies:

1. _____
2. _____
3. _____

Please see _____ for more information.

C Use the checklist to edit your writing. Check (✔) the true sentences.

Editing checklist	
1. I wrote about three problems in my school or classroom.	
2. I explained three school or classroom policies.	
3. The *To, From,* and *Subject (RE)* lines are complete.	
4. All sentences end with a period.	

D Exchange memos with a partner. Read and comment on your partner's work.

1. Point out one problem or policy that you think is interesting.
2. Ask your partner a question about one of the problems or policies.

TEST YOURSELF ✔

Write a new memo about something you want to change at home, at work, or at school. Share your memo with your classmates.

1 Learn comparisons

A Read the ads and the paragraph. Which computer would you buy?

Computer World
$1199.99
7.5 pounds
Speed: 1.8 GHz
Model 580

CHEAP TECH
$1499.99
7.5 pounds
Speed: 2 GHz
Model 680

I can't decide which computer to buy. The 580 laptop is less expensive than the 680. The 580 is as heavy as the 680, but it's not as fast as the 680. The 680 is faster than the 580, but it's more expensive than the 580. I also need to decide where to buy it. Other technicians aren't as experienced as the technicians at Computer World.

B Study the chart. Underline 1 example of each comparison with *as...as, (not) as...as, -er than, less...than,* and *more...than* in the paragraph above.

Comparisons with adjectives	
as...as	The 580 is **as** heavy **as** the 680.
not as...as	The 580 is **not as** fast **as** the 680.
-er than	The 680 is fast**er than** the 580.
less...than	The 580 is **less** expensive **than** the 680.
more...than	The 680 is **more** expensive **than** the 580.

Notes
• Add *-er than* to most adjectives with one syllable. (*fast-faster than*)
• For adjectives ending in *-y*, change the *y* to *i* and add *-er than*. (*friendly-friendlier than*)

C Complete the sentences with the comparisons and the adjectives in parentheses.

(NOT) AS...AS

1. The 580 laptop is _____*not as powerful as*_____ the 680 laptop. (powerful)

2. The 580 laptop is _____ the 680 laptop. (heavy)

-ER THAN/ LESS...THAN / MORE...THAN

3. The 580 laptop is _____ the 680 laptop. (cheap)

4. The 680 laptop is _____ the 580 laptop. (expensive)

5. Computer World's technicians are _____ CheapTech's technicians. (experienced)

✔ Use comparatives and superlatives to determine best prices, quality, and services

D Get the meaning. Work with your class. Which sentence has the same meaning? Circle *a* or *b*.

1. The salespeople are as helpful as the technicians.
   a. Some salespeople are more helpful than the technicians.
   b. Both the salespeople and the technicians are helpful.

2. Other salespeople are not as experienced as Computer World's salespeople.
   a. Other salespeople are more experienced than Computer World's salespeople.
   b. Other salespeople are less experienced than Computer World's salespeople.

3. Computer World's computers are less expensive than CheapTech's computers.
   a. Computer World isn't as expensive as CheapTech.
   b. CheapTech is as expensive as Computer World.

2 Review superlatives

A Study the ads. Then read the sentences in the chart with a partner.

Take Home a Digital Camera Today!

100X $99.99	180X $159.99	250 Z $399.99
Our least expensive camera!	Our most popular camera!	Our newest camera!

Superlatives: *-est, least, most*
The 100X is the **cheapest** camera.
The 100X is the **least** expensive camera.
The 250Z is the **most** expensive camera.

B Write the answers to the questions.

1. Which camera is the most expensive?
   The 250Z is the most expensive.

2. Which camera is the most popular?
   the 180x is the most popular

3. Which camera is the newest?
   The 250 is the newest

4. Which camera is the smallest?
   The 100X is the smallest

5. Which camera is the largest?
   The 250Z is the largest

3 Grammar listening

Listen to the story. Write the comparison words you hear.

My name is Lin. I'm an office manager for a large insurance company. I usually order all of our office supplies from Office Star or Business Max. For everyday items like paper and file folders, Office Star is usually _____less expensive_____
1
than Business Max. For special items like printer ink, Office Star is _____more expensive_____. But, I've noticed that the people
2
who work at Business Max are ___hot as Friendly___ as
3
the people who work at Office Star. The salespeople at Office Star are ___more Friendly___ than the salespeople at
4
Business Max. Oh, and I almost forgot! When I order from Office Star, my orders arrive _____Faster_____ than my orders from Business Max. They arrive in 48 hours or
5
less, or they're free!

4 Practice comparisons

A Think about your answers to these questions.

1. What are three stores you like?
2. Which store has the most helpful salespeople?
3. Which store is usually the least crowded?
4. Which store is the least expensive?

B Work with a partner. Ask and answer the questions in 4A.

C Talk about your answers with another pair. Does the other pair agree or disagree? Why or why not?

TEST YOURSELF ✔

Close your book. Write 5 sentences about the stores you discussed in section 4. Use *(not) as...as, -er than, less, more, -est, least,* or *most* in each sentence.

1 Learn to give and respond to feedback

STUDENT AUDIO **A** **Look at the pictures. Listen to the conversations. Then complete the sentences below with your classmates.**

1. The supervisor, Ms. Clark, wants Bill to ___Fixe storent___.
2. Ms. Clark wants Sue to ___be more concentrate (organize)___

STUDENT AUDIO **B** **Listen and read. What does Ms. Clark want Vicki to do?**

A: Vicki, can I see you for a moment?

B: Yes, Ms. Clark? What is it?

A: You're a good worker, Vicki. You're the most organized person in the office.

B: Thanks, Ms. Clark.

A: But Vicki, you're always late. You have to come to work on time.

B: I'm sorry, Ms. Clark. I'll try to do better.

A: Thank you, Vicki.

> **In other words...**
>
> **Responding to negative feedback**
>
> I'll try to do better.
> You won't have to tell me again.
> Thanks for letting me know.

C **Role-play giving and responding to feedback with a partner. Use the example in 1B to make a new conversation.**

Partner A: You're a school principal. Ask to see your office manager. Your office manager is the most experienced person at school, but he or she makes too many phone calls to friends. Tell him or her to spend less time on the phone.

Partner B: You are the office manager at a school. Listen to your principal's positive and negative feedback. Promise to change your behavior.

☑ Give and respond to positive and negative feedback   **39**

2 Review superlative forms

A Study the chart. Write the superlative forms of the words below in the correct columns.

angry   ~~big~~   efficient   ~~fast~~   ~~friendly~~   ~~great~~
~~happy~~   ~~hot~~   ~~kind~~   organized   ~~patient~~   thin

cvc

adjectives + *-est*	adjectives ending in y + *-est*	adjectives + *-est* (double the final consonant)	*most/least* + adjectives
kindest	happiest	biggest	most patient
greatest	angriest	hottest	least efficient
fastest	friendliest	thinnest	most organized

B Complete the sentences with the superlative form of the words in parentheses.

1. Al doesn't work quickly or carefully. He's the _____ *least efficient* _____ worker I know. (efficient)
2. Paulo is nice to everyone. He's the _____ kindest _____ person I know. (kind)
3. Lee isn't friendly. He's the _____ less friendly _____ person I know. (friendly)
4. Don is very happy. He's the _____ happiest _____ person I know. (happy)
5. Rosa never gets angry. She's the _____ most patient _____ person I know. (patient)

C Work with a partner. Ask and answer the questions.

1. Who is the friendliest student in class?
2. Who is the most organized person you know? My sister

3 Practice your pronunciation

  A Listen to the pronunciation of *v, b,* and *f* in these sentences.

1. **V**icki, can I see you for a moment?   3. You're the **f**riendliest student.
2. I'll try to do **b**etter.

B Listen to the names. Circle the sound you hear.

1. (v) f   2. (b) v   3. (f) b   4. v (b)   5. b (f)   6. f (v)

C Listen again. Repeat the names.

A Talk about the questions with your class.

1. What kinds of evaluations do students get?
2. What kinds of evaluations do workers get?
3. Do you ever have to evaluate other people?

B Listen to the conversations. Check the positive feedback for each worker.

1. Elizabeth is
   ☐ organized.
   ☐ kind.
   ☐ creative.
   ☑ on-time.

2. Ben is
   ☐ careful.
   ☐ helpful.
   ☑ organized.
   ☐ reliable.

3. Habib is
   ☐ careful.
   ☑ helpful.
   ☐ kind.
   ☐ confident.

C Listen again. Write what each worker needs to improve.

1. Elizabeth needs to _come to work on time_.
2. Ben needs to _be more organized_.
3. Habib needs to _be more helpful_.

5 Real-life math

Look at the student report card. Answer the questions. Talk about your answers with the class.

English	B	(3.0)
Math	A	(4.0)
History	B	(3.0)
Science	C	(2.0)
Art	B	(3.0)

1. What is this student's best subject? _Math_
2. What is this student's worst subject? _Science_
3. What is this student's average* grade, or grade point average (GPA)? _English, History, Art_

*To get the average, add the points for each grade.
 Then divide the total points by the number of grades.

TEST YOURSELF ✔

Role-play an evaluation. Partner A: You are the supervisor in a large factory. Your partner is a delivery driver at the factory. Give your partner positive and negative feedback. Partner B: Respond. Then change roles.

1 Get ready to read

A How do workers learn to use new machines at work?

B Read the definitions.

flexible: (adj.) able to change
production: (noun) the amount of products or services that a company makes or offers
train: (verb) to teach or educate

C Scan the article in 2A for percentages.

1. Production increased up to ____20____ % in companies with training programs.

2. Workers with a college degree earn ____77____ % more than workers with only a high school diploma.

2 Read and respond

A Read the article.

Workplace Training Spells Success

How do people describe the 21st century? "The digital age," "the information age," and "the technology[1] age" are popular descriptions. Whatever the name, one thing is sure; employees in the 21st century need to have more education and be more flexible than ever before. New technology means new machines, new ideas, and different jobs. Employees must learn new skills to prepare for new jobs.

More and more companies in the U.S. are providing training classes for their workers. The facts show that businesses with education programs are more successful. Here are some facts about worker education:

- Companies with training programs see production increase by 15 to 20%.

- Workers who learn more, earn more money. On average, college graduates' salaries are 77% higher than salaries for workers with only a high school degree.

- More than 57% of companies increased their worker education programs.

- Only two percent said they decreased their programs.

Today's workers need to be smarter, more creative, and more skilled than workers from the past. With the help of workplace training, they can be.

[1]technology: machines, computers

Source: *A Report of the U.S. Department of Commerce, U.S. Department of Education, U.S. Department of Labor, National Institute of Literacy, and the Small Business Administration*

✔ Identify the benefits of and sources for job training

B Listen and read the article again.

C Circle the correct words.

1. Companies see (employees / (production)) increase when they train their workers.

2. Workers need to learn new (salaries / skills).

3. Employees need to be (more / less) flexible in the 21st century.

4. When employees have training, their pay usually (increases / decreases).

5. High-school graduates earn 77% (more / less) than college graduates.

D Study the chart. Circle the correct words below.

> **Word Study: The suffix *-tion***
>
> Add *tion* to the end of some verbs to change them to nouns.
> produce — production   The company **produces** a lot. They have a high **production** rate.
> Note: The spelling may change when adding *-tion*.
>
> | describe | description | educate | education | dictate | dictation |
> | add | addition | invite | invitation | | |

1. People need more (educate / (education)) for new technology.

2. Computer World (produces / production) excellent computers.

3. My job (describes / description) is very clear.

4. (Add / Addition) and subtraction are not difficult.

5. Office managers (dictate / dictation) memos to their staff.

3 Talk it over

A Think about the questions. Make notes about your answers.

1. How do you think workers feel when they get good job training?
2. What are some reasons that a company might not give job training?

B Talk about the answers with your classmates.

BRING IT TO LIFE

Search the Internet, your local library, or your school office to find information on job training in your area. Bring the information to class.

1 Grammar

A Complete the sentences with the comparative form of the words in parentheses.

1. My sister is a graphic designer. She is _____more creative_____ than most people are. (creative)

2. Heather is __as friendly__ as Tracy. (friendly)

3. Today the technicians aren't __as busy__ as they were yesterday. (busy)

4. Digital cameras are usually __more expensive__ computers. (expensive)

B Read the sentences. Write a new sentence with the same idea. Use the words in parentheses.

1. Sue is not patient. Marta is patient.
   (not as...as)   _Sue is not as patient as Marta._

2. Mark and Fernando are both reliable.
   (as...as)   _Mark is as reliable as Fernan_

3. Ken is more efficient than Jack.
   (less)   _Jack is less efficient than Ken._

4. Ellen is not helpful. Tom is very helpful.
   (more)   _Tom is more helpful than Ellen._

5. Yanna is always creative. Jean isn't creative.
   (not as...as)   _Jean isn't as creative as Yan_

C Complete the sentences with the superlative form of the words in parentheses.

1. Bill has his papers everywhere. He's ___the least organized___ person at work. (organized)

2. Sheila doesn't talk much. She's __the most quiet__ student in class. (quiet)

3. Olga is not very organized. She's __the most disorganized__ person I know. (disorganized)

4. Yesterday it was 100 degrees outside. It was __the hottest__ day of the year. (hot)

5. Megan works very slowly. She's __the least efficient__ person in the office. (efficient)

2 Group work

A Work with 2–3 classmates. Write 6 sentences about the chairs. Use comparatives and superlatives. Share your sentences with the class.

The first chair is not as expensive as the third chair.
The second chair is more comfortable than the first one.

B Interview 3 classmates. Write their answers.

1. What's the most difficult thing about English? Why?
2. Which is the least difficult for you to learn—vocabulary, grammar, or pronunciation?
3. Is speaking English as easy as speaking other languages? Why or why not?

C Talk about the answers with the class.

PROBLEM SOLVING

A Listen and read about Omar.

Omar is looking for a job. He has two job offers. The first job is at Value Comp Computers. The second job is at Tech Time Electronics. The pay is a lot better at Value Comp, but the drive to work is longer. The medical benefits at Value Comp are not as good as the benefits at Tech Time, but the hours are more flexible. Omar can't decide what to do. Money, benefits, and travel time are all important to him.

B Work with your classmates. Answer the questions.

1. What is Omar's problem?
2. Which job is better for Omar? Make a list of the positive and negative things about each job.

UNIT 4

Good Work

FOCUS ON
- job interviews
- follow-up thank-you letters
- the present perfect
- job promotions
- employee skills

LESSON 1 Vocabulary

1 Learn job interview vocabulary

A **Talk about the questions with your class.**

1. What kinds of questions does an employer ask at an interview?
2. What kinds of questions can you ask the employer?

B **Work with your classmates. Match the words with the pictures.**

Interview Do not's

Interview Do's

_5_ arrive on time   _6_ greet the interviewer   _3_ (don't) dress inappropriately

_9_ bring your resume   _7_ look confident   _2_ (don't) look nervous

_8_ dress professionally   _1_ (don't) be late   _4_ (don't) use your cell phone

C **Listen and check. Then read the new words with a partner.**

D **Work with a partner. Write other job interview do's and do not's you know. Check your words in a dictionary.**

E **Work with a partner. Practice the conversation. Use the pictures in 1B.**

A: What should you do at a job interview?

B: You should dress professionally.

A: What shouldn't you do at a job interview?

B: You shouldn't look nervous.

2 Learn to describe your personal strengths

A **Read about different types of workers and their strengths. Check (✔) the strength(s) you have.**

This type of worker:	has this strength:	Is this you? (✔)
A problem-solver	is good at fixing problems.	☐
A team player	works well with other people.	☑
A self-starter	works well without much supervision.	☑
A creative thinker	has great ideas.	☑
A go-getter	sees what things need to be done and does them.	☐
A good leader	is good at supervising and showing people what to do.	☐

B **Work with a partner. Practice the conversation. Use the words in 2A.**

A: *Are you a problem-solver?*

B: *Yes, I am. I'm good at fixing problems.*

A: *Are you a team player?*

B: *Yes, I work well with other people.*

C **Talk about the questions with your class.**

1. What do you think are the three most important things to do at a job interview? Why?

2. What do you think are the three most important personal strengths to have? Why?

TEST YOURSELF ✔

Close your book. Categorize the new words in 3 lists: *Interview Do's, Interview Do not's,* and *Personal Strengths*. Check your spelling in a dictionary. Compare your lists with a partner.

1 Read an interview thank-you letter

A **Look at the picture. Talk about the questions with your class.**

1. When do you usually write thank-you letters?
2. Why is it important to write a thank-you letter after a job interview?

Thank you so much...

B **Listen and read about thank-you letters.**

Congratulations! You have finished the job interview. But, your work isn't finished yet. It's important to write a thank-you letter to the interviewer. Write the letter after your interview and send it by mail or email the next day. Here's a sample letter:

Ms. Paulina Reyes, Personnel Manager
Sherman's Auto Sales
1212 Willow Lane
Richmond, VA 23230

Dear Ms. Reyes:

Thank you for the opportunity to interview for the position of sales manager at Sherman's Auto Sales. I enjoyed learning more about your company.

I hope to have the chance to use my communication skills and sales experience at Sherman's.

If you have any questions, or need more information, please contact me at: tling@abc.us

Sincerely,
Tom Ling
Tom Ling

> **Writer's note**
>
> Use a colon (:) after the greeting in a formal business letter.

C **Check your understanding. Circle _a_ or _b_.**

1. What does the writer say in the first paragraph?
   a. Thank you.
   b. Please contact me.

2. Why does the writer talk about his skills in the letter?
   a. To show that he has other job offers.
   b. To show the employer that he's perfect for the job.

2 Write a thank-you letter

A **Talk about the questions with your class.**

1. What kinds of jobs do people have at your school?
2. Who do you think interviews people for jobs at your school?
3. Which of those jobs might be right for you? Why?

B **Imagine that you had a job interview at your school. Write a thank-you letter. Use the model in 1B and your answers to the questions in 2A.**

To start: What's your contact information? Who are you writing to?
            What is the interviewer's title and address?
Paragraph 1: What are you thanking the interviewer for?
Paragraph 2: What do you hope to have the chance to do?
Paragraph 3: What should the interviewer do if he or she has any questions?

> (your contact information)
> (interviewer's name, title)
> (interviewer's address)
>
> Dear _____:
> Thank you for the opportunity to interview for the position of...

C **Use the checklist to edit your writing. Check (✔) the true sentences.**

Editing checklist	
1. I wrote the name of the position I interviewed for.	
2. I talked about my skills for the job.	
3. I used a colon after the greeting.	
4. My phone number or email address is written clearly and correctly.	

D **Exchange letters with a partner. Read and comment on your partner's work.**

1. Point out one sentence that you think may help your partner get the job.
2. Ask your partner a question about his or her job skills.

TEST YOURSELF ✔

Congratulations! You had a job interview for the position of sales clerk at GBG Sportsmart with Ms. Vera Mills. The store is in your city, state, and zip code. The address of the store is 1320 Oak St. Write a new thank-you letter.

1 Learn the present perfect

A Read the paragraph and the job application. How many jobs did Jafar have before his current job?

Jafar is a messenger, but he wants a new job. Last year, he worked part-time in an office, and he has also worked as a sales representative. He has completed high school, but he hasn't finished college. He applied for the position of assistant manager at an automotive supply store last week. He had an interview this morning, but the manager hasn't called him back yet.

Job Application Form

Name: Jafar Fayez

Employment History:
List all jobs held starting with current or most recent.

Company	Position	FT or PT
Quicksilver Messengers	Messenger	Full-time
A1 Insurance Offices	Office Staff	Part-time
Joe's Men's Stores	Sales Representative	Full-time

B Study the chart. Circle the 4 examples of the present perfect in the paragraph above.

THE PRESENT PERFECT

Affirmative and negative statements			
Subject	*have/has*	past participle	
I You We They	have have not	worked	in an office.
He She	has has not		

Notes
- Use the present perfect to describe an event at a non-specific time in the past.
- To form the present perfect, use *have/has* and a past participle.
- Past participles of regular verbs have the same forms as the simple past (verb + *-d/-ed*).

C Complete the sentences with the present perfect. Use the words in parentheses.

1. Jafar _____has completed_____ his resume. (complete)

2. Mr. Baker ___has interviewed___ Jafar. (interview)

3. Jafar ___has written___ a thank-you letter. (write)

4. Mr. Baker ___hasn't read___ the letter. (not read)

5. Jafar ___has had___ three other interviews. (have)

Need help?

Some irregular verbs

Base form	Simple past	Past participle
be	was/were	been
do	did	done
go	went	gone
have	had	had
hear	heard	heard
read	read	read
write	wrote	written

☑ Use the present perfect to describe work, school, or life experiences

2 Learn the present perfect with *for* and *since*

A Study the chart and the time line. Then mark the statements below the time line T (true) or F (false).

The present perfect with *for* and *since*			
⌐Present perfect⌐	⌐*for* + period of time⌐	⌐ Present perfect⌐	⌐*since* + time activity began⌐
I have studied English	**for six months.**	I have been sick	**since Monday.**
He hasn't lived in Korea	**for a long time.**	Miguel has lived in Texas	**since 1994.**
They have worked here	**for many years.**	We haven't had a vacation	**since May.**

Note

Use the present perfect to describe activities that began in the past and continue to the present.
    I have been sick for 4 days. = I got sick four days ago and I'm still sick now.
    I have been sick since Monday. = I got sick on Monday and I'm still sick today.

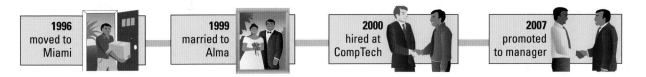

| 1996 moved to Miami | 1999 married to Alma | 2000 hired at CompTech | 2007 promoted to manager |

   __F__ 1. Carlos has been a manager since 2004.

   __T__ 2. He has worked at CompTech since 2000.

   __F__ 3. He has lived in Miami for only two years.

   __T__ 4. He has been married for more than five years.

B Complete the sentences with *for* or *since*.

1. He has worked here _____*for*_____ eight months.
2. Mrs. Min has been a teacher ____*Since*____ 1994.
3. They have studied every day ____*Since*____ Tuesday.
4. Sheila has been married ____*Since*____ 2001.
5. Rick has lived here ____*For*____ nine months.
6. We haven't seen our neighbors ____*For*____ a few weeks.

C Get the meaning. Work with your class. Read the sentences. Then mark the sentences T (true) or F (false).

1. They have been sick for a week.

   They're not sick now.   __F__

2. Carlos has worked in an office for three years.

   Carlos works in an office now.   __T__

3. Sheila has been married since 2001.

   Sheila got married in 2001.   __T__

3 Grammar listening

Listen to the story. Write the present perfect forms you hear.

My name is Sasha. I work for J & J Shipping Company.

I ____haven't worked____ here for very long, but
                    1

I _____have had_____ some great friends. My
             2

best friends at work are named Julie and Jenna. Both Julie

and Jenna _____have worked_____ here for 12 years.
                  3

They _____have working_____ in the same department since
              4

they started. Jenna helped me learn the company's computer

programs and Julie _____helped_____ me with all
                         5

kinds of things. I _____haven't had_____ a chance to
                    6

transfer to their department, but I hope I will someday.

4 Practice the present perfect

A **Look at the time line. When did you do these things or start to do these things? Write the correct date for each event.**

moved to this city	moved to my current address	studied English	attended this class
1 month ago	3 weeks ago	1 month ago	1 month ago

B **Work with a partner. Ask and answer the questions. Use *for* or *since*.**

1. How long have you lived in this city? I have lived here since January
2. How long have you lived at your current address? I have lived there for 3 weeks
3. How long have you studied English? I have studied english for a few wee
4. How long have you attended this class? I DEM

C **Talk about your answers with the class.**

I've lived in this city for 10 years. Elena has lived here since 2003.

TEST YOURSELF ✔

Close your book. Write 6 sentences about what you learned about people in your class. Use the present perfect.

Kemi has studied English since September.

1 Learn to interview for a promotion

STUDENT
AUDIO

A **Look at the pictures. Listen to the conversation. Then answer the questions below with your classmates.**

2003–2005

2005–present

1. What job does Beatriz have? *She's a server*
2. What job does she interview for? *for being a assistant chief*

STUDENT
AUDIO

B **Listen and read. What job does Ms. Ortiz want?**

A: How long have you been an assistant chef at Henri's Restaurant, Ms. Ortiz?

B: I've been an assistant chef here since 2005.

A: Why do you think you should be the new head chef?

B: I'm creative. I want to create delicious new dishes for Henri's customers.

A: Have you been a head chef before?

B: No, but I'm a fast learner.

A: That's terrific, Ms. Ortiz.

> **In other words...**
>
> **Ways to ask**
> Why do you think...?
> What makes you think...?
>
> **Ways to persuade**
> I'm creative.
> I'm a fast learner.
> I'm hard-working.
> I know I can do it.

C **Role-play a promotion interview with a partner. Use the example in 1B to make a new conversation.**

Partner A: You are a manager at Discount Mart. Interview your best salesperson for the job of assistant manager.

Partner B: You are the best salesperson at Discount Mart. You've been a salesperson for five years. You're hard-working. You want to teach other employees what you've learned. You know you can do it.

2 Learn contractions with the present perfect

A Study the chart. Who has learned a lot?

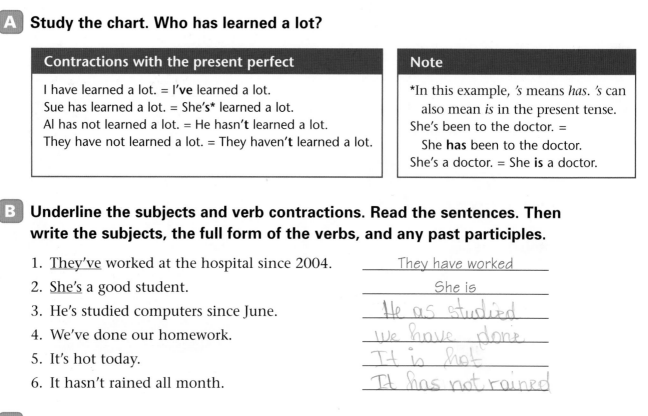

Contractions with the present perfect	Note
I have learned a lot. = I**'ve** learned a lot. Sue has learned a lot. = She**'s*** learned a lot. Al has not learned a lot. = He hasn**'t** learned a lot. They have not learned a lot. = They haven**'t** learned a lot.	*In this example, *'s* means *has*. *'s* can also mean *is* in the present tense. She's been to the doctor. = She **has** been to the doctor. She's a doctor. = She **is** a doctor.

B Underline the subjects and verb contractions. Read the sentences. Then write the subjects, the full form of the verbs, and any past participles.

1. <u>They've</u> worked at the hospital since 2004.   _They have worked_
2. <u>She's</u> a good student.   _She is_
3. He's studied computers since June.   _He as studied_
4. We've done our homework.   _We have done_
5. It's hot today.   _It is hot_
6. It hasn't rained all month.   _It has not rained_

C Work with a partner. Follow the directions.

1. Tell your partner three places you've gone this week. Use contractions.
2. Tell your partner three things you've done at home since Sunday.

3 Practice your pronunciation

A Listen to the pronunciation of *th* in these sentences. Underline the *th* sounds you hear.

1. How long have you been a salesperson at this store?
2. I want to teach other employees what I've learned.
3. That's terrific!

B Listen. Do you hear *th* in any of these sentences? Circle *yes* or *no*.

1. yes (no)   3. yes (no)   5. (yes) no
2. (yes) no   4. yes (no)   6. (yes) no

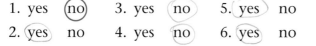

C Ask and answer the questions with a partner. Then listen to the questions and repeat.

1. Is the weather better this week than it was on the weekend?
2. Is this the only clothing that you thought about wearing today?

4 Focus on listening

A **Talk about the questions with your class.**

1. What kind of information do job applications usually ask for?
2. Do you think most people like to complete job applications? Why or why not?

B **Read the questions. Then listen to the conversation and circle *a* or *b*.**

1. Where does Miguel work now?
   a. Center Street Hospital
   b. Springfield General Hospital

2. Why does he want a new job?
   a. He wants to work at a better hospital.
   b. He wants to work closer to home.

C **Listen again and complete Miguel's job application.**

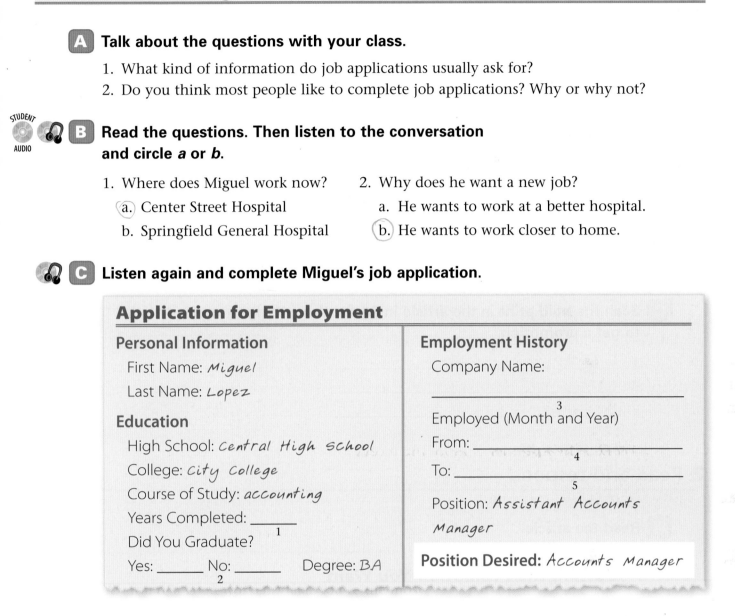

Application for Employment

Personal Information

First Name: *Miguel*

Last Name: *Lopez*

Education

High School: *Central High School*

College: *City College*

Course of Study: *accounting*

Years Completed: _____
1

Did You Graduate?

Yes: _____ No: _____ Degree: *BA*
2

Employment History

Company Name:

_____
3

Employed (Month and Year)

From: _____
4

To: _____
5

Position: *Assistant Accounts Manager*

Position Desired: *Accounts Manager*

5 Real-life math

Read about Miguel's job and answer the question.

The Springfield General Hospital manager has offered Miguel a job. The hours for the job are Tuesday through Saturday from 8:30 to 3:30. The pay will be $23.50 per hour. What is the gross pay* for one week? _____

*gross pay = the money you make before taxes

> **TEST YOURSELF ✔**
>
> Role-play a workplace conversation. Partner A: You're the manager at a restaurant. Interview your best server for a promotion to night manager. Partner B: You're the best server in the restaurant. Tell the manager why you should get the promotion. Then change roles.

1 Get ready to read

 A **Has someone you know received a promotion at work? Why?**

B **Read the definitions.**

honest: (adj.) truthful
interpersonal skills: (noun) the ability to work and communicate well with other people
market: (verb) to sell or promote
network: (verb) to talk, or communicate, with other people at work

C **Scan the bold print in the article in 2A for three things you need to do to get a promotion.**

1. _____

2. _____

3. _____

2 Read and respond

A **Read the article.**

Getting the Promotion You Want

Do you like the company you work for? Are you ready for more responsibility? If you answered "yes," you might be ready for a promotion. To get a promotion, you need a plan. First, you need to make sure you have the job skills to get the promotion you want. Then you need to market yourself and your skills to your supervisor.

Improve Your Skills
- Take classes or study at home.
- Accept extra work with a smile. Employees who do this often learn new skills and make their supervisors happy. Think about what you are learning while you are working.

Market Yourself and Your Skills
- Dress for success. Clothing, shoes, and haircut can make a big difference in how your supervisor sees you. Conservative[1] choices are usually best.
- Network, or communicate, with people in other departments. Eat lunch with other employees. Attend company events. You'll be surprised how much you learn and how much people learn about you.

---

[1]conservative: traditional

☑ Identify ways to get a promotion

Know your Personal Strengths
- What are your top qualities? What makes you the best person for the promotion?
- Look at the Top Qualities list. Be sure that these qualities describe you. Be sure you know your personal strengths and job skills. Be ready to talk confidently about them.

Top 5 Qualities Supervisors look for:
1. Good communication skills
2. Honesty
3. Strong interpersonal skills
4. Good teamwork skills
5. Flexibility

Source: *Job Outlook and The National Association of Colleges and Employers*

 B Listen and read the article again.

C Mark the sentences T (true), F (false), or NI (no information).

__T__ 1. To get a promotion, you need to have job skills.

____ 2. You shouldn't network with other people if you want a promotion.

____ 3. Honest employees get promoted 50% of the time.

____ 4. A good way to market yourself is to study at home.

____ 5. Flexibility isn't a quality that supervisors look for.

____ 6. Conservative clothing is usually best for work.

____ 7. Don't worry about qualities supervisors look for.

____ 8. It's important to know your personal strengths.

3 Talk it over

A Think about the questions. Make notes about your answers.

1. Do you think it's easier to get a promotion or to get a new job at a different company? Why?
2. Look at the Top Qualities list in the article. What other qualities are important to have at work or at school?

B Talk about the answers with your classmates.

BRING IT TO LIFE

Talk to a neighbor or family member who has a job. Ask the question:
What do you think the top 3 employee qualities are for your job? Write the answers. Bring the information to class.

1 Grammar

A **Complete the sentences. Use past participles.**

1. Don hasn't ____made____ his bed yet.
2. Suki has _____ several movies this summer.
3. We haven't _____ a vacation since July.
4. We've never _____ at that restaurant.
5. Leo has _____ two cups of coffee since this morning.

> **Need help?**
>
> **More irregular verbs**
>
> | Base form | Simple past | Past participle |
> | --- | --- | --- |
> | drink | drank | drunk |
> | eat | ate | eaten |
> | get | got | gotten |
> | make | made | made |
> | see | saw | seen |
> | take | took | taken |

B **Complete the sentences. Use the present perfect of the verbs in parentheses.**

1. Adela _____has lived_____ here for a long time. (live)
2. She _____ at a hospital since 2003. (work)
3. Her brothers _____ high school. (complete)
4. They _____ jobs this month. (not get)
5. She _____ a headache all day. (have)

C **Complete the sentences with *for* or *since*.**

1. We've been here ____for____ 20 minutes.
2. Have you talked to Marta _____ yesterday?
3. Khan hasn't visited Mexico _____ 2001.
4. I haven't used my car _____ two weeks.
5. Antonio and Esteban haven't lived here _____ last May.

D **Look at the underlined subjects and verb contractions. Write the subject and the full forms of the contracted verbs *is* or *has*.**

1. <u>Mark's</u> the new assistant manager. _____Mark is_____
2. <u>He's</u> worked in this office since last year. _____
3. <u>Mark's</u> not here right now. _____
4. <u>He's</u> at a meeting in Toronto. _____
5. <u>He's</u> been to other meetings in Canada before. _____

2 Group work

A Work with 2–3 classmates. Write a conversation between the people in the picture. Share your conversation with the class.

A: *Tell me about your personal strengths.*

B: *I am a team player...*

B Interview 3 classmates. Write their answers.

1. Do you have a job now? What do you do?
2. How long have you been a _____?
3. How many jobs have you had?
4. How long have you been at this school?

C Talk about the answers with your class.

PROBLEM SOLVING

A Listen and read about Hector.

It's 10 p.m. Hector has a job interview in the morning. He's been at work all day. He hasn't had time to prepare for the interview. He hasn't learned much about the company. He hasn't written a list of questions to ask the interviewer, and he hasn't decided what to wear. He needs to go to bed by 11:30. Hector is worried that he is unprepared. He's getting nervous about tomorrow.

B Work with your classmates. Answer the questions.

1. What is Hector's problem?
2. What is the best way for Hector to spend his time tonight? Make a list of the top 3 things he should do.

Community Resources

FOCUS ON
- community resources
- reporting safety problems
- the present perfect
- taking action in the community
- protecting the environment

LESSON **1**   Vocabulary

1 Learn community resource vocabulary

A Talk about the questions with your class.

1. Where are the government offices in your city or town?
2. What types of services do people in your city or town need?

B Work with your classmates. Match the words with the picture.

_5_ animal shelter

_1_ city hall

_4_ community clinic

_6_ Department of Motor Vehicles (DMV)

_8_ employment agency

_3_ recreation center

_2_ recycling center

_7_ senior center

C Listen and check. Then read the new words with a partner.

D Work with a partner. Write other community resource words you know.
Check your words in a dictionary.

E Work with a partner. Practice the conversation. Use the picture in 1B.

A: What's next to the clinic?

B: The animal shelter is next to the clinic.

2 Learn about community services

A Look at the community website. Match the services and the places below.

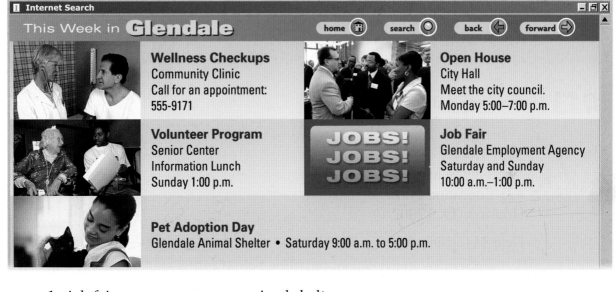

- _c_ 1. job fair
- _a_ 2. pet adoption
- _e_ 3. volunteer program
- _b_ 4. open house
- _d_ 5. wellness checkup

- a. animal shelter
- b. city hall
- c. employment agency
- d. community clinic
- e. senior center

B Work with a partner. Practice the conversation. Use the words in 2A.

A: I'm interested in the job fair. Where should I go?

B: You should go to the employment agency this weekend from 10:00 to 1:00.

A: Thanks.

C Talk about the questions with your class.

1. Which community resources would you like near your home? Why?
2. Where can you find information about community services and events?

TEST YOURSELF ✔

Work with a partner. Partner A: Read the vocabulary words in 1B to your partner. Partner B: Close your book. Write the words. Ask your partner for help with spelling as necessary. Then change roles. Partner B: Use the words in 2A.

1 Read about community action

A **Look at the picture. Talk about the questions with your class.**

1. What is a safety problem at this school?
2. Who could you ask to help you with school safety problems?

B **Listen and read the letter.**

Sally Hunter
Mid-City School Board
473 Education Plaza
Houston, TX 77002

Dear Ms. Hunter:

I am writing to the school board on behalf of the students in my English class. We have been students at Mid-City Community Center for seven months. Mid-City is a wonderful school, but we are worried about a safety problem.

The problem is that there are no lights in our parking lot. It's dangerous to walk there after class because it's too dark. We've discussed the problem with our school principal, but she says there's no money for lights at this time. Can you help us put lights in our parking lot?

We invite you to visit our school from Monday to Thursday between 7 and 9 p.m. so you can see the problem. Thank you for helping us make our school safe.

Sincerely,

Marta Alvarez
Marta Alvarez ◄

Writer's note

Sign and print your name at the end of a formal or business letter.

C **Check your understanding. Mark the statements T (true), F (false), or NI (no information).**

__T__ 1. The letter is to the school board.

__T__ 2. The parking lot is dangerous because it's dark.

__T__ 3. The students want the school board to put lights in the parking lot.

____ 4. There are only classes in the evening at Mid-City Community Center.

__F__ 5. The students don't like their school.

2 Write a letter to a school board member

A **Talk about the questions with your class.**

1. Choose a school problem. Why is it a problem for you and your classmates?
2. What do you want your school board member to do about the problem?

B **Write a letter to your school board member. Use the model in 1B and your answers to the questions in 2A.**

_____

_____

_____

_____

Dear _____:

   I am writing on behalf of the students in my English class.

_____

_____

   The problem is that _____

_____

_____

   We invite you to visit our school _____
so you can see the problem. _____

_____

Sincerely,

_____

_____

C **Use the checklist to edit your writing. Check (✔) the true sentences.**

Editing checklist	
1. I described the problem.	
2. I asked for help.	
3. All my sentences start with capital letters and end with periods.	
4. I signed and printed my name at the end of the letter.	

D **Exchange letters with a partner. Read and comment on your partner's work.**

1. Point out the sentences that you think describe the problem.
2. Ask your partner a question about the problem.

TEST YOURSELF ✔

Imagine that there's a dangerous intersection with no stop sign in your neighborhood. Write a new letter to a city official at city hall to ask for help. Or write to a school or government official about a different problem.

1 Learn *Yes/No* questions with the present perfect

A Read the conversation and the project report. When will the electrician arrive?

A: Have you painted the cafeteria?
B: Yes, I have.
A: Has the electrician fixed the air-conditioning?
B: No, he hasn't.
A: When will he fix it?
B: He'll be here tomorrow.

Senior Center Project Report:

	yes	no
1. paint cafeteria	✔	
2. fix air-conditioning		✔
3. buy lunch tables	✔	
4. repair stove		✔
5. advertise programs	✔	
6. start lunch program		✔

B Study the charts. Underline the 2 present perfect questions in the conversation above.

YES/NO QUESTIONS WITH THE PRESENT PERFECT

Yes/No Questions		
Have	I you we they	repaired the stove?
Has	he she	

Answers					
Yes,	I you we they	have.	No,	I you we they	haven't.
	he she	has.		he she	hasn't.

C Complete the questions and answers. Use the project report in 1A.

1. ____Have____ the workers ___painted___ the cafeteria?   ___Yes, they have.___
2. ____Has____ the office manager _seen the_ new lunch tables?   _Yes, he has_
3. ____Has____ the electrician ___fixed___ the air-conditioning?   _no, he hasn't_
4. ____Has____ the office manager _given you_ the lunch program?   _Yes, he has._
5. ____Has____ the office manager _shown you_ the center programs?   _no, he hasn't_
6. ____Have____ they ___bought___ the stove?   _yes, they have_

D **Work with a partner. Talk about class activities.**

A: *Have you completed exercise C?*
B: *Yes, I have.*
A: *Has Maria written the answers on the board?*
B: *No, she hasn't.*

> **Need help?**
>
> **Class activities**
> done the homework
> read ___
> talked to ___
> learned ___

2 Learn the present perfect with *ever, already,* and *yet*

A **Study the chart. Circle the correct words in the sentences below.**

Present perfect with *ever, already,* and *yet*	Notes

A: Have you **ever** volunteered at an animal shelter?
 B: No, I haven't. OR
  No, I've never volunteered before.
	ever = at any time (not ever = never)
	  Use *ever* in Yes/No and information
	  questions and in negative statements.

A: Have you **already** served lunch to the seniors?
 B: Yes, I have. They've **already** eaten.
	already = some time before now
	  Use *already* in questions when you expect
	  a *yes* answer and in affirmative statements.

A: Have you called the clinic **yet**?
 B: No, I haven't. I haven't found the number **yet**.
  I'll call tomorrow.
	yet = at any time until now
	  Use *yet* in Yes/No questions and in
	  negative statements.

1. We haven't (already / (ever)) used that new copy machine.
2. Have you (yet / (ever)) visited city hall?
3. I haven't signed the paper ((yet) / ever).
4. Has Sam ((already) / yet) painted the kitchen?

B **Match the questions and the answers. Then practice them with a partner**

___d___ 1. Has Maria been to New York yet?   a. No, I haven't ever been there.

___b___ 2. Has George already been to Miami?   b.) Yes, he went twice last year.

___c___ 3. Have they ever gone to Russia?   c. No, they plan to go next year.

___a___ 4. Have you ever been to Mexico?   d. No, she's going next week.

C **Get the form. Work with your class. Correct the sentences.**

1. Marisol hasn't never volunteered.   Marisol hasn't ever volunteered.
2. I haven't done my homework already.
   I'll do it tonight.   ... homework yet
3. Natasha went to the DMV yet. She got
   her license last week.   DMV already
4. Michael has ever been to a job fair.
   Maybe he'll go next week.   ... hasn't ever

3 Grammar listening

 Listen and circle _a_ or _b_.

1. (a.) Mark has been to Los Angeles.
   b. Mark has never been to Los Angeles.

2. a. He's been to the recreation center three times.
   b. He's taken three classes at the recreation center.

3. a. She has gotten a new dog.
   b. She's planning to get a new dog.

4. a. Toshi has already started working.
   b. Roberto has already started working.

5. a. She's never written a letter to the school board.
   b. She wrote three letters to the school board.

6. a. He hasn't been to the job fair.
   b. He's been to the job fair twice.

4 Practice the present perfect

A **Work with a partner. Complete the questions.**

1. Have you ever been to _____? (place in your state)
2. Have you ever read _Alice au pays_...? (name of a book)
3. Have you ever visited _____? (name of a community resource)
4. Have you eaten _____ yet today? (a meal you eat every day)
5. Have you spoken* to _____ yet today? (name of a person in your class)

*speak-spoke-spoken

B **Work with another pair. Ask and answer the questions in 4A. Give as much information as possible.**

A: _Have you ever been to Miami?_
B: _No, I haven't. I'd like to go there some day._
A: _Have you ever read "Romeo and Juliet"?_
B: _Yes, I have. But, I haven't read it in English yet._

Miami

TEST YOURSELF ✔

Close your book. Write 6 sentences using the information you learned about your classmates. Use the present perfect, _ever, already,_ and _yet._
   Yana hasn't ever visited city hall.

1 Learn to improve your community

STUDENT AUDIO **A** Look at the pictures. Listen to the conversations. Then answer the questions below with your classmates.

1. What are the apartment residents doing?
2. Do you think the woman will sign the petition?

STUDENT AUDIO **B** Listen and read. What do the residents want?

A: Hi Anya. Did you go to the residents' meeting Wednesday night? I didn't see you there.

B: No, I didn't, John. I'm sorry. I forgot all about it!

A: That's OK. By the way, have you signed the petition for a security camera yet?

B: No, I haven't. What's it about?

A: The parking garage is dark. We're asking the building owners to put in a security camera.

B: A security camera in the parking garage? That's a great idea. Where do I sign?

> **In other words...**
>
> **Apologizing**
> I'm sorry.
> I'm so sorry.
> I apologize.

C Role-play a conversation between two neighbors with a partner. Use the example in 1B to make a new conversation.

Partner A: Ask your neighbor about the neighborhood meeting last night. Ask if he or she has signed a petition for a traffic light. Explain that the intersection by the school is dangerous. You are asking the city council to put in a traffic light.

Partner B: You had to go to work and didn't go to the neighborhood meeting last night. Ask your neighbor what the petition is about. Say you will or won't sign it, and say why.

☑ Give an opinion on a community or local issue **67**

2 Review the simple past and the present perfect

A Study the chart. Then circle the correct answers in the sentences below.

The simple past
Don **worked** last night.
He **didn't go** to the meeting.
A: **Did** he **go** to the meeting last month?
B: No, he **didn't**.

The present perfect
Don **has worked** nights for many years.
He **hasn't signed** the petition yet.
A: **Has** he ever **been** to a meeting?
B: No, he **hasn't**.

Note
The simple past tense describes completed actions or situations, often with a specific time reference (*last night, yesterday, in 2001*). The present perfect tense describes past experiences, often without a specific time reference.

1. Has Abdul ever (sign / (signed)) a petition?
2. Did Beth ((sign) / signed) the petition yesterday?
3. Toshi (didn't go / (hasn't gone)) to the new park yet.
4. Maria (was / (has been)) to that clinic before.

B Work with your classmates. Ask and answer the questions.

1. Have you ever gone to a neighborhood meeting? If so, did you enjoy it?
2. Have you ever been to the DMV? If so, how long did you wait in line?
3. Have you had a wellness checkup since last year? If so, when did you have one?

3 Practice your pronunciation

STUDENT AUDIO

A Listen to the pronunciation of *y, w,* and *j* in the conversation.

A: Hi Anya. Did you come to the residents meeting Wednesday night?
B: No, I didn't, John.

STUDENT AUDIO

B Listen and write the missing words.

1. The _____woman_____ volunteers at the senior center.
2. Check the _____ for the next _____.
3. I haven't signed the petition _____.
4. Alex _____ in line for two hours _____.
5. We've completed the class _____ already.

C Listen again and check. Repeat the sentences in 3B.

4 Focus on listening

A **Talk about the questions with your class.**

1. Do you recycle glass, newspaper, and cans in your home?
2. Is it convenient or difficult to recycle in your community?

B **Listen to the news interview. Circle _a_ or _b_.**

1. People in the U.S. have recycled paper, glass, and metal ____.
   a. since 1590
   b. for a long time

2. The speaker says we need to recycle because ____.
   a. we produce a lot of trash
   b. the population is growing

C **Read the sentences. Then listen again and complete them.**

1. The first paper recycling in the U.S. began in the year _____.
2. A recycling center was built in New York City in _____.
3. In _____, 6.5 percent of the U.S. population recycled.
4. In 2005, the percentage of people in the U.S. who recycled was _____.

5 Real-life math

Use the graph to complete the sentences.

1. About 32 percent of the U.S. population recycled in __2005__.
2. Recycling increased by 1 percent between 1960 and _____.
3. Recycling increased by _____ percent between 1980 and 2000.
4. Between 1960 and 2005, recycling increased by _____ percent.

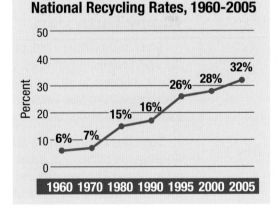

National Recycling Rates, 1960-2005

TEST YOURSELF ✔

Role-play a conversation. Partner A: Ask your partner to sign a petition for new computers at your school. Partner B: Ask for more information and decide if you want to sign it. Then change roles.

LESSON 5 — Real-life reading

1 Get ready to read

A How do you help keep your neighborhood clean?

B Read the definitions.

environment: (noun) the world around you
natural resources: (noun) things produced by the earth that people use
pollution: (noun) things that make the environment dirty or dangerous
litter: (noun) paper, cans, or other trash that is left in a public place

C Look at the definitions in 1B and the picture in 2A. What do you think Earth Day is about? Circle the answer.

a. celebrating the earth's birthday
b. taking care of the earth
c. studying how the earth began

2 Read and respond

A Read the article.

Happy Earth Day!

Every year on April 22nd, people around the world celebrate Earth Day. On that day, people volunteer to pick up litter, clean up the environment, and plan ways to take care of the earth's natural resources.

Earth Day began in 1970 when a group of Americans became upset about pollution in the air and water. They worried that too much of the earth's water and air was unclean, unsafe, and unhealthy. So, they started an event to help people think about creating a cleaner, healthier, and safer earth. Now, over 174 countries around the world and hundreds of millions of people celebrate Earth Day each year.

Here are a few Earth Day success stories from communities around the world.

- **Amelia, Ohio, USA:** 300 volunteers collect more than 700 bags of litter, 46 tires, 1 refrigerator, and over 100 other items from the Ohio River.

China's 2005 Earth Day stamp made people think about protecting the environment.

- **Toronto, Canada:** hundreds of volunteers plant thousands of trees and bushes[1] in Rouge Park. Volunteers have planted more than 100,000 trees and bushes in the area since 1989.

- **Vera Cruz, Brazil:** a special bus visits 1,500 school students to teach students what they can do today to make the environment healthier for the future.

[1]bush: a plant, smaller than a tree, usually 3–5 feet tall.

Source: *www.earthday.net*

☑ Identify ways to reduce trash and protect the environment

B **Listen and read the article again.**

C **Mark the statement T (true), F (false), or NI (no information).**

_T_ 1. On Earth Day, people try to make a healthier, cleaner earth.

____ 2. Five thousand people participated in the first Earth Day.

____ 3. Over 174 countries celebrate Earth Day.

____ 4. Volunteers in Canada have planted many trees since 1989.

____ 5. In Brazil, students learn how to improve the environment for the future.

D **Study the chart. Complete the sentences below.**

> **Word Study: The prefix un-**
>
> The prefix un- means not. Add un- to the beginning of some adjectives to make its meaning negative.
> clean–unclean   People want a **clean** environment.
>   **Unclean** air and water can be dangerous.
>
> | healthy | unhealthy | happy | unhappy |
> | safe | unsafe | important | unimportant |

1. Many volunteers work on Earth Day to create a _____clean_____ environment.

2. Some people worry that the earth's water is _____, _____ and

   _____.

3. Earth Day began because people were _____ about pollution.

4. On Earth Day, it's _____ to work together to take care of the earth.

3 Talk it over

A **Read the statistics. Think about the questions. Make notes about your answers.**

1. Where does all that trash go?
2. What are some ways people can produce less trash?

B **Talk about your answers with your classmates.**

Trash Statistics

The average American throws away 4.4 pounds of trash every day. That means a family of four throws away 6,424 pounds of trash every year.

BRING IT TO LIFE

Look around your neighborhood. Write an idea for an environmental improvement you and your neighbors could make. Talk about your idea with your classmates.

1 Grammar

A Complete the sentences with the present perfect. Use the verbs in parentheses.

1. I _____haven't been_____ to the new clinic yet. (be)
2. Tom _____ at the DMV for ten years. (work)
3. The students _____ their homework yet. (do)
4. We _____ already _____ a letter to the school board. (write)

B Complete the questions and answers. Use the verbs in parentheses.

1. _Have_____ they _planted_ the trees? (plant)   Yes, _they have_____.
2. _____ the mayor _____ his speech? (finish) No, _____.
3. _____ the celebration _____? (start)   Yes, _____.
4. _____ you _____ Ramon? (see)   No, _____.
5. _____ you _____ to city hall? (go)   No, _____.

C Complete the sentences with *ever, already,* or *yet*.

1. Victor hasn't _____ever_____ been to the new movie theater, but he plans to go there this weekend.
2. I haven't seen the new movie _____. I'm going to see it with Victor this weekend.
3. We've _____ bought the tickets. We bought them yesterday.
4. Min hasn't _____ gone with us before, but she's going with us tomorrow.
5. She hasn't bought her ticket _____. She will buy it in the morning.

D Complete the sentences with the past or present perfect. Use the verbs in parentheses.

1. I _____have worked_____ here for two months. Last year, I
   _____worked_____ in a clinic. (work)
2. Tom _____ home from work again yesterday. He
   _____ home for three weeks now. (stay)
3. We _____ many times about Tom's health. We
   _____ about it yesterday, too. (talk)
4. He _____ to the clinic several times. Last month
   I went with him. (go)

2 Group work

A Work with 2–3 classmates. Write a paragraph about the picture. Share your paragraph with the class.

Every year in April, the people in my neighborhood celebrate Community Clean-Up Day...

keeping our environm clean and safe.

B Interview 3 classmates. Write their answers.

1. Have you ever helped with a neighborhood project? What was it?
2. Have you ever seen a problem in your neighborhood? What did you see?
3. Have you ever gone to a town or neighborhood meeting? Why or why not?

C Talk about the answers with your class.

PROBLEM SOLVING

A Listen and read about Paulina.

Paulina has lived in Lake City for two weeks. She wants to get involved in the community. She hasn't met many people yet. She hasn't had time to learn much about the city yet. She hasn't ever volunteered for community work before, but she thinks it might be a good opportunity to meet some nice people. Unfortunately, Paulina doesn't know where to begin. She doesn't know how or where to volunteer.

B Work with your classmates. Answer the questions.

1. What is Paulina's problem?
2. What can Paulina do? Make a list of places she can go or call to get involved.

Every 3th September, citizens in my country celebrate community clean-up day for keeping our enviroment clean and safe.

UNIT 6

What's Cooking?

FOCUS ON
- food preparation
- recipes
- phrasal verbs
- restaurant service and tipping
- food safety

LESSON 1 Vocabulary

1 Learn kitchen vocabulary

A **Talk about the questions with your class.**

1. Do you like to cook? Why or why not?
2. Has anyone in your family ever worked in a restaurant kitchen?

B **Work with your classmates. Match the words with the picture.**

____	boil	____	fork	____	pan	____	pour
____	bowl	____	glass	____	plate	____	spoon
_1_	chop	____	knife	____	pot	____	stir

 C **Listen and check. Then read the new words with a partner.**

D **Work with a partner. Write other kitchen words you know. Check your words in a dictionary.**

Work with a partner. Practice the conversation. Use the picture in 1B.

A: *Where are the plates?*
B: *They're in the sink.*

2 Learn more kitchen vocabulary

A **Look at the pictures. Name the foods and actions you see.**

peel

steam

beat

grate

mix

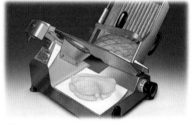

slice

B **Underline the verbs in the sentences below. Then change the verbs to nouns and complete the sentences.**

1. <u>Peel</u> the carrots with a vegetable _____*peeler*_____.
2. Steam the vegetables in a _____.
3. Beat the eggs with a _____.
4. Grate the cheese with a cheese _____.
5. Mix the ingredients with a _____.
6. Slice the ham with a knife or a _____.

> **Need help?**
>
> Add *-r* or *-er* to the end of some verbs to change them to nouns.
> *Peel + er = peeler*
> Use the peeler to peel the carrots.

C **Talk about the questions with your class.**

1. Which foods do you slice? Which foods do you peel?
2. How do you prepare vegetables at home?
3. What is the most useful tool in the kitchen? Why?

TEST YOURSELF ✓

Close your book. Categorize the new words in 2 lists: *Kitchen Activities* and *Things in the Kitchen*. Check your spelling in a dictionary. Compare your lists with a partner.

1 Read about a family recipe

A **Look at the picture. Talk about the questions with your class.**

1. Who usually prepares meals in your family?
2. What are some of your family's favorite foods?

STUDENT
AUDIO

B **Listen and read the story about a family recipe.**

My Favorite Dish

When I was a child in El Salvador, my grandfather was the best cook in the family. On Sundays, he cooked a big meal for everyone. I usually helped him. In the morning, we picked up ingredients from the market. At home, Papi cooked and I put away the groceries and cleaned up the kitchen.

Papi's chicken and rice was my favorite dish. It was sweet, sour, and spicy all at the same time. First, he cooked the chicken with onions, garlic, and a few chilies to make the chicken spicy. Then he chopped up tomatoes and vegetables and stirred everything together. He put in a tablespoon of lemon juice to make it a little sour. He added the last ingredient, fruit juice, to make it sweet. Then he mixed everything together. Finally, he poured everything over the rice. The fruit juice was his secret ingredient. He never forgot it. Sorry, I can't tell you what kind or how much. It's a family secret.

> **Writer's note**
>
> This story has two paragraphs.
> A paragraph is two or more sentences about an idea or topic. Indent the first word of each paragraph.

C **Check your understanding. Complete Papi's recipe.**

Cook the ___chicken___ with the ___onions___ , ___garlic___ , and ___a few chilies___ .
             1   2   3   4
Chop up the ___tomatoes___ and vegetables. Put in a tablespoon of ___lemon___ juice and
                 5   6
some fruit juice. ___Mixe___ everything together. Pour everything over ___the rice___ .
                   7   8

2 Write about a family recipe

A **Talk about the questions with your class.**

1. What were your favorite foods when you were a child?
2. When did your family have special meals?

B **Write about a family recipe. Use the model in 1B and the questions below to help you.**

Paragraph 1: Who was the best cook in your family when you were a child?
When did this person cook special meals?
Did you help the person cook? How? If not, what did you do?

Paragraph 2: What was your favorite food that he or she cooked?
How did the person prepare the food? (List three important ingredients.)
Was there a secret ingredient? If so, what was it?

My Favorite Dish
When I was a child the best
cook in my family was...

C **Use the checklist to edit your writing. Check (✔) the true sentences.**

Editing checklist	
1. I wrote about a favorite family recipe.	
2. I listed three or more ingredients and how to prepare them.	
3. My story has two paragraphs.	
4. I indented the first word of each paragraph.	

D **Exchange stories with a partner. Read and comment on your partner's work.**

1. Point out one sentence that you think is very interesting.
2. Ask your partner a question about his or her favorite dish.

TEST YOURSELF ✔

Work with a new partner. Listen to the first paragraph of your partner's story.
Then use your own words to write the story you heard.

Adolfo's mother was the best cook in his family. On Friday nights, she cooked...

1 Learn separable phrasal verbs

A **Read the story. What ingredient did Joel and Ming forget?**

Joel and Ming have been classmates since September. They decided to make a cake together at Ming's house for their class party. Joel wrote down a recipe. Ming put in the eggs, flour, and milk. She mixed the ingredients well. Joel turned on the oven and put the cake in. They waited patiently. When they opened the oven and took out the cake, it looked great. They brought the cake to the party and everyone tasted it. Everyone figured out the mistake right away. The cake was missing an important ingredient.

B **Study the chart. Underline the 6 phrasal verbs in the story above.**

Separable phrasal verbs	
She **put in** the eggs.	They **figured out** the mistake.
She **put** the eggs **in**.	They **figured** the mistake **out**.
She **put** them **in**.	They **figured** it **out**.

Notes
• Phrasal verbs are verbs + short words (*put in, figure out, write down*).
• Many phrasal verbs are separable. They can be separated by other words in the sentence.
• Other separable verbs are: *write down, turn on, turn off, take out, leave out, pick up*.

C **Separate the phrasal verbs to write the sentences another way.**
Use the pronouns *it* or *them* for the underlined words.

1. Mia wrote down <u>the recipe</u>.   *She wrote it down.*

2. She picked up <u>the ingredients</u> at the store.   _____

3. She put in <u>the flour</u>.   _____

4. She always leaves out <u>the salt</u>.   _____

5. She turned off <u>the oven</u>.   _____

6. She took out <u>the cake</u>.   _____

2 Learn inseparable phrasal verbs

A **Study the chart. Look at the pictures. Then complete the sentences with an inseparable phrasal verb.**

Inseparable phrasal verbs	
I **looked for** the recipe.	Joel **came over** to my house.
I **looked for** it.	Joel **came over** there.

Notes
• Some phrasal verbs are inseparable. They cannot be separated.
*I **looked** the recipe **for**. (INCORRECT)
I looked for the recipe.
• Other inseparable verbs are: *get on, get off, come over, look after.*

get on   get off   look after   get over

1. When you _____ the bus, give the money to the driver.

2. I _____ my baby brother from 4:00–5:00 every day.

3. When the doors open, stand up and _____ the train.

4. When did Ali _____ his cold?

B **Complete the conversation. Use the words in the box.**

look for   get off   get on   ~~come over~~

A: Do you want to ____*come over*____ to my house for dinner?

B: Sure. How do I get there?

A: You live on 1st Street, so _____ the #5 bus. _____ at the 12th Street stop. _____ my house across the street. It's the only blue house on the street.

3 Grammar listening

Listen to the sentences. Which sentence is true? Circle *a* or *b*.

1. a. She is sick.
   b. She doesn't like winter.

2. a. He wants a salad with onions.
   b. He doesn't want any onions.

3. a. She is looking for the trash.
   b. She is going to put the trash outside.

4. a. He's looking for a piece of paper.
   b. He's looking in the phone book.

5. a. She is going to her friends' home.
   b. Her friends are coming to her home.

6. a. He stayed on the bus.
   b. He did not stay on the bus.

4 Practice phrasal verbs

A **Think about a dish you can make. How do you prepare it? Write the steps.**

B **Work with 2 partners. Follow the directions. Then change roles.**

Partner A: Explain to your classmates how to cook a dish.
                         Use as many of the verbs in the list as you can.

Partners B and C: Check (✔) the verbs in the list that you hear.

Phrasal verb list	Partner A's recipe	Partner B's recipe	Partner C's recipe
put in			
chop up			
leave out			
turn on			
turn off			
take out			

C **Work with another group. Tell them about one of the recipes.**

TEST YOURSELF ✔

Write 3 sentences about one or more of the recipes you discussed above.
Use a phrasal verb in each sentence.

For Julio's scrambled eggs, chop up one onion and put it in the eggs.

1 Learn to order a meal

A Look at the pictures and listen to the conversations. Then answer the questions below with your classmates.

1. What does the first customer order?
2. What does the second customer order?

B Listen and read. What is a Denver Omelet?

Customer: Excuse me. I have a question about the menu. I've never heard of a "Denver Omelet". What is it?

Server: It's an egg dish with cheese, tomatoes, peppers, and ham.

Customer: Sounds good. OK. I'll try it.

Server: Excellent. Ours is the best in town.

Customer: I'd also like some coffee cake. Is yours sweet?

Server: No, it isn't. Our cook doesn't use much sugar.

Customer: Good. I'm trying to cut down on* sugar.

*Idiom note: trying to cut down on = not eating much

C Role-play a restaurant conversation with a partner. Use the example in 1B to make a new conversation.

Partner A: You are the customer. You've never heard of a chili dog. Ask the server about it. You also want some vegetable soup. Ask if it is salty. You are trying to cut down on salt.

Partner B: You are the server. Tell the customer that a chili dog is a hot dog with a spicy meat sauce. Also tell the customer that the cook doesn't use much salt.

2 Learn possessive pronouns

A **Study the charts. Then work with a partner. Partner A: Say a possessive adjective. Partner B: Say the matching possessive pronoun.**

Possessive adjectives	Possessive pronouns	Notes
my	mine	• A possessive pronoun replaces a possessive adjective and a noun:
your	yours	I'd like some coffee cake. Is yours sweet?
his	his	(*yours* = your coffee cake)
her	hers	• Never use a possessive pronoun with another noun:
our	ours	Ours is the best in town.
your	yours	Our Denver Omelet is the best in town.
their	theirs	*Ours Denver Omelet is the best in town. (INCORRECT)

B **Circle the correct possessive adjectives or possessive pronouns.**

1. ((Their) / Theirs) dinner was good, but (our / ours) was terrible.
2. Juanita and I both ate sandwiches today. (My / Mine) was delicious, but (her / hers) was too spicy.
3. I tried Sonya's recipe for chicken soup today. (Hers / Her) recipe is much better than (me / mine).
4. I went over to Helen's house today. (Her / Hers) kitchen is very organized. (My / Mine) kitchen isn't. Is (your / yours)?
5. (Your / Yours) dessert looks delicious. Can I try some of (your / yours)?

3 Practice your pronunciation

 A **Listen to the linking of the phrasal verbs in these sentences.**

1. I can't figure out something on the menu.
2. Please turn on the oven.

B **Listen to the conversations. Complete the phrasal verbs you hear.**

1. look _____   3. get _____   5. came _____
2. turn _____   4. turn _____   6. get _____

C **Listen again and check. Repeat the phrasal verbs in 3B.**

4 Focus on listening

A Talk about the questions with your class.

1. When you eat at a restaurant, do you usually look at the bill carefully before you pay?
2. Do most restaurants include the tip in the bill?

Can we have the bill, please?

B Listen to the conversation. Mark the sentences T (true) or F (false).

_____ 1. The customers enjoyed their lunch.

_____ 2. The service was not good.

_____ 3. There was a mistake on the bill.

_____ 4. The tip is included in the total.

C Listen again and complete the information on the bill.

BILL		
_____	hamburgers @ $6.00 each =	_____
_____	turkey burgers @ $5.50 each =	_____
_____	lemonades @ _____ each =	_____
_____	coffee @ _____ each =	$1.50
	Sub-total =	$36.50
	Tax =	$3.19
	Total =	_____

5 Real-life math

Use the bill in 4C to answer the questions.

The Kim family in 4C is very happy with their meal. They want to leave a good tip.

1. How much money should they leave for a 15% tip?

    $36.50 × .15 = _____

2. If the Kims leave a 20% tip, how much will they pay for the food, tax, and tip? _____

Need help?

Tipping
Most people only tip on the total of the food. It's not necessary to tip on any tax.

┌─ TEST YOURSELF ✔ ─

Role-play a restaurant conversation. Partner A: You are the customer. Order something and ask for help with a menu item. Partner B: You are the server. Tell your customer about the menu item. Then change roles.

1 Get ready to read

A **Has someone you know ever gotten sick from bad food? What happened?**

B **Read the definitions.**

bacteria: (noun) very small living things that sometimes make people sick
food poisoning: (noun) illness people get by eating food that has dangerous bacteria
leftovers: (noun) extra or uneaten food from a meal that people eat at a later meal
throw out: (phrasal verb, separable) to put in the garbage

bacteria

C **Look at the title of each section of the pamphlet in 2A. Name the five ways to protect against food poisoning.**

2 Read and respond

A **Read the pamphlet.**

Protect Yourself from Food Poisoning

Follow these steps to stay safe:

Clean

Wash your hands for 20 seconds with soap and warm water before and after you touch food.

Dry your hands with paper towels or a clean dishtowel. Clean counters and dishes with hot, soapy water every time you use them.

Cook

Cook food long enough to kill bacteria. Different foods have different cooking temperatures.

To check food temperatures, put a cooking thermometer deep[1] in the center of the food.

---

[1]deep: far inside
[2]spread: to move

Use the Safe Temperatures chart to cook foods to a safe temperature.

Safe Temperatures
145° F - beef, steaks, and roasts
160° F - ground beef, pork, and eggs
170° F - chicken and turkey breasts
180° F - chicken and turkey (whole)

Separate

Bacteria can spread[2] from food to food. Separate uncooked beef, chicken, and fish from fruits and vegetables in your shopping cart and in your refrigerator.

☑ Identify methods of safe food preparation

Refrigerate

Bacteria grows very fast. Refrigerate leftovers within two hours after you cook them. Keep your refrigerator set at 40°F or less to keep food safe from bacteria. Check the temperature with a thermometer every few months.

Check "use by" and expiration dates

Always check the "use by" dates on the things in your refrigerator. "Use by" dates are suggestions. If there is an expiration date on a food product, don't eat or drink it after the date. Expiration dates are there for your safety.

When in Doubt, Throw It Out!

Cooked vegetables:
  keep 3 to 4 days

Poultry, fish, or
ground meat:
  keep 2 days (cooked) or
  1 to 2 days (uncooked)

Other cooked meats:
  keep 3 to 4 days

Milk: keep 5 to 7 days

Eggs: keep 3 weeks

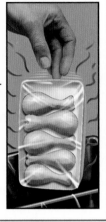

Source: *State of California Department of Health Services*

B Listen and read the pamphlet again.

C Complete the sentences. Use the information in the pamphlet.

1. Use _____soap_____ and _____water_____ to clean your hands and kitchen counters.
2. Check the food temperature with a _____.
3. You should cook ground beef until the temperature is _____.
4. _____ grows very fast and can spread from food to food.
5. Of the foods in the food chart, you can keep _____ the longest.
6. After two days in the refrigerator, you should _____ ground meat.
7. _____ dates tell you when you must use or throw away a food product.

3 Talk it over

A Think about the questions. Make notes about your answers.

1. Do you think eating in restaurants is as safe as eating in your home? Why or why not?
2. Name 3 foods not listed in the food storage chart. How long do you think it's safe to keep them in the refrigerator? Where can you look to check your answers?

B Talk about the answers with your classmates.

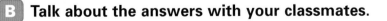

BRING IT TO LIFE

Look at the "use by" dates in the dairy section of a market. Bring a list of 3 items and dates to class. How many days are there between today's date and the "use by" dates on each item? Talk about your answers with the class.

1 Grammar

A **Complete the answers with separable phrasal verbs. Change the underlined nouns to pronouns.**

1. **A:** Can you pick up <u>Mark</u>?

   B: Yes, I can _____ _pick him up_ _____.

2. **A:** Who can figure out <u>these problems</u>?

   B: I can _____.

3. **A:** Did Danielle leave out <u>the eggs</u> again?

   B: Yes, she _____.

4. **A:** Who took out <u>the trash</u>?

   B: Elsa _____.

5. **A:** Did you write down <u>the recipes</u>?

   B: Yes, I _____.

B **Complete the sentences. Use the phrasal verbs in the box. Use pronouns for the underlined nouns.**

turn off   look after   ~~take out~~   put in   look for

1. Why is the <u>trash</u> still here? Can you _____ _take it out_ _____?

2. I need a babysitter for the <u>kids</u> on Saturday. Can you _____?

3. Is the <u>stove</u> still on? Can you _____?

4. I can't find my <u>keys</u>. Can you help me _____?

5. Here are the <u>carrots</u> for the soup. Can you peel them and _____?

C **Circle the correct possessive pronouns or adjectives.**

A: Did you remember to bring in ((your) / yours) favorite recipe?
   ₁

B: Yes, I did. This is (my / mine). It's actually my grandmother's recipe—tomato salad.
                          ₂

A: You're kidding! (My / Mine) is for tomato salad, too. But it's (my / mine) father's recipe.
                          ₃   ₄

B: That's interesting. What's in (your / yours)?
                                      ₅

A: (His / He) salad uses tomatoes and onions. It also has sugar and vinegar.
      ₆

B: My grandmother just uses tomatoes, but (his / hers) also has vinegar and sugar.
                                              ₇

A: (Their / Theirs) recipes are almost the same.
      ₈

2 Group work

A Work with 2–3 classmates. Write a conversation between the people in the picture. Share your conversation with the class.

Server: *Are you ready to order?*
Customer: *Yes, but I have a question about the menu...*

B Complete the sentences. Then interview 3 classmates. Write their answers.

1. My favorite restaurant is _____. What's yours?
2. I like my favorite restaurant because _____. Why do you like yours?
3. My favorite dish is _____. What's yours?
4. I use _____ to prepare my favorite dish. What do you use to prepare yours?

C Talk about the answers with your class.

PROBLEM SOLVING

A Listen and read about Dora and Jorge.

Today is Dora and Jorge's 25th wedding anniversary. They went out to a nice restaurant for dinner. Unfortunately, the chicken was too salty, the fish was dry, the vegetables were cold, and the dessert was too sweet. Dora and Jorge are upset. The service was good, but the food was terrible, and the meal was expensive. They don't really want to leave a tip for a terrible meal, but the server was very nice. They don't know what to do.

B Work with your classmates. Answer the questions.

1. Why are Dora and Jorge upset?
2. What should they do? Make a list of 3 or 4 things that they can do.

Money Wise

FOCUS ON
• banking
• financial planning
• real conditionals
• billing errors
• identity theft

LESSON 1 **Vocabulary**

1 Learn banking vocabulary

A **Talk about the questions with your class.**

1. Do you usually do your banking at the bank, at the ATM, or on your computer?
2. What are some services that banks offer?

B **Work with your classmates. Match the words with the picture.**

CASHIER'S CHECK
State Bank **SB**

Remitter

Carlos Pena   Date June 3, 2007

Pay to the
order of: — Joe's Automobiles $ 7,500.00

Seven Thousand Five Hundred Dollars and 00/100

David Chen
Authorized Signature

LOAN
CENTER

NEW
ACCOUNTS

State Bank **SB**   LOAN APPLICATION

Loan Amount: LoanType:
                          ☐ Individual
$10,000.00   ☑ Joint with Spouse
                          ☐ Joint with no Spouse
Name: Antonio Ramirez
Name: Beatriz Ramirez
Address _____

State Bank **SB**   NEW ACCOUNT
                    APPLICATION

Account Type: ☑ Individual
Checking   ☐ Joint with Spouse

Primary Account Owner Nikita Federov
Address _____

____ accounts manager   ____ security guard   ____ apply for a loan
____ account services desk   ____ teller   _1_ get a cashier's check
____ loan officer   ____ teller window   ____ open an account

 C **Listen and check. Then read the new words with a partner.**

D **Work with a partner. Write other banking words you know.**
Check your words in a dictionary.

   Identify banking vocabulary

E Work with a partner. Practice the conversation. Use the picture in 1B.

A: Excuse me, I need to open an account. Where should I go?

B: Go to the account services desk and talk to the accounts manager.

A: Great. Thank you.

2 Learn about banking services

A Look at the bank's website. What kind of accounts, services, and tips do you know about? Which ones are new to you?

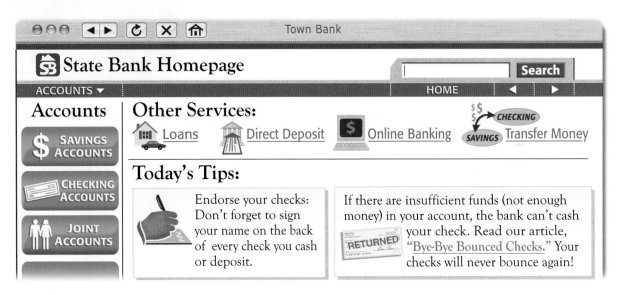

B Work with a partner. Partner A: Read the questions. Partner B: Look at the website in 2A. Tell your partner where to click to find the information.

A: *How can my spouse and I share a savings account?*

B: *Click on joint accounts.*

1. How can my paycheck go directly into my account?
2. How can I use banking services from my home computer?
3. How do I move money from one account to another?
4. How can I avoid bounced checks?

C Talk about the questions with your class.

1. Name at least three bank jobs. What do these employees do?
2. Name at least two important bank services. Why are they important?

TEST YOURSELF ✓

Close your book. Categorize the new words in 3 lists: *Banking, Bank Employees,* and *Bank Services.* Check your spelling in a dictionary. Compare your lists with a partner.

1 Read about financial planning and goals

A Look at the picture. Talk about the questions with your class.

1. What is Kim and her husband's goal?
2. What can they do to reach their goal?

 STUDENT AUDIO

B Listen and read the story about financial planning.

Financial Planning for the Future ←
By: Kim Sanchez

    My husband and I are hoping to buy a new car next year. The one we have now is very old, needs many repairs, and uses a lot of gas. We have a plan. My husband and I have a joint account. We're saving money in our account so we can buy the car of our dreams.

    We've learned a lot about saving money. My husband doesn't drive to work alone anymore. He rides with a co-worker, and they share the cost of gas. We never buy our lunch at work anymore. It's cheaper to bring it from home. I plan my grocery shopping carefully. I go to the supermarket once a week. I always make a list, and I use coupons. Saving money isn't easy, but if we work hard, we can reach our goal. With a new car, we'll save money on gas and repair bills. We'll also feel safer on the road.

> **Writer's note**
>
> In a title, use capital letters for all words except articles (*the, a/an*) and prepositions (such as *for, in, on, at*).

C Check your understanding. Mark the statements T (true), F (false), or NI (no information).

  _F_ 1. Kim is single.

  _____ 2. Kim and her husband are happy with the car they own now.

  _____ 3. They have a joint account.

  _____ 4. They saved $100 last month.

  _____ 5. Kim uses coupons at the supermarket.

☑ Describe a personal financial plan

2 Write about a financial plan

A **Talk about the questions with your class.**

1. What are some places that people put the money they save?
2. Is saving money easier for you now than it was in the past? Why or why not?

B **Write about your financial plan. Use the model in 1B and the questions below to help you.**

Paragraph 1: What are you hoping to buy in the future? Why?
What's your plan for saving the money you'll need?

Paragraph 2: What things do you do now to save money?
(Write about three or more things.)
When do you think you will you reach your goal?
How will your new purchase help you?

> **My Financial Plan**
>
> I'm hoping to buy a house in two
> years. I live in an apartment now.

C **Use the checklist to edit your writing. Check (✔) the true sentences.**

Editing checklist	
1. I wrote about something I plan to buy and why I want to buy it.	
2. I wrote about three or more ways I save money.	
3. I used the rules on page 90 for capital letters in the title of my story.	
4. There are two paragraphs in my story.	

D **Exchange stories with a partner. Read and comment on your partner's work.**

1. Point out one way that your partner saves money.
2. Ask your partner a question about his or her financial plan.

TEST YOURSELF ✔

Write a paragraph about your partner's savings plan. Use the information you learned from 2D.

Paulo is hoping to buy a new TV.

1 Learn real conditionals

A Read the conversation. Will the customer buy the coat today?

Customer: I'd like to buy this coat, please.

Salesperson: You know, tomorrow we're having a big sale. If you wait until tomorrow, it'll probably be twenty percent off.

Customer: That's a good deal. But if I wait until tomorrow, someone else might buy it!

Salesperson: You could come in early. You'll save an extra ten percent if you come in before 9 a.m.

Customer: That's perfect! What time do you open?

B Study the chart. Underline the 3 *if* clauses in the conversation above.

Real Conditionals			
⎯⎯⎯*If* clause⎯⎯⎯	⎯Main clause⎯	⎯Main clause⎯	⎯*If* clause⎯
If **I buy** the coat tomorrow, **I'll save** money.		**I'll save** money if **I buy** the coat tomorrow.	
If **she buys** the coat today, **she won't save** money.		**She won't save** money if **she buys** the coat today.	

Notes
• Real conditionals describe possible events in the future.
• Use the simple present in the *if* clause and *will/won't* in the main clause.
• The *if* clause can come before or after the main clause.

C Complete the sentences. Use the verbs in parentheses.

1. If she ____buys____ the coat tomorrow, she ___will save___ money. (buy, save)

2. If she _____ to the store before 9:00, she _____ ten percent less. (go, pay)

3. I _____ to the bank if I _____ a cashier's check. (go, need)

4. If they _____ enough money, they _____ a car loan. (save, not need)

5. Ali _____ to a loan officer if he _____ a car loan. (speak, want)

6. If you _____ money to your checking account, the check _____. (transfer, not bounce)

7. If we _____ our money in a joint checking account, we _____. money faster. (put, save)

8. The bank _____ free checks if we _____ an account today. (give, open)

D **Get the form. Work with your class. Read the sentences. Then circle *a* or *b*.**

a. If I buy the coat tomorrow, I'll save thirty percent.

b. I'll save thirty percent if I buy the coat tomorrow.

1. Which sentence has a comma?

   a. sentence a

   b. sentence b

2. Complete the rule: Use a comma when ____.

   a. the *if* clause is first.

   b. the main clause is first.

2 Learn questions with real conditionals

A **Study the chart. Then match the questions and answers below.**

Questions and answers with real conditionals	
A: Will you buy a new jacket if it's on sale? **B:** Yes, I will. OR No, I won't.	**A:** How much will they save if they bring their lunch? **B:** They'll save $20 a week.
A: What will you do if you get a loan? **B:** I'll celebrate.	**A:** Where will you go if you need a new computer? **B:** I'll go to Computer World.

_e_ 1. What will Ben do if he needs a loan?

____ 2. What will you buy if you save enough money?

____ 3. How much will Mateo deposit if he gets paid today?

____ 4. Where will you go if you want to open a new account?

____ 5. Will he buy the coat if it's on sale?

a. He'll deposit $500.

b. I'll go to the new accounts desk.

c. I'll buy a computer.

d. Yes, he will.

e. He'll talk to a loan officer.

B **Complete the questions.**

1. **A:** What will Safiya do _if she gets the job_____?

   B: If Safiya gets the job, she will open a new bank account.

2. **A:** What will Jose do _____?

   B: If he finds the right house, Jose will apply for a loan.

3. **A:** How much _____?

   B: If they take the bus, they will save $10.00 a week.

4. **A:** Where _____?

   B: If they need a new TV, they'll go to Atlas Electronics.

3 Grammar listening

 Listen to the questions. Circle *a* or *b*.

1. a. I'll look for a car this weekend.
   b. I'll get a loan.

2. a. I'll buy a new jacket.
   b. I'll withdraw $200.

3. a. No, I won't.
   b. I'll use the ATM.

4. a. I'll deposit money.
   b. I'll go to the mall.

5. a. Yes, he will.
   b. Yes, I will.

6. a. I'll reach it by the end of the year.
   b. Yes, I will.

4 Practice talking about future plans

A **Work with 3 classmates. Talk about what you see in the picture.**

B **What do you think will happen? Write 5 sentences with your group.
Use an *if* clause and a main clause in each sentence.**

If the manager sees the security guard, he'll be angry.

C **Read your sentences with another group.**

TEST YOURSELF ✔

Close your book. Write 5 sentences about what you will do if you have free
time this weekend. Use an *if* clause and a main clause in each sentence.

1 Learn to report a billing or banking error

STUDENT AUDIO 🎧 **A**   **Look at the picture. Listen to the conversation. Then mark the sentences below T (true) or F (false).**

_____ 1. Min is upset about her credit card bill.

_____ 2. She lives in Pacific City.

_____ 3. She doesn't have to pay her bill
this month.

STUDENT AUDIO 🎧 **B**   **Listen and read. What is the problem with the bill?**

Customer:	I'm calling to report a problem on my credit card bill.
Customer Service:	What seems to be the problem?
Customer:	It says I spent $100 at Tom's Market last week, but that's impossible. I've never been to Tom's Market.
Customer Service:	OK. I'll talk to my supervisor and ask him to review it before we send your next bill.
Customer:	So, do I have to pay the $100 charge this month?
Customer Service:	Let's wait and see what my supervisor says. When you receive your next bill, you'll see your new balance.

> **In other words...**
>
> **Asking about problems**
> What seems to be the problem?
> What's the problem?
> How can I help you?

C   **Role-play a telephone conversation with a partner. Use the example in 1B to make a new conversation.**

Partner A: You are a customer. Call customer service at your cell phone company and report a problem on your cell phone bill. You received a bill that says that you owe $300 for phone calls to India. You don't know anybody in India.

Partner B: You are a customer service representative for the cell phone company. Ask the customer to tell you the problem. Say that your supervisor will review the charge before you send the next bill.

☑ Report a billing or banking error; listen for automated account information   **95**

2 Learn future events with time clauses

A Study the chart. Then match the clauses below to make complete sentences.

Describing future events with time clauses	Notes
Main clause — **Time clause**	• Time clauses give information about when things happen.
We'll review the statement **before** we send the next bill.	• A time clause can come before or after the main clause.
You'll see your new balance **when** you receive your next bill.	• Use *will* in the main clause and the simple present in the time clause.
I'll pay the bill **after** I get my next statement.	

_b_ 1. The bank will review the statement   a. we'll apply for a home loan.

____ 2. I will sign the check   b. before they send the next one.

____ 3. We will know how much to pay   c. before I deposit it.

____ 4. After we find a house,   d. when we receive our bill.

B Complete the sentences with your own ideas. Practice your sentences with a partner.

1. If I have time this weekend…

2. Before I leave class today…

3. After I finish this class…

4. When I go home today…

3 Practice your pronunciation

A Look at the chart. Listen to the pronunciation of the linked words in these sentences.

Sentence	Linked words	Note
I'll ask her.	ask ~~her~~	When two words are linked, speakers often don't pronounce the beginning "h" sound in the second word.
What's his name?	What's ~~his~~	
Come here now!	Come ~~here~~	

B Listen. Circle the linked words.

1. Your sister (brought her) friend. (What's her) friend's name?
2. Tim will brush his teeth before he goes to bed.
3. He'll go to the bank before he comes home.
4. When he gets his paycheck, Jack will buy a new TV.

C Listen again and check. Repeat the sentences.

4 Focus on listening

A Talk about the questions with your class.

1. What kind of information can you get about your bank accounts over the phone?
2. Is it easy or difficult to get account information over the phone?

B Listen to the account information. Mark the sentences T (true) or F (false).

_____ 1. The recording has information for two kinds of accounts.

_____ 2. The customer is listening to information about a savings account.

_____ 3. The customer wrote these checks after March 15th.

C Listen again. Complete the account information.

Checking Account			
1.	3/07	#266	$44.73
2.	3/07	#_____	$106.50
3.	3/09	#267	_____
4.	_____	#270	_____
5.	_____	_____	_____

5 Real-life math

Read about Town Bank's Savings Accounts. Answer the questions below. Then compare your answers with the class.

1. Sara wants to open a savings account with $500. Which account can she get?

_____

2. Adam has $10,000 in a Premiere Savings Account. How much interest will he earn this year?

10,000 × .05 = _____

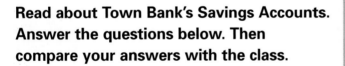

🖳 Internet Search _ □ x

Address `http://www.townbanksavings.mypage.com` ▼ Go

Town Bank Savings Accounts Compare our accounts.	Interest rate	Minimum balance
Basic Savings Click to Apply	2%	None
Gold Savings Click to Apply	4.03%	$2,500
Premiere Savings Click to Apply	5%	$8,000

TEST YOURSELF ✓

Role-play a conversation in a bank. Partner A: There's a mistake on your bank statement. Talk to the teller. Partner B: You're the teller. Help the customer. Then change roles.

1 Get ready to read

A Has anyone ever used your name or credit card number to buy something without your permission?

B Read the definitions.

crime: (noun) an action that breaks the law

criminal: (noun) a person who breaks the law

identity theft: (noun) the crime of using another person's name, social security number, credit card number, or other personal information without permission

C Look at the title and pictures in the article. What is the article is about?

2 Read and respond

A Read the article.

Identity Theft: Are You Safe?

Identity theft is a growing problem in the U.S. This crime affects 10 million people a year. A criminal can use your personal information to apply for credit cards, take money from your bank account, or even buy a new home!

Unfortunately, it can be easy for the wrong person to get your information. The U.S. Department of Justice lists the most common[1] ways people steal information and how you can protect yourself.

If you are a victim of identity theft, you should contact the Federal Trade Commission at *www.ftc.gov* or look in the government pages of your phone book.

---

[1]common: usual, popular

Shoulder surfing

Be careful with your information in public places. A person behind you can listen to you or watch over your shoulder and get your information

Dumpster diving

Some criminals look in trash cans outside of homes to get information. Always cut up papers with your personal information before you throw them away.

Phishing

Criminals can pretend to be your bank or credit card company. They send an email that looks real and asks you for personal information such as your social security or credit card numbers. If you get an email with your bank's name on it and it asks you to send personal information, don't do it.

Source: *U.S. Federal Trade Commission*

☑ Identify ways to avoid becoming a victim of identity theft

B Listen and read the article again.

C Mark the sentences T (true), F (false), or NI (no information).

 _F_ 1. Ten billion people a year are victims of identity theft.

 ____ 2. Fortunately, it's very difficult for a criminal to get your personal information.

 ____ 3. Criminals won't look for information in a trash can.

 ____ 4. A criminal can listen to you in public and steal your information.

 ____ 5. If an email asks for your bank password, you shouldn't give it.

 ____ 6. The author of the article was a victim of identity theft.

D Study the chart. Circle the correct words in the sentences below.

> **Word Study: The suffix -al**
>
> Add –al to some nouns to form adjectives.
> person + -al = personal   You should protect your **personal** information.
>
> | accident | accidental | music | musical |
> | nation | national | profession | professional |

1. Identity theft is a (nation / (national)) problem.
2. It can be easy for a (person / personal) to steal your identity.
3. Sandra is very (music / musical). She can sing, play the piano, and play the guitar.
4. There was a car (accident / accidental) on the corner yesterday.
5. When Eli has a job interview, he always wears (profession / professional) clothing.

3 Talk it over

A Think about the questions. Make notes about your answers.

1. How can you say "no" if someone asks for your personal information on the telephone?
2. Why do you think there is more and more identity theft in the U.S. every year?

B Talk about the answers with your classmates.

BRING IT TO LIFE

Look around your home for two letters, papers, or other things that you should cut up before you throw away. Tell the class what you found.

1 Grammar

A Match the clauses to make complete sentences.

_____ 1. When I save enough money,   a. if I don't have time tonight.

_____ 2. I'll pay the bills   b. I'll go to the gym before work.

_____ 3. I'll do my homework in the morning   c. I'll buy a house.

_____ 4. If the bus comes on time,   d. when I get my paycheck.

B Circle the correct words to complete the sentences.

1. If Inez and Rubin (won't spend /(don't spend)) all their money, they'll put it in the bank.
2. If Jorge needs help with his homework, (he'll call / he calls) a classmate.
3. If Alma's husband (forgets / will forget) her birthday, she'll be upset.
4. I (go / will go) to the bank if I need a cashier's check.
5. Yukio will be a little nervous if he (applies / will apply) for a home loan.

C Write answers to the questions.

1. What will you do when you complete this class?

   _____

2. How will you feel when you speak fluent English?

   _____

3. Where will you go if you take a vacation?

   _____

4. What will you do if it rains tomorrow morning?

   _____

D Complete the sentences with *before, when,* or *after.*

1. Ella will fill out the application _____ she gives it to the loan officer.
2. I'll ask a supervisor _____ I need help.
3. Jamal will mail the letters _____ he buys stamps.
4. _____ you deposit a check, you will need to endorse it.
5. We'll open an account _____ we talk to the accounts manager.
6. _____ I have enough money, I'll buy a car.

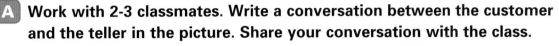

A Work with 2-3 classmates. Write a conversation between the customer and the teller in the picture. Share your conversation with the class.

Customer: Excuse me, there's a mistake on my bank statement. Could you check my account?

Teller: Sure. What seems to be the problem?

B Interview 3 classmates. Write their answers.

1. Do you enjoy financial planning? Why or why not?
2. Do you have a financial goal right now? What is it?
3. When you reach your goal, what will you do next?

C Talk about the answers with your class.

PROBLEM SOLVING

A Listen and read about Li.

　　Li is thinking about getting a credit card. Every week he receives 3 or 4 credit card offers in the mail. All the offers are a little different. For example, one card offers 0% interest for 6 months and 12% interest after that. Another card offers 7% interest all the time. Another card offers no annual fee and only 5% interest on balance transfers. All the cards promise to be the best. Li isn't sure what to think. They can't all be the best.

B Work with your classmates. Answer the questions.

1. What is Li's problem?
2. What should Li do? Think of 2–3 things that Li should do before he decides which credit card to get.

Living Well

FOCUS ON
• the body and health care
• wellness
• past actions with *used to*
• following doctor's advice
• drug safety

LESSON **1** Vocabulary

1 Learn parts of the body

A **Talk about the questions with your class.**

1. Do you think scientists and doctors know a little or a lot about the human body?
2. Do you think the study of the human body is interesting? Why or why not?

B **Work with your classmates. Match the words with the pictures.**

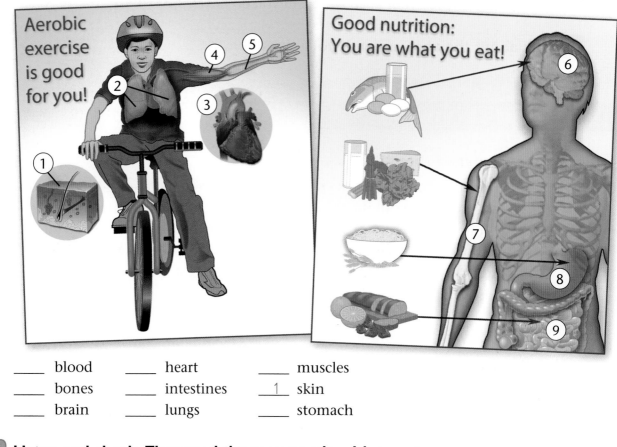

Aerobic exercise is good for you!

Good nutrition: You are what you eat!

____ blood	____ heart	____ muscles
____ bones	____ intestines	_1_ skin
____ brain	____ lungs	____ stomach

C **Listen and check. Then read the new words with a partner.**

D **Work with a partner. Write other parts of the body you know.
Check your words in a dictionary.**

E Work with a partner. Practice the conversation. Use the pictures in 1B.

A: What are milk and cheese good for?

B: They're good for your bones.

A: What is aerobic exercise good for?

B: It's good for your heart and lungs.

2 Learn about medical departments

A Look at the hospital directory. Write the department names next to the sentences below.

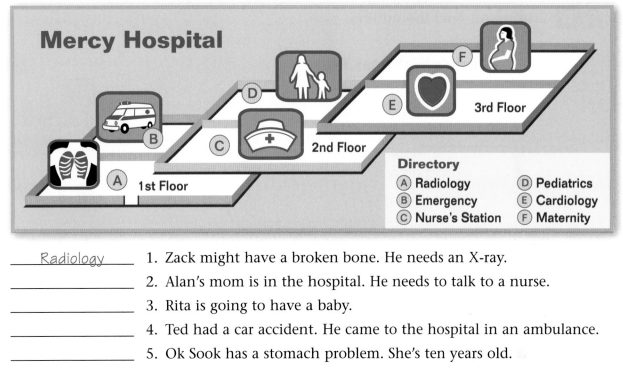

Mercy Hospital

3rd Floor

2nd Floor

1st Floor

Directory
(A) Radiology   (D) Pediatrics
(B) Emergency   (E) Cardiology
(C) Nurse's Station (F) Maternity

_____Radiology_____ 1. Zack might have a broken bone. He needs an X-ray.

_____ 2. Alan's mom is in the hospital. He needs to talk to a nurse.

_____ 3. Rita is going to have a baby.

_____ 4. Ted had a car accident. He came to the hospital in an ambulance.

_____ 5. Ok Sook has a stomach problem. She's ten years old.

_____ 6. Habib needs to have some tests done on his heart.

B Work with a partner. Practice the conversation. Use the words in 2A.

A: Excuse me. Where is Maternity?

B: It's on the third floor, near Cardiology.

A: Thank you.

C Talk about the questions with a partner.

1. Which medical departments have you been to?
2. Which parts of the body do doctors need to learn more about? Why?

TEST YOURSELF ✔

Close your book. Work with a partner. Make a list of as many new words from the lesson as you can. Alphabetize your list.

1 Read an outline about staying healthy

A Look at the pictures. Talk about the questions with your class.

1. What things do you do to take care of your health?
2. What do you think is the most important thing people can do to stay healthy?

B Listen and read the outline.

Maria's Wellness Plan

I. Improve Eating Habits
   A. Eat less fast food
   B. Eat low-fat ice cream
   C. Eat more fresh vegetables at lunch and dinner

II. Get in Shape
   A. Do aerobics three times a week
   B. Lift weights for strong bones and muscles

III. Stay Well
   A. Make medical and dental appointments
      1. See the doctor for a physical exam
      2. See the dentist for a cleaning
      3. Get an eye exam
   B. Manage Stress
      1. Relax with my family
      2. Don't worry about little things

C Check your understanding. Circle *a* or *b*.

1. Maria plans to eat less ____.
   a. fast food
   b. fresh vegetables
2. Maria will ____ three times a week.
   a. do aerobics
   b. get an eye exam

3. The three main parts of Maria's plan are about ____.
   a. nutrition, doctors, and stress
   b. nutrition, exercise, and staying well
4. Maria has only two details about ____.
   a. eating habits
   b. managing stress

2 Write an outline about staying healthy

A **Talk about the questions with your class.**

1. What food is healthy?
2. What kind(s) of exercise do you do?
3. Why do people see the doctor and dentist?
4. What are some ways to manage stress?

B **Write an outline of your plan for good health. Use the model in 1B and your answers to the questions in 2A.**

My Wellness Plan

I. _____
   A. _____
   B. _____
   C. _____

II. _____
   A. _____
   B. _____

III. _____
   A. _____
      1. _____
      2. _____
   B. _____
      1. _____
      2. _____

C **Use the checklist to edit your writing. Check (✔) the true sentences.**

Editing checklist	
1. I wrote at least three points about good eating habits.	
2. I wrote two different ways to stay well, and I wrote details for each one.	
3. I used a dictionary to check the spelling of words I wasn't sure about.	
4. All lines in my outline begin with a capital letter.	

D **Exchange outlines with a partner. Read and comment on your partner's work.**

1. Point out one part of the plan that you think is very interesting.
2. Ask your partner a question about his or her wellness plan.

TEST YOURSELF ✔

What wellness advice do you think a doctor or other healthcare worker would give? Write a new outline.

1 Learn *used to*

 A **Look at the pictures and read the paragraph. What changes do you see in Sam?**

Sam wants to take better care of his health, so he has made some changes in his life. He used to eat a lot of junk food. He doesn't eat it anymore. He didn't use to eat fruit and vegetables. Now, he eats more healthy food. Sam used to watch a lot of TV. He didn't use to exercise. Now, he walks every day. Sam didn't use to have many friends. Now, he feels great and has made many new friends.

Before   After

B **Study the charts. Underline the 5 examples of *used to* in the paragraph above.**

USED TO

Affirmative statements					
I You He She	**used to**	eat junk food.	We You They	**used to**	eat junk food.

Negative statements					
I You He She	**didn't use to**	exercise last year.	We You They	**didn't use to**	exercise last year.

Note
Use *used to* + verb to talk about a habit or situation that was true in the past but is not true now.

C **Read the sentences about the things that Sam used to do, but doesn't do now. Rewrite the sentences with the correct forms of *used to*.**

1. Sam watched a lot of TV last year.   _Sam used to watch a lot of TV._
2. Sam didn't go outside very often.   _____
3. Sam drank too much soda.   _____
4. Sam didn't lift weights.   _____
5. Sam stayed inside a lot.   _____

2 Learn questions with *used to*

A Study the chart. Then match the questions below with the answers.

Questions and answers with *used to*	
A: Did Jim **use to smoke**? **B:** Yes, he did. OR No, he didn't.	**A:** Did they **use to see** Dr. Jones? **B:** No, they **didn't use to see** Dr. Jones.
A: When did you **use to exercise**? **B:** We **used to exercise** after work.	**A:** What doctor did they **use to see**? **B:** They **used to see** Dr. Green.

<u>b</u> 1. What did Mia use to eat all the time?   a. No, she didn't.

____ 2. Where did Mia use to eat?   b. She used to eat fast food.

____ 3. What problem did Mia use to have?   c. She used to eat in her car.

____ 4. Did Mia use to take care of herself?   d. She used to have stomach problems.

____ 5. Why did Mia use to eat fast food?   e. Yes, she does.

____ 6. Does Mia take care of herself now?   f. She used to be too busy to cook.

B Get the form. Work with your class. Circle the correct words in the sentences.

1. Write (*used to* / *use to*) + *verb* for affirmative sentences.
2. Write *didn't* (*used to* / *use to*) + *verb* for negative sentences.
3. Write (*used to* / *use to*) in questions with *did*.

C Complete the questions and answers. Use the correct form of *used to* and the words in parentheses.

1. **A:** How often <u>did Tom use to get a physical exam</u>? (Tom, get a physical exam)

   B: He used to get a physical exam once a year when he was younger.

2. **A:** Did _____ in Mexico? (Mr. and Mrs. Diaz, live)

   B: Yes, they did. They _____ in Mexico City 5 years ago. (live)

3. **A:** Did _____? (Sara, study)

   B: Yes, she used to study a lot when she was a student.

4. **A:** When _____? (Bill, lift weights)

   B: He used to lift weights when he was in college.

5. **A:** When she was a child, how often _____? (Fatima, eat breakfast)

   B: She used to eat breakfast every day when she was a child.

3 Grammar listening

 A Listen to the health habits of the Martinez family. Mark the sentences T (true) or F (false).

   _F_ 1. Livia eats white bread now.

    ____ 2. Carlos didn't use to go to the park.

    ____ 3. Tomas used to save a lot of money.

    ____ 4. Paulo didn't use to exercise on the weekend.

    ____ 5. Elena can't play basketball because she hurt her knee.

B Listen and check (✔) *used to, didn't use to,* or Question with *use to*.

	used to	*didn't use to*	Question with *use to*
1.			✔
2.			
3.			
4.			
5.			

4 Practice *used to*

A Think about your answers to these questions.

1. What exercise did you use to do that you don't do now?
2. What food did you use to eat that you don't eat anymore?
3. What places did you use to go that you don't go now?
4. What habit did you use to have that you don't have anymore?

B Work with 3 classmates. Compare your answers from 4A.

A: *I used to play at the playground when I was in elementary school.*
B: *I used to play volleyball, but now I don't have time.*

C Talk about your answers with the class.

Nadia and I used to eat beef, but we don't eat it anymore.

TEST YOURSELF ✔

Close your book. Write 4 sentences about yourself and 4 sentences about your classmates. Use *used to* and the information you learned in 4B and 4C.
Ali used to play soccer, but he doesn't anymore.

1 Learn to follow a doctor's advice

A   **Look at the pictures. Listen to the conversation. Then check the correct patient.**

Patient 1

Patient 2

1. Which patient used to go to the gym?   ☐ Patient 1   ☐ Patient 2
2. Which patient used to jog?   ☐ Patient 1   ☐ Patient 2

B   **Listen and read. What does the doctor suggest for this patient?**

Doctor: I'm a little concerned about your blood pressure.

Patient: I've been under a lot of stress recently.

Doctor: Have you been getting enough exercise?

Patient: Well, I used to go to the gym, but it was too expensive.

Doctor: Heart disease runs in your family,* so you need to exercise. Why don't you walk in the park?

Patient: OK. I can do that. I'll start today.

*****Idiom note:** run in the family = to be common in a family

> ### **In other words...**
>
> **Making suggestions**
> Why don't you...
> You might...
> You could...
>
> **Accepting suggestions**
> I can do that.
> Good idea. I'll try it.
> I'll give it a try.

C   **Role-play a doctor/patient conversation with a partner. Use the example in 1B to make a new conversation.**

Partner A: You are a doctor. You are concerned about your patient's heart. Ask about the patient's exercise habits. Suggest that your patient ride a bike to work.

Partner B: You're the patient. You've been tired a lot recently. You used to ride your bike after work, but now you don't have time. Accept your doctor's suggestion.

2 Learn present perfect continuous

A Look at the time line and study the chart. Then read the sentences with a partner.

Tomas has been working at a restaurant for two years.

The present perfect continuous		
⌐Subject¬	⌐have/has + been + verb + *ing*¬	
I	**have been walking**	to work since April.
They	**haven't been getting**	enough exercise recently.
He	**has been working**	at a restaurant for two years.
She	**hasn't been feeling**	well this week.

Note

Use the present perfect continuous to talk about actions or situations that began in the past and are continuing now.

B Complete the sentences. Use the words in parentheses.

1. Stan _____ has been waiting _____ to see the doctor for an hour. (wait)

2. We _____ for 30 minutes. (walk)

3. I _____ since 4:30. (cook)

4. They _____ well recently. (not feel)

5. Roya _____ three times a week. (not exercise)

3 Practice your pronunciation

A Listen to the pronunciation of *use* in each sentence. Which *use* has the *z* sound? Which has the *s* sound?

1. I **use** the microwave to cook vegetables.   2. I didn't **use** to eat a lot of vegetables.

B Listen and complete the sentences. Use *use, didn't use,* or *didn't use to.* Then read the sentences with a partner.

1. What do most people _____ to cook vegetables?

2. These days, they _____ steamers and microwaves.

3. There was a time when people _____ eat a lot of vegetables.

4. They _____ microwaves, because there weren't any!

C Listen again and check. Repeat the sentences.

4 Focus on listening

A Talk about the questions with your class.

1. What are some reasons people don't get enough exercise?
2. What do you think is the best kind of exercise?

B Listen to the radio program. Circle the correct words.

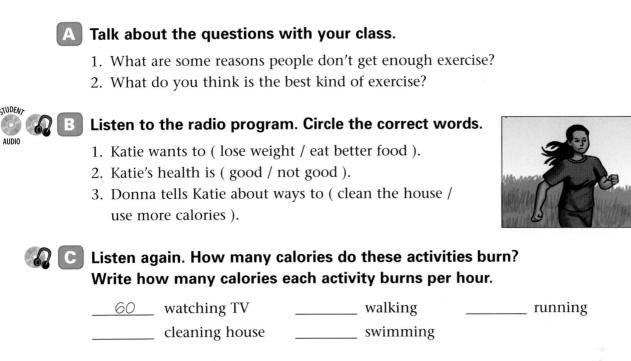

1. Katie wants to (lose weight / eat better food).
2. Katie's health is (good / not good).
3. Donna tells Katie about ways to (clean the house / use more calories).

C Listen again. How many calories do these activities burn? Write how many calories each activity burns per hour.

_____60_____ watching TV   _____ walking   _____ running

_____ cleaning house   _____ swimming

5 Real-life math

Read about Mario. Use the chart to answer the questions.

Mario had a busy weekend. On Saturday, he played soccer for three hours. After that, he came home and vacuumed his apartment for thirty minutes. Then he played the guitar for an hour.

On Sunday, he went for a 1-hour bike ride. Then he played soccer again for 90 minutes.

Activity	Calories/hour
bike riding	350
playing guitar	175
playing soccer	400
vacuuming	200

1. How many calories did Mario burn on Saturday? _____
2. How many calories did he burn on Sunday? _____
3. On which day did Mario burn the most calories? _____

TEST YOURSELF ✔

Role-play a conversation between a doctor and a patient. Partner A: Ask about your patient's exercise habits. Make a suggestion to increase your patient's exercise. Partner B: Accept your doctor's suggestion. Then change roles.

1 Get ready to read

A **What kinds of medication do people take most often?**

B **Read the definitions.**

generic drug: (noun) a drug with no brand name that has the same ingredients as a more expensive drug with a brand name. For example: *Aspirin is a generic drug.*

side effect: (noun) something uncomfortable that happens when a patient takes medication. For example: *Headaches are a side effect of this heart medication.*

C **Look at the title of the brochure in 2A. Talk about the questions with your classmates.**

1. What are some questions you should ask before taking a new medication?
2. What kind of information is usually on a prescription label?

2 Read and respond

A **Read the brochure.**

Using Medication Safely

In a study, 63 percent of Americans say they have taken vitamins in the last six months. 59 percent say they have taken over-the-counter (OTC) medication. 54 percent say they have taken a prescription medicine. Here are some ways to be sure you are using medication correctly and safely.

Ask the doctor or pharmacist these questions about the medication:

- Does this medicine have any side effects?
- What should I do if I have side effects?
- Is it safe to take this medicine with other medications or vitamins I take?
- Can I use a less expensive, generic drug?
- When should I start to feel better?

[1]dosage: the amount of medicine to take
[2]quantity: how many or how much of something

Read and understand the label:

Follow the directions:

- Each time you take the medicine, read the label again.
- Take the exact dosage.[1]
- Take the medicine until the directions tell you to stop.

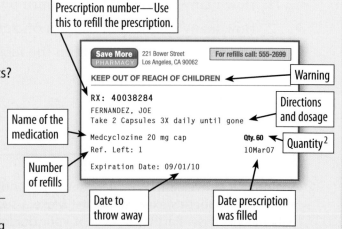

Prescription number—Use this to refill the prescription.

| Save More PHARMACY | 221 Bower Street Los Angeles, CA 90062 | For refills call: 555-2699 |

KEEP OUT OF REACH OF CHILDREN ← Warning

RX: 40038284
FERNANDEZ, JOE
Take 2 Capsules 3X daily until gone → Directions and dosage

Name of the medication

Medcyclozine 20 mg cap   **Qty. 60** → Quantity[2]
Ref. Left: 1   10Mar07

Number of refills

Expiration Date: 09/01/10

Date to throw away   Date prescription was filled

Source: *National Council on Patient Information and Education © 2002–2006*

✔ Interpret a medicine label; ask a health care provider about medication

B Listen and read the brochure again.

C Mark the sentences T (true), F (false), or NI (no information).

 T   1. It's important to ask your doctor about possible side effects.

____ 2. You should throw away all medicine after six months.

____ 3. Vitamin C is the most popular vitamin that people take.

____ 4. It's important to take the correct amount of medicine.

D Study the chart. Complete the sentences below.

> **Word Study: The prefix re-**
>
> Add re- to the beginning of some verbs to mean *do the action again*.
> fill - refill
> The pharmacist filled my prescription last month. I took all the pills, so the pharmacist will **refill** the prescription this month.
>
> print   reprint | read   reread | use   reuse | write   rewrite

1. I can't read the number you wrote. Please ____rewrite____ it.
2. You should _____ a medicine label each time you take the medicine.
3. There was a mistake on the label. The pharmacist has to _____ the label.
4. Don't throw that away! I think we can _____ it.

3 Talk it over

A Read the statistics. Think about the questions. Make notes about your answers.

1. Do these statistics surprise you? Why or why not?
2. Why do you think some people take too much medication?

Medication Statistics

- Of all the over-the-counter medications people buy, 78 percent are pain relievers.
- About 33 percent of people in the U.S. say they take more medication than the directions recommend.

Source: *National Council on Patient Information and Education © 2002–2006*

B Talk about the answers with your classmates.

BRING IT TO LIFE

Look for an over-the-counter medicine at the pharmacy or in your home.
Write down the name, use, dosage, any side effects, and the expiration date.
Bring the information to class.

1 Grammar

A Complete the sentences with *used to* and the correct form of the verbs in parentheses.

1. Now Greg eats healthy food. He _____used to eat_____ junk food. (eat)
2. We _____ home every evening, but now we take a walk. (stay)
3. Rita _____ the doctor often. Now she goes every year. (not see)
4. I _____ about my health, but now I think about it. (not think)

B Complete the questions and answers with the correct form of *used to*.

1. **A:** _Did_____ you _____use to_____ live in Florida?
   B: No, I didn't. I _____used to live_____ in New Jersey.
2. **A:** Where _____ you _____ live?
   B: I _____ in Cleveland, Ohio. (live)
3. **A:** What _____ they _____ study?
   B: They _____ Spanish. (study)
4. **A:** Where _____ your sister _____ work?
   B: She _____ at the bank. (work)

C Complete the sentences. Use the present perfect continuous and the verbs in parentheses.

1. My brother _____has been driving_____ since he was 17. (drive)
2. He _____ this week. (not drive)
3. He _____ to work instead. (walk)
4 The mechanic _____ his car all week. (fix)

D Complete the questions and answers.

1. **A:** _Where have_____ you been working?
   B: _I've been working_____ in a drugstore.
2. **A:** _____ John been studying English?
   B: _____ English for two years.
3. **A:** _____ Marcia and Lucy been swimming?
   B: _____ since they were in elementary school.
4. **A:** _____ Alma been buying these delicious vegetables?
   B: _____ them at the farmers market downtown.

2 Group work

A Work with 2–3 classmates. Write 5 sentences about the woman's life *before* and *after* she made some changes. Share your sentences with the class.

Before

After

She used to be tired. Now she feels great.

B Interview 3 classmates. Write their answers.

1. What's a quick, healthy meal you like to eat or prepare?
2. Do you think that most people eat well every day? Why or why not?
3. Is it easy or difficult for most people to exercise every day? Why?

C Talk about the answers with your class.

PROBLEM SOLVING

A Listen and read about Juan and Anita.

   Juan and his wife, Anita, were riding their bicycles in a large state park. Anita fell off her bike and hurt her ankle. She can't move it, and it really hurts. Juan and Anita think it might be broken. It doesn't look like Anita can walk. Juan has a cell phone, but they don't know where they are in the park. Juan used to have a map of the park, but he doesn't have it now.

B Work with your classmates. Answer the questions.

1. What is Juan and Anita's problem?
2. What should they do? Outline a plan or make a list of what they should do.

Hit the Road

FOCUS ON
- parts of a car
- describing travel
- time clauses
- buying a car
- lemon laws

LESSON 1 **Vocabulary**

1 Learn automobile vocabulary

A **Talk about the questions with your class.**

1. Have you ever changed the oil in a car before?
2. What is Quick Change's recommendation for oil changes? Do you agree?

B **Work with your classmates. Match the words with the picture.**

____ bumper	____ hood	____ trunk
____ gas tank	____ license plate	____ turn signal
____ headlight	____ tire	_1_ windshield

C **Listen and check. Then read the new words with a partner.**

D **Work with a partner. Write other automobile words you know. Check your words in a dictionary.**

☑ Identify interior and exterior parts of cars

E **Work with a partner. Practice the conversation. Use the words in 1B.**

A: *Where's the windshield?*
B: *The windshield is on the front of the car, near the hood.*

A: *Where are the tires?*
B: *The tires are under the car. There are two in the front and two in the back.*

2 Learn about the interior of a car

A **Look at the picture from an owner's manual. Match the definitions and the words below.**

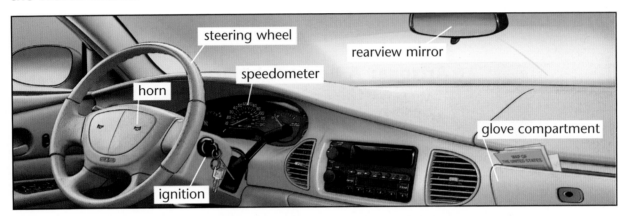

steering wheel
rearview mirror
speedometer
horn
glove compartment
ignition

<u>d</u> 1. Use this to check the road behind you.   a. ignition

____ 2. Use this to check your speed as you drive.   b. horn

____ 3. Use this to steer the car.   c. steering wheel

____ 4. Use this to start the car.   d. rearview mirror

____ 5. Use this to keep the owner's manual safe.   e. speedometer

____ 6. Use this to warn other drivers.   f. glove compartment

B **Work with a partner. Practice the conversation. Use the owner's manual in 2A.**

A: What's the steering wheel for?
B: You use it to steer the car.

A: What's the rearview mirror for?
B: You use it to see behind you.

C **Talk about the questions with your class.**

1. Have you ever owned a car? Do you own one now?
2. Which parts of the car are most important for safety or protection? Why?
3. Can you name three or more parts of a car that hold or store things?

TEST YOURSELF ✔

Close your book. Work with a partner. Make a list of as many new words from the lesson as you can. Alphabetize your list.

1 Read about a road trip

A Look at the pictures. Talk about the questions with your class.

1. Does this kind of vacation look fun to you?
2. Have you ever taken a driving vacation before?

B Listen and read the story about a road trip.

Arizona: A Beautiful Place to Visit

My family likes to take driving trips. We love to put our bags in the trunk and hit the road!* My wife reads the maps while I drive. We haven't gotten lost yet! We all like road trips because we can stop any time we want to.

Last summer my family took a road trip through Arizona. First, we went to Phoenix. We stayed there for two days. After we visited Phoenix, we drove through the Sonora Desert. It was beautiful, but it was very hot during the day. We didn't see any gas stations for miles. We stayed one night in the desert at a comfortable motel. The next day, we went to the Grand Canyon. The Grand Canyon is incredible! You should see it sometime. It was definitely my favorite part of the trip.

Arizona is a beautiful place, but take my advice. If you drive through the desert, be sure you have enough gas and water in the car before you go. It's hot and there aren't many places to stop.

*Idiom note: hit the road = to leave, or go away in a car

C Check your understanding. Mark the statements T (true), F (false), or NI (no information).

_F_ 1. The writer's family drove to Arizona last spring.

____ 2. They drove through the Sonora Desert.

____ 3 The desert is usually cool during the day.

____ 4. They stayed at a motel.

____ 5. The writer's favorite part of the trip was the Grand Canyon.

____ 6. Their car didn't have enough gas and water.

2 Write about a trip

A Talk about the questions with your class.

1. Think about your last trip. Was it for a vacation, work, or family business?
2. Are vacations and travel important for good health, why or why not?

B Write about a trip you have taken. Use the model in 1B and the questions below to help you.

Paragraph 1: How do you and your family or friends like to travel?
What do you like about traveling?

Paragraph 2: Where did you go on your last trip?
When did you go?
How long did you stay?
What was your favorite part?

Paragraph 3: Whatadvice do you have for somebody who wants to take the same trip?

Our Trip across Canada
My friends and I like to travel by train.
We all like trains because we can relax...

C Use the checklist to edit your writing. Check (✔) the true sentences.

Editing checklist	
1. I gave my story a title.	
2. I gave some advice to help someone who wants to take this trip.	
3. I used capital letters for the names of places in my story.	
4. My story has three paragraphs.	

D Exchange stories with a partner. Read and comment on your partner's work.

1. Point out one sentence that you think is very interesting.
2. Ask your partner a question about his or her trip.

> **TEST YOURSELF** ✔
>
> Write a paragraph about your partner's trip. Describe where your partner went and what he or she did.

1 Learn to describe events with time clauses

A **Read the story. What is the mechanic going to do?**

Peter had a car problem this morning. When he started the car, the engine made a strange noise. Before he got to work, a red light came on near the speedometer.

He took the car to the garage and talked to his mechanic. Peter said, "When I start the car, the engine makes a strange noise."

The mechanic asked, "Have you changed the oil recently?" Peter said, "Yes. I changed the oil before I drove to Denver last week." The mechanic replied, "OK. I'll take a look at it tomorrow." Peter said, "OK. After I finish work, I'll call you."

B **Study the chart. Underline the 5 examples of time clauses in the story above.**

Describing present, past, and future events with time clauses	
Present	**When I start the car**, the engine makes a strange noise. The engine makes a strange noise **when I start the car**.
Past	**Before I drove to Denver last week**, I changed the oil. I changed the oil **before I drove to Denver last week**.
Future	**After I finish work**, I'll call you. I'll call you **after I finish work**.

Note
Time clauses give information about when things happen or happened. A time clause can come before or after the main clause.

C **Match the clauses to make sentences.**

   _e_   1. Peter talked to the mechanic,   a. before we go on vacation.

        2. We always buy maps   b. when she drives.

        3. Tina always listens to the radio   c. we take the car to the mechanic.

        4. We'll go shopping   d. after we go to the bank.

        5. When we hear a strange noise,   e. after he finished work.

Get the form. Work with your class. Read the sentences. Then circle the correct word.

When I have car problems, I take my car to a mechanic.
After the mechanic looked at the car, he told me what was wrong.
Before I go on vacation, I'll ask him to fix the car.

1. If both things happen in the present, both clauses are in the (present / past) tense.
2. If both things happen in the past, both clauses are in the simple (present / past) tense.
3. If both things happen in the future, the time clause is in the simple present tense. The main clause is in the (present / future).

E **Get the meaning.** Work with your class. Write *1st* or *2nd* to put the events in each sentence in order. If the events happen at the same time, write *same.*

1. <u>Mel learned to drive a car</u> after <u>he came to Los Angeles.</u>

    _____2nd_____   _____1st_____

2. <u>Min puts on her seat belt</u> before <u>she starts the car.</u>

    _____   _____

3. After <u>we take a long trip,</u> <u>we're always happy to come home.</u>

    _____   _____

4. When <u>I listened carefully,</u> <u>I heard a strange noise under the hood.</u>

    _____   _____

2 Compare time clauses

A **Circle the correct words.**

1. Marta and I studied together before we (take / (took)) the driving test.
2. We were both nervous before we (took / will take) the test.
3. I was tired after I (leave / left) the DMV.
4. Marta (bought / will buy) a new car after she passes the test.

B **Write answers to the questions.**

1. When you get in a car, what should you do first?

    You should put on your seat belt when you get in a car.

2. What things do people usually check before they take a road trip?

    _____

3. When should you use your turn signals?

    _____

4. After you leave class today, where will you go?

    _____

3 Grammar listening

Listen to the sentences. Which event happens first? Circle *a* or *b*.

1. a. We called the mechanic. *(a circled)*
   b. We took the car to the garage.

2. a. Ana stopped at the gas station.
   b. Ana picked me up.

3. a. I stopped the car.
   b. I saw my friend on the corner.

4. a. Mr. Chen took his driving test.
   b. Mr. Chen was nervous.

5. a. Susan will buy a new car.
   b. Susan will sell her old car.

6. a. Anthony will move to Los Angeles.
   b. Anthony will learn to drive.

7. a. I got an oil change.
   b. I went on a trip.

8. a. Karla starts the car.
   b. Karla adjusts the rearview mirror.

4 Practice time clauses

A **Work with a partner. Choose 1 of the topics below and take notes on your ideas.**

Topic 1: Vacation time: List 5 things you do before and after you take a trip.

OR

Topic 2: Moving day: List 5 things you do before and after you move to a new place.

B **Talk about your ideas with your class.**

A: *We lock all the doors of our houses before we take a trip.*
B: *We fill out change of address cards before we move.*

C **Work with your classmates. Make a "Top 5" list for each topic in 4A.**

vacation time

moving day

TEST YOURSELF ✔

Close your book. Think about the last trip you took or the last time you moved. Write 5 sentences about the experience. Include a time clause in each sentence.

1 Learn to negotiate price

STUDENT AUDIO

A **Look at the picture. Listen to the conversation. Then answer the questions below with your classmates.**

1. How many miles does the car have on it?
2. Name two things on the car that are new.
3. How much is the car?

STUDENT AUDIO

B **Listen and read. What's wrong with the car?**

Car dealer:	This is a great car. It only has 15,000 miles on it, and it has a one-year warranty.
Customer:	It sure is beautiful. How much is it?
Car dealer:	It has new tires and a beautiful interior, too.
Customer:	Uh-huh. And how much is it?
Car dealer:	It's going for $10,000. It's a fantastic price.
Customer:	$10,000! But the radio doesn't work, and the CD player doesn't either!
Car dealer:	Uhhh...Let me talk to my manager. I'm sure we can work something out.

> **In other words...**
>
> **Making a deal**
> I'm sure we can work something out.
> We're flexible.

C **Role-play a conversation between a car dealer and a customer with a partner. Use the example in 1B to make a new conversation.**

Partner A: You are a car dealer. Your customer is looking at a stylish car. It has 17,000 miles and a two-year warranty. Tell the customer it has a new stereo and CD player. You want to sell it for $8,000.

Partner B: You're the customer. You like the car you're looking at, but it's too expensive. The rearview mirror is broken, and the turn signals don't work.

☑ Identify features and defects in a product; negotiate for a lower car price   **123**

2 Learn *and...too, and...not either, but*

A Study the chart. Complete the sentences below with *and, too, either,* or *but.*

Conjunctions: *and...too, and...not either, but*	
and...too	I like the red car. Tom likes the red car. I like the red car, **and** Tom does, **too**.
and... not either	The radio doesn't work. The CD player doesn't work. The radio doesn't work, **and** the CD player doesn't **either**.
but	I don't like the blue car. My wife likes the blue car. I don't like the blue car, **but** my wife does.

1. This door doesn't lock, and the trunk doesn't ____either____.

2. That's a nice car, _____ it's a great price, too!

3. We don't need gas, _____ we need some oil.

4. I don't like to fly, and my friends don't _____.

B Use *and, too, not either,* or *but* to make a new sentence for the two sentences.

1. Jun doesn't drive. Mary doesn't drive.

   Jun doesn't drive, and Mary doesn't either.

2. I enjoy road trips. Josh doesn't enjoy road trips.

   _____

3. Lee drives carefully. Karen drives carefully.

   _____

4. Miguel doesn't like to travel. Naomi doesn't like to travel.

   _____

3 Practice your pronunciation

A Study the chart. Listen to the pronunciation of the schwa sound in these words.

STUDENT AUDIO

The schwa sound
We pronounce some vowels (a,e,i,o,u) in certain words as "uh". This is the *schwa sound*. It is the most common sound in English. Dictionaries show the schwa sound as the symbol (ə). manager   CD player   warranty

STUDENT AUDIO

B Listen and circle the letters with the schwa sounds.

1. sign(a)l   3. mirror   5. the   7. Arizona
2. either   4. travel   6. computer   8. Grand Canyon

C Listen again and check. Repeat the words.

4 Focus on listening

A Read the statement. Talk about the questions with your class.

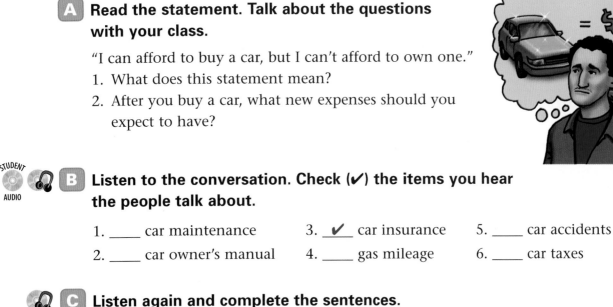

"I can afford to buy a car, but I can't afford to own one."
1. What does this statement mean?
2. After you buy a car, what new expenses should you expect to have?

B Listen to the conversation. Check (✔) the items you hear the people talk about.

1. ____ car maintenance   3. _✔_ car insurance   5. ____ car accidents

2. ____ car owner's manual   4. ____ gas mileage   6. ____ car taxes

C Listen again and complete the sentences.

1. Most people pay car insurance every ___month___.
2. The average person drives _____ miles per year.
3. Good mileage means anything above _____ miles per gallon.
4. In many states, people pay car taxes every _____.
5. An example of car maintenance is an oil change every _____ miles.

5 Real-life math

Read the problems about car expenses. Write the answers.

1. Josh gets the oil changed in his car every three months. The price of an oil change is $36.99, but every 4th one is free. How much does he pay for oil changes every year?

   _____

2. Eva drives 16,000 miles per year. Her car gets 32 miles per gallon. The average price of gas last year was $2.50 per gallon. How much did she spend for gas last year?

   _____

   > **Need help?**
   >
   > Total cost = Total miles ÷ miles per gallon x price

TEST YOURSELF ✔

Role-play a conversation at a used car lot. Partner A: You're the car dealer. Tell the customer about the mileage, warranty, and price of one car. Partner B: You're the customer. You think the price is too high. Talk about the car's problems. Then change roles.

1 Get ready to read

A What do you do when you buy something that doesn't work?

B Read the definitions.

consumers: (noun) customers, people who buy things
defect: (noun) something that is wrong with, or missing from, a product
lemon: (noun) 1. a sour, yellow fruit
       (noun) 2. a product that has a defect that is difficult or impossible to fix

C Look at the picture in 2A. Which definition of *lemon* is this article about?

2 Read and respond

A Read the article.

ℹ Internet Search   _ □ x

Address `http://www.lemonlaws.site` ▾ Go

Lemon Laws

Have you ever bought a car with a defect that the mechanics couldn't fix? If your car was under warranty,[1] you bought a lemon. You aren't alone. To protect consumers, most states have lemon laws. Lemon laws say that a car company has to fix a car that is under warranty. If the car cannot be fixed, then the company must give the customer another car or a refund.

In general, if the car can't be fixed after three or four repairs for the same defect, it is a lemon.

Frequently asked questions (FAQs) about lemon laws:

Do lemon laws protect used-car buyers?
Sometimes. Some states have lemon laws for used cars. For example, in New York, when you buy a used car with fewer than 100,000 miles, you are probably protected.

Am I protected when I buy a car from a friend or neighbor?
No. When you buy a car from a neighbor, friend, or other private individual, there are no lemon laws. You must buy the car from a car dealer for the laws to protect you.

When I buy a car, is there anything I need to do to be sure I'm protected?
Yes. Be sure you receive a warranty with the car. After you buy the car, write down all repairs and maintenance. Here is a sample of a Repair and Maintenance Log.

---

[1]under warranty: protected by a written promise that a product is reliable and in good condition

Repair and Maintenance Log

License plate #: 2NNU 636   Date of Purchase: 01-08-05

Date In	Date out	Mileage	Mechanic or Garage	Description of problem	Work Performed	Price
12-11-06	12-13-06	51, 274	Mid-City Auto	regular maintenance	tune-up	$149.99
03-22-07	03-22-07	54,890	Quick Change		oil Change	$39.95
06-07-07	06-08-07	56,122	Mid-City Auto	left headlight not working	repaired headlight	no charge

Source: *The Center for Auto Safety*

B **Listen and read the article again.**

C **Complete the sentences. Circle *a* or *b*.**

1. A car is a lemon if _____.
   a. it has problems that can't be fixed
   b. it can be fixed after two repairs

2. Ms. Jones is my co-worker. If I buy a car from her, lemon laws _____.
   a. protect me
   b. do not protect me

3. To be protected by lemon laws, _____.
   a. keep a record of all maintenance and repairs
   b. only buy a used car

4. Based on the information in the Repair and Maintenance Log in 2A, the car _____.
   a. is a lemon
   b. isn't a lemon

5. The main idea of the article is: lemon laws can help you _____.
   a. if you buy a car with defects from a dealer
   b. if you buy a car with defects from a neighbor

3 Talk it over

A **Think about the questions. Make notes about your answers.**

1. Has someone you know ever bought a lemon? If so, what happened?
2. Is it better to buy a car from a dealer or a private individual? Why?

B **Talk about the answers with your classmates.**

BRING IT TO LIFE

Look in magazines, in newspapers, or online. Find a picture of your dream car. Bring the picture to class. Tell your classmates why it's the perfect car for you.

1 Grammar

A Circle the correct words.

1. The mail arrived before Fernando (comes /(came)) home.
2. When Raisa calls, we always (talk / talked) for a long time.
3. Paul stopped for gas after he (goes / went) to the market.
4. Before I decided on my new car, I (asked / ask) a lot of questions.
5. Alex leaves the house after the kids (go / went) to school.

B Match the clauses to make sentences.

__e__ 1. Before I got my driver's license,   a. after she finishes school.

_____ 2. I fill the gas tank   b. when they were in Florida.

_____ 3. Before we go on a trip,   c. he will drive to school.

_____ 4. Raquel will visit us   d. when it's empty.

_____ 5. After he fixes the car,   e. I usually took the bus.

_____ 6. They went to Orlando   f. we often check the oil and tires.

C Circle the correct words.

1. Marco wears his seat belt and Esteban does, ((too)/ either).
2. Kwan likes to read maps, (either / but) Angelo doesn't.
3. I always wash my windshield, (and / but) Alan never does.
4. My car gets good gas mileage, (and / but) Taka's car does, too.
5. I don't have my license yet, and Juanita doesn't, (too / either).

D Complete the paragraph. Use the words in the box.

and	before	tires	too	after	but	~~trip~~	when

   Vicky took a _____trip_____ to San Diego last summer. _____ she went, she took
                      1   2
her car to the mechanic. The mechanic told Vicky that the car was in good condition,

_____ it needed new _____. He also wanted $75 to fix the radio. Vicky
        3   4
wasn't sure if she had enough money, but _____ she checked her account, she
                                                  5
decided to buy the tires _____ fix the radio, _____. Vicky was happy she
                                6   7
did. She didn't have any problems with the car _____ she went on her trip and
                                                        8
she had a great time.

2 Group work

A Work with 2–3 classmates. Write a conversation between the people in the picture. Share your conversation with the class.

Customer: *How many miles does this car have on it?*
Car dealer: *It only has 20,000 miles on it.*

B Interview 3 classmates. Write their answers.

1. In your city, do you think it's easy to go places by car? Why or why not?
2. What's the worst problem people have when they shop for a car?
3. What's the worst problem people have after they buy a car?

C Talk about the answers with your class.

PROBLEM SOLVING

A Listen and read about Frank.

Every day, Frank takes his kids to school before he drives to work. This morning, after he took the kids to school, his car made a strange noise and stopped in the middle of a busy intersection. Now, cars are honking, and people are getting angry. Frank's car won't start. He doesn't know what to do.

B Work with your classmates. Answer the questions.

1. What is Frank's problem?
2. Make a list of things Frank can do. Put the list in order.
   Start with what Frank should do first.

Crime Doesn't Pay

FOCUS ON
- crime and safety
- home security
- gerunds as subjects
- reporting a crime
- careers in public safety

LESSON **1** Vocabulary

1 Learn safety vocabulary

A **Talk about the questions with your class.**

1. How do you stay safe in your home?
2. How do you stay safe when you are out at night?

B **Work with your classmates. Match the words with the pictures.**

_____ arrest a suspect

_____ commit a crime

_____ don't walk alone at night

_1_ lock the doors

_____ protect your wallet or purse

_____ report a crime

_____ walk in well-lit areas

_____ witness a crime

 C **Listen and check. Then read the new words with a partner.**

D **Work with a partner. Write other safety words you know. Check your words in a dictionary.**

Work with a partner. Practice the conversation. Use the pictures in 1B.

A: *What are they doing in the first picture?*

B: *They're leaving their apartment. She's locking the door.*
He's protecting his wallet. He's putting it in his jacket.

2 Learn about the criminal justice system

A **Look at the picture. Complete the article about the picture.**

Maple Lane Trial Begins

courtroom   judge   attorney

witness

jury

defendant

Everyone inside the _____courtroom_____ was quiet. The _____

                                    1   2

listened to the case. Mary Gold (standing), an _____, questioned

                                                                          3

the _____. All twelve people on the _____ listened

            4   5

carefully, too. The _____ sat quietly next to his attorney.

                              6

B **Talk about the questions with your class.**

1. What does an attorney do?
2. How many people are on a jury?
3. Who do you think has the most difficult job in the courtroom? Why?
4. How would you feel about being a witness to a crime?

TEST YOURSELF ✔

Work with a partner. Partner A: Read the vocabulary words in 1B to your
partner. Partner B: Close your book. Write the words. Ask your partner for help
with spelling as necessary. Then change roles. Partner B: Use the words in 2A.

1 Read about home security

A Look at the pictures. Talk about the questions with your class.

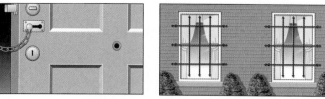

1. What home security features do you see in the pictures?
2. How many home or auto security features can you name?

B Listen and read the story about home security.

Home Security: Safe at Home
by Sandi Lopez

   I live in an apartment downtown. My neighborhood is a great place to live. It's clean, convenient, and it's usually pretty safe. Even so, sometimes I think of ways to make my home safer. The other day, I decided to look around and check the security of my home.

   I'm happy with the deadbolt locks on the doors in my apartment. I also have a chain lock. I'd like to get a peephole for the front door so I can see who's at the door before I open it. I'm going to ask the landlord to install one. The lights in my building's hallways are fine, but my neighbors and I would like to have better lighting on the sides of the building.

   Last week, one of my neighbors said, "We should have a neighborhood email group to make the neighborhood safer." Now we write emails if we see something strange or unusual in the neighborhood. Keeping a neighborhood safe takes a little work, but I think people sleep better at night when they feel safe at home.

> **Writer's note**
>
> Use quotation marks (" ") to show a person's exact words. Use a comma before you begin the quotation.

C Check your understanding. Complete the sentences.

1. The writer's neighborhood is usually pretty _____ _safe_ _____.
2. The writer wants to make her home _____.
3. The writer wants the landlord to put a _____ in the front door.
4. Her neighbors want more lights on the _____ of the building.
5. Neighbors can use email to report anything _____ or

_____.

2 Write about home security

A **Talk about the questions with your class.**

1. Do you ever think about how safe your home is?
2. Have you added any security features to your home since you've lived there?

B **Write a story about security in your home and your neighborhood. Use the model in 1B and the questions below to help you.**

Paragraph 1: Where do you live? Why do you like living there?
Do you ever think about home security?

Paragraph 2: What security feature(s) in your home are you happy with?
What other security features would you like to have? Why?

Paragraph 3: Whathave your neighbors or family members suggested to make the
neighborhood safer? If possible, include a quotation about safety from a
family member or neighbor. Why is it important to work together?
Does it take a little work or a lot of work to keep a neighborhood safe?
Why do you think people want to feel safe?

	My Home Security
	I live in ...

C **Use the checklist to edit your writing. Check (✔) the true sentences.**

Editing checklist	
1. I wrote about one or more good security features in my home.	
2. I wrote about one or more security features I would like to have.	
3. I followed the rules on page 132 for quotations.	
4. There are three paragraphs in my essay.	

D **Exchange stories with a partner. Read and comment on your partner's work.**

1. Point out one security feature that you think is very important.
2. Ask your partner a question about his or her neighborhood.

TEST YOURSELF ✔

Think about safety and security at your school. Write a new story about the
security features at your school and any security features you would like to
have at school.

1 Learn gerunds as subjects

A Read the article. What crime happened at Millie's house?

"Locking the doors is more important than it used to be," says Millie Olsen, age 82. Millie knows because she was at home last night when two men broke into her house and tried to take her TV. Millie was not sleeping, so she quietly called 911 from another room. Calling was the right thing to do. It saved Millie's TV, and maybe even her life. What's Millie going to do next? "Thanking the police will be the first thing on my list. Buying newer, stronger locks is the second. I guess my old locks weren't as strong as I thought they were."

B Study the chart. Underline the 4 examples of gerunds as subjects in the article above.

Gerunds as subjects		Notes
⌐Gerund⌐		• Form a gerund by adding *-ing* to the base form of a verb.
Calling was the right thing to do.		• A gerund acts as a singular noun in a sentence.
Locking the doors is important.		
Thanking the police will be the first thing I do.		

C Complete the sentences. Use the verbs in the box to make gerunds. Then read your sentences to a partner.

call	walk	~~lock~~	protect	report	park

1. ___Locking___ your car doors is a good idea.
2. _____ a crime quickly can save lives.
3. _____ alone at night is not a good idea.
4. _____ near a streetlight is safer than parking on a dark street.
5. _____ the police to report crimes can make everyone safer.
6. _____ our neighborhood is important to everyone.

134 ✔ Use gerunds as subjects to discuss personal safety issues

D Get the form. Work with your class. Read the sentence. Then circle the correct words.

Adding streetlights makes a neighborhood safer.

1. In this sentence, the gerund is (*neighborhood* / *Adding*).
2. The gerund is the (subject / verb) in the sentence.
3. When a gerund is the subject of a sentence in the simple present tense, the verb is singular and ends with (*-s* / *-er*).

2 Compare gerunds and the present continuous

A Study the charts. Then read the sentences below. Write *G* for gerund or *P* for present continuous.

Gerunds
Reporting crime is the right thing to do.
Walking alone isn't safe.

Present continuous
Irina **is reporting** the crime to the police.
Jack **isn't walking** alone now.

  P   1.   Michelle is installing new locks on her windows.

_____ 2.   The attorneys are speaking with the judge.

_____ 3.   Protecting your wallet is easy to do.

_____ 4.   Dana is walking in a well-lit area.

_____ 5.   Listening carefully is the jury's job.

B Complete the sentences. Use a gerund or present continuous form.

A: My neighborhood is very safe. Why should I **lock** the door?

B: _____Locking_____ the door protects you and your home.
           1

A: OK, I _'m locking____ the door right now.
           2

B: And you should **put** your wallet in your purse.

A: I know, I know. _____ my wallet in my
                      3
purse will keep it safe.

B: Right! Look, I _____ my wallet in my purse.
                4

A: And now, you're going to tell me how to **walk**.

B: Well, _____ in the dark isn't smart.
          5

A: Hah! I _____ not _____. I plan
            6   7
to **drive**!

B: I guess _____ in the dark is OK, but don't forget to turn your lights on.
        8

3 Grammar listening

🎧 **Listen to the sentences and check (✔) *Gerund* or *Present continuous*.**

	Gerund	Present continuous
1.		✔
2.		
3.		
4.		
5.		
6.		

4 Practice gerunds

A **Read the chart. Check (✔) *Safe* or *Dangerous* for each situation.**

Is the situation dangerous or safe?	Safe	Dangerous
1. sleeping with the windows open		
2. talking to people you don't know		
3. going out alone		
4. driving alone at night		
5. opening the front door to a stranger		
6. giving out your phone number to a stranger		

B **Work with 3 classmates. Compare your answers to the survey.**

A: *I think sleeping with the windows open is safe.*
B: *I agree. Sleeping with the windows open is safe if you keep the doors locked.*
C: *I disagree. Sleeping with the windows open is dangerous. Someone could come in through the windows.*

C **Take a class poll. How many students think each situation in 4A is safe? How many think each situation is dangerous?**

TEST YOURSELF ✔

Close your book. Write 4 sentences about situations that are safe and 4 sentences about situations that are dangerous. Use a gerund in each sentence.

1 Learn to report a crime

STUDENT AUDIO **A** **Look at the pictures. Listen to the conversation. Then answer the questions below with your classmates.**

1. What did the witness see?
2. What did the man do when he saw the witness?

STUDENT AUDIO **B** **Listen and read. What did the person witness?**

Desk Officer:	Police department. How can I direct your call?
Witness:	I'd like to report a crime I witnessed.
Desk Officer:	OK. Please tell me what happened.
Witness:	Well, while I was waiting for the bus, I saw a man across the street. First, he broke a car window. Then he opened the car door.
Desk Officer:	What happened after that?
Witness:	I think he saw me because, all of a sudden, he ran away.
Desk Officer:	OK. Hold on. An officer will fill out a complete report. Reporting this was the right thing to do.
Witness:	Thank you.

> **In other words...**
>
> **Sequencing events**
> first
> then
> after that
> next
> all of a sudden
> suddenly

C **Role-play a conversation between a witness and a police officer with a partner. Use the example in 1B to make a new conversation.**

Partner A: You're the witness. Call and report a crime. While you were walking to work, you saw some teenagers behind a building. First, they painted some words on the building. Then, they broke a few windows. After that, they ran away.

Partner B: You're a desk officer at the police station. Ask the witness about the crime.

✔ Report a crime to police   **137**

2 Learn to use infinitives and gerunds

A Study the chart. Circle the correct words below.

Gerunds and infinitives		Note
Gerund	**Infinitive**	The infinitive form of a verb is *to* + the base form of the verb.
Reporting crime is important.	It's important **to report** crime.	
Walking alone isn't safe.	It isn't safe **to walk** alone.	
Locking your car is a good idea.	It's a good idea **to lock** your car.	

1. It's important ((to listen) / listening) to the judge in a courtroom.

2. (Go / Going) out alone at night isn't always a good idea.

3. (Talk / Talking) to neighbors is good for the neighborhood.

4. It's a good idea (to walk / walking) in well-lit areas.

B Underline the gerunds or infinitives in the sentences. Then write a new sentence with the same idea. Use a gerund or an infinitive.

1. <u>Walking</u> down a dark street is dangerous.

   It's dangerous to walk down a dark street.

2. It isn't safe to leave the garage door open at night.

   _____

3. Understanding the criminal justice system is important.

   _____

4. It's important to make sure your home is safe.

   _____

3 Practice your pronunciation

A Study the chart. Listen to the words that are stressed in these sentences.

Stressed words in sentences	
He broke the car window.	**He** broke the window. She didn't do it.
He broke the **car** window.	He broke a **car** window, not a house window.
He broke the car **window**.	He broke the **window**, not the horn or door.

B Listen and circle the sentences you hear.

1. a. **I** called the police.
   b. I called the **police**.

2. a. **They** ran that way.
   b. They ran **that** way.

3. a. We walk every **evening**.
   b. We **walk** every evening.

C Listen again and check. Repeat the sentences.

4 Focus on listening

A **Talk about the questions with your class.**

1. Have you ever reported a crime?
2. What are some reasons people might not want to report a crime?

B **Read the questions. Then listen to the telephone conversation. Answer the questions.**

1. Where was Ms. Aziz? _____
2. Was the victim a man or a woman? _____
3. What happened to the victim? _____
4. What should the women do now? _____

C **Listen to the conversation. Put the events in the correct order. Number the items from 1–6.**

_____ A woman ran by and said the purse was hers.

_____ The woman asked Ms. Aziz to call the police.

_____ The police officer sent a police car.

_____ The man fell down and dropped the purse.

__1__ Ms. Aziz was sitting in the park.

_____ A man ran by carrying a lady's purse.

5 Real-life math

Study the survey. Answer the questions.

A survey asked 200 people what crimes they were worried about. Here's what they said.

1. Which crime were people most worried about?

   _____

   Which crime were people least worried about?

   _____

3. How many people in the survey were worried about
   school safety? __200__ x _____ % = _____

Source: Loveland, Colorado Police Department

┌─────────────────────────────────┐
What are you worried about?

Mugging — 17%
Park Safety — 31%
School Safety — 36%
Identity Theft — 60%

0% 20% 40% 60% 80%

TEST YOURSELF ✔

Role-play reporting a crime. Partner A: You're the witness. Tell the police officer about a crime you witnessed. Partner B: You're the police officer. Ask for more information. Then change roles.

1 Get ready to read

A Name some jobs that help keep the public safe.

B Read the definitions.

options: (noun) things to choose from
law enforcement: (noun) police officers, and others who make sure that people obey the laws
rewarding: (adj.) giving a feeling of happiness

C Look at the first sentence in the article. What is the article about?

2 Read and respond

A Read the article.

Where the Jobs Are

Thinking about a career in public safety or law enforcement? Statistics show that these careers are growing, have great benefits, and can be very rewarding. Police officer, paramedic, and firefighter are some of the most popular jobs in this field; but there are hundreds of public safety jobs to think about—everything from police officers who protect people to driver's license examiners who test driving skills.

For example, Angela Bloom is an animal control worker for the city. She and her co-workers pick up animals that are lost, sick, or dangerous. They also

Angela Bloom has been an animal control worker for 16 years. Animal control is one of many careers in public safety.

investigate reports of animal abuse.[1] Being in good physical condition is important for this job. People with a high school diploma or GED can usually apply for this job.

Martin Lee is a health inspector. He looks for health problems in places where people prepare and serve food. There are many kinds of jobs for inspectors. Public safety inspectors look for safety violations

Occupation	Average Annual Salary (2004)	Growth Rate (2014)
animal control worker	$17,420	18–26%
building inspector	$43,670	18–26%
fire inspector	$46,340	18–26%
police officer	$45,210	9–17%

[1] abuse: the act of hurting or injuring someone or something

or dangerous workplaces. Fire inspectors look for problems in buildings that could cause fires. Problem solving skills are important for these jobs. A college degree is often necessary.

These are only a few of the job options available. So remember, if you like working with the public, and are looking for a good job, a career in public safety might be perfect for you.

Source: *U.S. Department of Labor*

B **Listen and read the article again.**

C **Read the sentences. Circle *a* or *b*.**

1. A driver's license examiner tests people's driving skills.

   a. They make sure that unsafe drivers don't get licenses.

   b. They make sure that people can cross the street.

2. Health inspectors look for problems in places where people serve food.

   a. They might inspect hospitals and schools.

   b. They might inspect banks and pharmacies.

3. Public safety employees often feel good because they protect and help people.

   a. They feel good because they make a lot of money.

   b. They feel good because their jobs are rewarding.

4. Fire inspectors look for problems in buildings that could cause fires.

   a. They can check the plumbing in the building.

   b. They can check the electrical system in a building.

3 Talk it over

A **Think about the questions. Make notes about your answers.**

1. What do you think are the three best things about a job in public safety?
2. Which job in the chart do you think is the best? Why?

B **Talk about the answers with your classmates.**

BRING IT TO LIFE

Choose one of the public safety jobs from the article in 2A. Talk to someone who has this job or search online to learn what education and training is required for the job. Bring the information to class.

1 Grammar

A **Unscramble the sentences.**

1. in the neighborhood / everyone / helps / talking / to neighbors

   Talking to neighbors helps everyone in the neighborhood.

2. locked / keeping / is / doors and windows / important

   _____

3. at night / is not / alone / walking / safe

   _____

4. a light on / a good idea / leaving / is / at night

   _____

B **Complete the sentences with a gerund or the present continuous.**
Use the verbs in parentheses.

1. To me, _____ working _____ with my neighbors is fun and rewarding. (work)
2. _____ the building is a big job. (manage)
3. The landlord _____ some new lights in the hallways. (install)
4. _____ time for safety is important. (take)
5. Our neighborhood group _____ a new project. (start)
6. _____ money for a safer playground is our goal. (raise)

C **Circle the correct words.**

1. It's important (working / (to work)) together.
2. (Helping / To help) others makes you feel good.
3. It is possible (making / to make) our neighborhood safer.
4. It's difficult (stopping / to stop) all crime.
5. (Living / To live) in that old building is dangerous.
6. It's not smart (walking / to walk) down that dark street at night.

D **Rosa is reporting a crime to the police. Put the events in the correct order.**

_____ After that, a man ran out of a building.

_____ I saw two teenagers break a car window.

__1__ It was about 8:00, and I was walking home from the bus stop.

_____ The two kids drove away and I called the police.

_____ Next, they got into the car and tried to start it.

_____ The man yelled, "They're stealing my car."

2 Group work

A Work with 2–3 classmates. Write a conversation between the people in the picture. Share your conversation with the class.

Witness: *I'd like to report what I witnessed.*

Police officer: *OK. Please tell me what happened.*

B Interview 3 classmates. Write their answers.

1. What safety problems have you seen in your neighborhood?
2. Which public safety workers do you see most often in your neighborhood?
3. If you were a safety worker, what kind would you be?

C Talk about the answers with your class.

PROBLEM SOLVING

A Listen and read about Delia.

    Some people broke into two houses in Delia's neighborhood last week. Delia is feeling a little nervous. This evening, she saw something strange on her street. A truck drove slowly up and down the street. It didn't have a license plate. Delia doesn't think the people in the truck are neighbors. Now the truck has been parked on the street for 20 minutes, but the people are still inside. Delia is worried. Forgetting about it doesn't feel right, but she doesn't want to call the police.

B Work with your classmates. Answer the questions.

1. What is the problem?
2. What can Delia do? Make a list and discuss your ideas. What is the best thing for Delia to do?

UNIT **11**

FOCUS ON
* life events
* attending social events
* the present passive voice
* responding to news
* buying or renting a home

That's Life

1 Learn life-event vocabulary

A **Talk about the questions with your class.**

1. Look at the picture. How many of these life events have you experienced?
2. Life events are exciting but sometimes stressful. Which are the most stressful?

B **Work with your classmates. Match the words with the pictures.**

__1__ be born	____ get engaged	____ have a baby
____ become a grandparent	____ get married	____ retire
____ get a promotion	____ graduate	____ start a business

 STUDENT AUDIO **C** **Listen and check. Then read the new words with a partner.**

D **Work with a partner. Write other life-event words you know. Check your words in a dictionary.**

144 ✔ Identify life events

E Work with a partner. Practice the conversation. Use the words in 1B.

A: I just heard from my friend. His first child was born last week!

B: Hey! That's great news!

2 Learn about life events and special occasions

A Look at the newspaper announcements. Ask and answer the questions below with a partner.

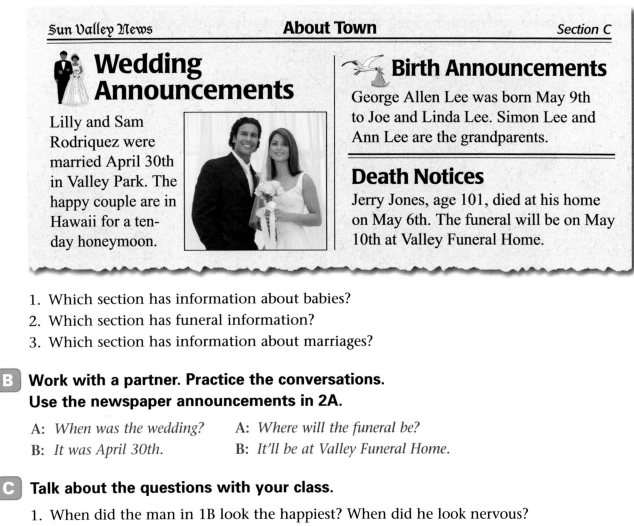

Sun Valley News — **About Town** — *Section C*

Wedding Announcements

Lilly and Sam Rodriquez were married April 30th in Valley Park. The happy couple are in Hawaii for a ten-day honeymoon.

Birth Announcements

George Allen Lee was born May 9th to Joe and Linda Lee. Simon Lee and Ann Lee are the grandparents.

Death Notices

Jerry Jones, age 101, died at his home on May 6th. The funeral will be on May 10th at Valley Funeral Home.

1. Which section has information about babies?
2. Which section has funeral information?
3. Which section has information about marriages?

B Work with a partner. Practice the conversations. Use the newspaper announcements in 2A.

A: *When was the wedding?*

B: *It was April 30th.*

A: *Where will the funeral be?*

B: *It'll be at Valley Funeral Home.*

C Talk about the questions with your class.

1. When did the man in 1B look the happiest? When did he look nervous?
2. Which life events are family events? Which are work events?

TEST YOURSELF ✓

Work with a partner. Partner A: Read the vocabulary words in 1B to your partner. Partner B: Close your book. Write the words. Ask your partner for help with spelling as necessary. Then change roles. Partner B: Use the words in 2A.

1 Read responses to an invitation

A **Look at the pictures. Talk about the questions with your class.**

1. What are some ways people respond to invitations?
2. What kinds of invitations have you received recently? How did you respond?

B **Listen and read the invitation and the responses.**

Nate and Julia
Invite You to a
Housewarming
Party!

Date: Sunday, October 9th
Time: 2:30 – 5:30 p.m.
Place: 2121 Lucky Lane

Dear Nate and Julia,
Congratulations on your new home!
Thanks so much for inviting me to your
housewarming party.
   Unfortunately, I can't make it*. I'm going
to be out of town for a business trip.
   I wish you all the best in your new home.
I'd love to see the place when I get back
to town.
   Have a great party!

   Sincerely,
   Meg

Dear Nate and Julia,
Congratulations on your new home! I'm sure
it's beautiful. Thanks for thinking of us.
   Maria and I are so excited to come to the
party next week. Let us know if we can bring
anything. We look forward to seeing you.
   Love,
   Uncle Peter

*Idiom note: make it = to attend

C **Check your understanding. Circle the correct words.**

1. ((Nate and Julia) / Uncle Peter and Meg) are having a housewarming party.
2. (Nate / Peter) is invited to the party.
3. Peter is (happy / sorry) to come to the party.
4. Meg (can / cannot) come to the party.
5. Meg is going (to another party / out of town).

2 Write responses to invitations

A Talk about the questions with your class.

1. What are some of the special events you have celebrated in your life?
2. What was the last event you were invited to? Did you go? Why or why not?

B Read the two invitations. Choose one party that you will attend and one that you won't attend. Write responses to both invitations. Use the model in 1B and the suggestions below to help you.

1. Congratulate the person.
2. Tell the person if you will or will not attend.
3. Ask the person if you can bring something.
4. Suggest meeting at a later date if you can't attend.

Dear Anna,
    Congratulations on your
retirement...

'Goodbye Work!
Hello Fun!
Anna's Retirement Party!
Date: Saturday, May 19th
Time: 5:30–10:00 p.m.
Place: Eastside Banquet Hall
703 Lake Ave

You are Invited
What? Paolo's Graduation Party
When? Saturday, May 19th
What Time? 5:30–10:00 p.m.
Where? Paolo's Apartment:
307 River Road, Apt. B

C Use the checklist to edit your writing. Check (✔) the true sentences.

Editing checklist	
1. I congratulated Anna and Paolo.	
2. I thanked them for the invitations.	
3. I used a comma after the greetings and the closings.	
4. My handwriting is neat and easy to read.	

D Exchange responses with a partner. Read and comment on your partner's work.

1. Point out one sentence that you think is interesting.
2. Ask your partner a question about his or her response.

TEST YOURSELF ✔

Write an invitation for a party this weekend. Include the date, time, and location. Exchange invitations with a classmate. Write a response to your classmate's invitation.

1 Learn the present passive

A Read the flyer. How is this retirement community different
from an apartment building?

Welcome to Oak View Apartments Retirement Community!

Please pay attention to the following information. If you have any questions or need assistance, please call the office.

- We serve delicious meals daily. Dinner is served in the dining room from 5 p.m. to 7 p.m. every day.

- Swimming is not permitted after 10 p.m.

- Trash is picked up every Thursday.

- Mail is picked up and delivered before 12 p.m.

- A monthly calendar of events is kept next to the reception desk.

B Study the chart. Underline the 5 examples of the present passive
in the flyer above.

THE PRESENT PASSIVE

The present passive		
be + past participle		
Dinner	**is served**	between 5 p.m. and 7 p.m.
Mail	**is delivered**	before 12 p.m.

Notes
• We usually use the active voice in English. We say what people or things do. We serve delicious meals daily.
• We use the passive voice when we do not know who performed the action, when it is not important who performed the action, or when it is clear who performed it. Dinner is served between 5 p.m. and 7 p.m.

C Complete the sentences. Use the present passive and the words
in parentheses.

1. My family _____is invited_____ to Ernesto's graduation party. (invite)

2. Usually, food _____ at graduation parties. (serve)

3. Party invitations _____ to guests a month in advance. (mail)

4. Transportation to graduation parties _____. (not provide)

5. A party _____ for Julio's graduation, too. (plan)

D Get the meaning. Work with your class. Read the sentences. Then circle the correct words.

The mail carrier works very quickly. The mail is always delivered before 12 p.m. Oak View Apartments were built in 1975. They've been in this neighborhood a long time.

1. We (know / don't know) who delivers the mail.
2. We (know / don't know) who built Oak view apartments.

2 Learn the passive with *by*

A Study the chart. Match the parts of the sentences below.

The present passive with *by*	
Active Voice	The bride's parents send the wedding invitations. (The focus is on the bride's parents.)
Passive Voice	The wedding invitations are sent by the bride's parents. (The focus is on the wedding invitations.)

Note
Use *by* + person/thing when you want to say who performs the action in a passive sentence.

_b_ 1. Wedding invitations are sent   a. by friends and family.

____ 2. Dinner is served   b. by the bride and groom.

____ 3. Music is performed   c. by a professional photographer.

____ 4. Photos are taken   d. by an excellent band.

____ 5 Presents are given   e. by experienced servers.

B Write the answers. Then ask and answer the questions with a partner.

1. When is the mail delivered in your neighborhood?

   In my neighborhood, mail _____.

2. When is the trash picked up?

   Trash _____.

3. When are newspapers delivered?

   Newspapers _____.

4. When are the streets cleaned?

   The streets _____.

3 Grammar listening

 **Listen to the sentences. Circle the letter of the sentence with the same idea.**

1. (a.) You can't smoke in the restaurant.
   b. You can smoke in some sections.

2. a. They haven't planned a reception.
   b. The reception is after the wedding.

3. a. The hospital has good nurses.
   b. The hospital doesn't have good nurses.

4. a. Tina and Lim are having a party.
   b. Tina and Lim are going to a party.

5. a. The guests welcome the bride.
   b. The bride welcomes the guests.

6. a. Announcements aren't in the paper.
   b. The paper has announcements.

4 Practice the present passive

A **Work with 3 classmates. What types of parties do you like to attend? What happens at these parties? Use the present passive. Complete the chart with your group.**

Types of parties	What happens at parties?
Birthday party	Food is served

B **Talk about the chart with your classmates.**

A: *What types of parties do you like to attend?*
B: *I like to attend New Year's parties.*
A: *What happens at New Year's parties?*
B: *Music is played.*

TEST YOURSELF ✔

Close your book. Write 5 sentences about what happens at parties. Use the information in 4B.
Food is served at parties.

---

1 Learn to talk about life events

A Look at the pictures. Listen to the conversation. Then answer the questions below with your classmates.

1. What is Min's bad news?
2. What is her good news?
3. What does her friend want to do?

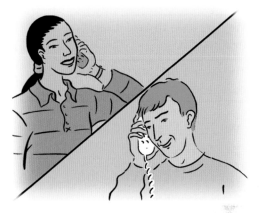

B Listen and read. What's the good news?

A: Hello, Dan? It's Maria. I've got some good news and some bad news.

B: Oh, no. What's the bad news?

A: Well, I took my driving test today. It was really difficult.

B: Oh, no. That's too bad.

A: Yes, but the good news is that I passed. I'll be able to get my license right away.

B: Congratulations! That's fantastic! Let's celebrate tonight.

A: That sounds great. I'm on my way home now.

> **In other words...**
>
> **Responding to good news**
> Congratulations!
> That's fantastic!
> That's great news!
> That's terrific!

C Role-play a good news/bad news conversation with a partner. Use the example in 1B to make a new conversation.

Partner A: Call a friend and tell him or her your good news and bad news. The boss asked to talk to you this morning. You got very nervous. You got a promotion and a raise! You'll be able to pay all your bills.

Partner B: Respond to the bad news. Congratulate your friend on the good news. Invite him or her to celebrate.

✔ Respond to good and bad news appropriately **151**

2 Learn *be able to* + verb for ability

A Study the chart. Then complete the sentences below. Use the words in parentheses.

BE ABLE TO+VERB FOR ABILITY

Future
I will **be able to** drive next year.
Ben won't **be able to** retire.
We'll **be able to** take a vacation next month.
They won't **be able to** start college in June.

Note

In the present, it is more common to use *can* for ability, not *be able to*.
 	
  I can drive. (more common) = I am able to drive. (less common)
 	
In the past, it is more common to use *could* for ability.
  I couldn't drive last year. (more common) =
  I wasn't able to drive last year. (less common)

1. We ____will be able to attend____ Frank's graduation next week. (attend)

2. Jack is sorry, but he _____ be able to attend the graduation. (not go)

3. They're happy because they _____ this June. (get married)

4. Sue's sorry, but she _____ at their wedding. (not sing)

B Complete the sentences with *be able to* + verb. Use your own ideas.

1. Last year, _I wasn't able to use a computer_____ .

2. Last week, _____ .

3. Next year, _____ .

4. In twenty years, _____ .

5. In 100 years, doctors _____ .

3 Practice your pronunciation

A Study the chart. Listen to intonation in these sentences.

Showing excitement
Congratulations! Let's celebrate tonight. That's great! I'm so happy for you. Terrific! I knew you could do it.

Note
Use an exclamation point (!) to show excitement when you write. Use rising intonation to show excitement when you speak.

B Listen to the sentences. Is the speaker excited? Check (✔) *yes* or *no*.

1. ☑ yes ☐ no   3. ☐ yes ☐ no   5. ☐ yes ☐ no
2. ☐ yes ☐ no   4. ☐ yes ☐ no   6. ☐ yes ☐ no

C Listen again and check.

4 Focus on listening

A Talk about the questions with your classmates.

1. What happens at the weddings you go to?
2. Have you ever been to a wedding with traditions that were new to you? Describe what you saw or did.

B Listen to the story. Then mark the statements T (true) or F (false).

___T___ 1. The story talks about wedding traditions in different countries.

_____ 2. The story talks about weddings in the U.S.

_____ 3. The story talks about things that brides and grooms do.

_____ 4. The story talks about the age that people marry in different countries.

_____ 5. The story talks about weddings in China.

C Listen again. Match the traditions with the places.

___d___ 1. The groom gives the bride 13 gold coins.   a. China and India

_____ 2. Dishes are broken for good luck.   b. The U.S.

_____ 3. People throw rice.   c. Greece

_____ 4. A red gown is worn by the bride.   d. Mexico and Panama

5 Real-life math

Read about Jorge and Gina. Answer the questions.

1. Jorge and Gina are planning their wedding reception. The band will cost $400. The reception hall will cost $300 to rent. Dinner will cost $25 per person including the tip. Jorge and Gina plan to spend $3,200 for their reception. How many people will they be able to invite? _____

2. After the wedding, Jorge and Gina want to go to San Francisco for three nights and four days for their honeymoon. The plane tickets are $300 each and the hotel is $175 per night. They plan to spend $150 a day on food and entertainment. How much will the trip cost? _____

> **TEST YOURSELF** ✔
> Role-play a conversation. Partner A: Tell your partner some bad news and good news that happened to you recently. Partner B: Respond and suggest a time to celebrate. Then change roles.

1 Get ready to read

A How many times have you moved in your life?

B Read the definitions.

disability: (noun) a mental or physical condition that makes it difficult for a person to do some things

discrimination: (noun) unequal treatment based on race, religion, or something else

fair: (adj.) equal

rights: (noun) things you are allowed to do

C Look at the title and the picture's caption in the article. What do you think the article is about?

2 Read and respond

A Read the article.

MOVE☐ Moving On

In an average year, 14 to 20 percent of the U.S. population moves to a new home. Some people move to new cities to start a career or to enjoy retirement. Others move across town to be closer to family. There's a good chance that you will move in the future. Whatever your reason for moving, it's important to know your rights and to be careful when you buy or rent a home.

The U.S. government has laws to protect people from discrimination. When you buy or rent a home, the Fair Housing Act says that discrimination is not permitted based on race, religion, familial status,[1] or disability. When you buy a home, the Equal Opportunity Credit Act protects you and your credit application from discrimination. If you have experienced housing discrimination, contact the U.S. Department of Housing and Urban Development (HUD).

[1]familial status: married, divorced, or with children

First, read the lease. Then unpack.

When you rent an apartment or a house, it's your job to read and understand the lease[2] before you sign it. Are utilities included? When can the landlord raise the rent? How much is the security deposit? Don't be afraid to ask questions if something isn't clear. Never sign a lease if information is missing. You might be in for a surprise. Finally, you should get a copy of the lease immediately after you sign it. Moving can be stressful. However, if you know your rights and understand your lease, moving may be easier!

[2]lease: a rental agreement

Source: *U.S. Department of Justice, HUD*

B **Listen and read the article again.**

C **Choose the best heading for each paragraph of the article.**

1. Paragraph 1
   a. Buying a Home
   b. Reasons People Move
   c. Enjoying Retirement

2. Paragraph 2
   a. Understanding Housing Laws
   b. Preparing to Move
   c. Renting or Buying

3. Paragraph 3
   a. Preparing to Move
   b. Signing and Security
   c. Understanding the Lease

3 Talk it over

A **Read the information. Think about the questions. Make notes about your answers.**

1. What are some reasons a person might want to spend only 25 to 30 percent of his or her salary on rent?
2. Is this easy, difficult, or impossible, to do in your city?

How much should you spend on your home?

Financial professionals recommend that you spend between 25 and 30 percent of your total income on your rent or mortgage.

B **Talk about the answers with your classmates.**

BRING IT TO LIFE

Read the small print from your lease or mortgage agreement (homeowner's contract). Write 3 rules that you think are important. Bring the information to class.

1 Grammar

A Complete the sentences. Use the present passive and the verbs in parentheses.

1. You _____are invited_____ to a party next month. (invite)
2. A large meal _____ for the guests. (plan)
3. Coffee and tea _____ with dinner. (include)
4. This party _____ every year. (hold)
5. The invitations _____ on the first of the month. (mail)

B Match the parts of the sentences.

_d_ 1. A birth announcement is usually written   a. by the employer.

____ 2. Cards are often sent to the graduate   b. by a moving company.

____ 3. A retirement present is given   c. by friends and family.

____ 4. Furniture is taken to a new house   d. by the parents.

C Complete the sentences with the past of *be able to*. Use the verbs in parentheses.

1. Jack _____was able to clean_____ the garage but not the pool. (clean)
2. We _____ the grass because it rained. (not cut)
3. I tried, but I _____ the lights. (not fix)
4. We _____ the kitchen. (paint)
5. Our neighbor _____ us with the garden. (help)

D Complete the sentences with the future of *be able to*. Use the verbs in parentheses.

1. Next year, we _____will be able to swim_____ in the new pool. (swim)
2. When the new parking lot is finished, we _____
   closer to the building. (park)
3. The kids _____ in the field after the parking lot
   is built over it. (not play)
4. In a few years, everyone _____ in the mall next
   to the apartments. (shop)
5. In a few months, seniors _____ the new senior
   center. (use).

2 Group work

 A **Work with 2–3 classmates. Write a conversation between the people in the picture. Share your conversation with the class.**

A: *Congratulations on your retirement, Jack.*
B: *Thank you.*

B **Interview 3 classmates. Write their answers.**

1. Have you received any invitations or gone to any parties recently?
2. What events do you celebrate with your friends or family every year?
3. How do you celebrate these events?

C **Talk about the answers with your class.**

PROBLEM SOLVING

A **Listen and read about Soo.**

   Soo received a wedding invitation from her cousin many weeks ago. She wanted to go to the wedding, but she needed to ask her boss for a vacation day. Her boss said that he wasn't able to give Soo a day off. Soo didn't want to say no to her cousin, so she didn't respond to the invitation right away. She wanted to think about her response. She just looked at the invitation again. The wedding is next week! Soo is embarrassed, and she doesn't know what to do now.

B **Work with your classmates. Answer the questions.**

1. What is Soo's problem?
2. What can Soo do? Make a list of things that Soo can do.

Doing the Right Thing

FOCUS ON
- civic rights and responsibilities
- community involvement
- infinitives and gerunds after verbs
- protecting your rights
- the Civil Rights Movement

LESSON 1 Vocabulary

1 Learn civics vocabulary

A Talk about the questions with your class.

1. Look at the pictures. Which things apply to all U.S. residents?
2. Which things apply to U.S. citizens only?

B Work with your classmates. Match the words with the pictures.

Rights and Freedoms In The United States

____ freedom of peaceful assembly

____ freedom of speech

____ freedom of the press

____ the right to carry a U.S. passport

____ the right to a fair trial

_1_ the right to vote

STUDENT AUDIO

C Listen and check. Then read the new words with a partner.

D Work with a partner. Write other civics words you know. Check your words in a dictionary.

☑ Identify civic rights, freedoms, and responsibilities

E **Work with a partner. Talk about the questions. Use the pictures in 1B.**

1. In your opinion, which freedom is the most important? Why?
2. In your opinion, which right is the most important? Why?

2 Learn about civic responsibilities

A **Look at the pamphlet. Complete the paragraph.**

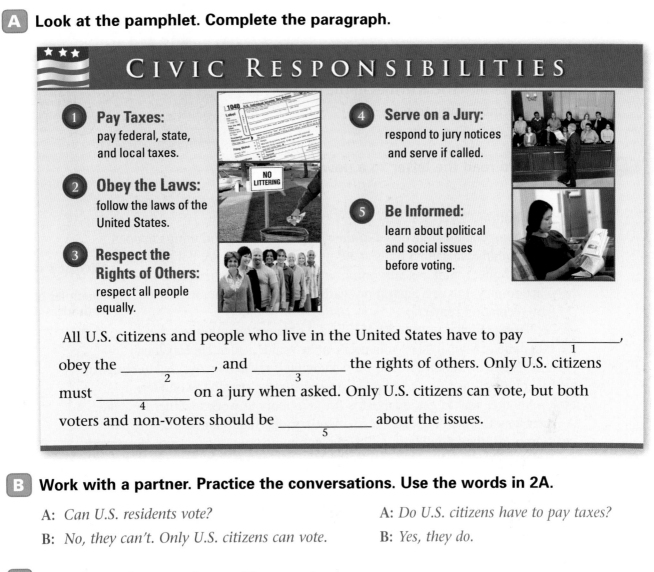

CIVIC RESPONSIBILITIES

1 **Pay Taxes:** pay federal, state, and local taxes.

2 **Obey the Laws:** follow the laws of the United States.

3 **Respect the Rights of Others:** respect all people equally.

4 **Serve on a Jury:** respond to jury notices and serve if called.

5 **Be Informed:** learn about political and social issues before voting.

All U.S. citizens and people who live in the United States have to pay _____ ,
                                                                              1
obey the _____ , and _____ the rights of others. Only U.S. citizens
              2   3
must _____ on a jury when asked. Only U.S. citizens can vote, but both
          4
voters and non-voters should be _____ about the issues.
                                       5

B **Work with a partner. Practice the conversations. Use the words in 2A.**

A: *Can U.S. residents vote?*   A: *Do U.S. citizens have to pay taxes?*

B: *No, they can't. Only U.S. citizens can vote.*   B: *Yes, they do.*

C **Talk about the questions with your class.**

1. How can people stay informed about the issues?
2. The voting age in the U.S. is eighteen. Do you agree or disagree with this age limit? Why?

TEST YOURSELF ✔

Close your book. Work with a partner. Make a list of as many new words from the lesson as you can. Alphabetize your list.

1 Read about civic involvement

A Look at the picture. Talk about the questions with your class.

1. Have you ever written a letter to a newspaper?
2. Which of the civic activities in the picture is more interesting to you?

B Listen and read the letter to a newspaper.

STUDENT
AUDIO

Dear Editor,

When people get involved in their communities, good things happen.

One thing we can all do is stand up for* the things we believe in. For example, I think it's very important to give children a safe ← place to play. I have a sign in my yard telling people to vote for the new recreation center.

There are other ways to get involved. Volunteer opportunities are everywhere. My neighbor volunteers at the senior center. He eats lunch and visits with seniors. He has been studying English. He says that his English has improved, and he's heard great stories since he started to volunteer.

Another way to get involved is for neighbors to work together to make their neighborhoods great. I read about a group that planted trees together to improve their neighborhood. I'm planning to try it this spring. If we work together, we can all make positive changes for the future.

Ernie Rodriguez
Freehold, New Jersey

> **Writer's note**
>
> Examples help make your ideas clear.

*__Idiom note:__ stand up for = to show you agree with something

C Check your understanding. Mark the statements T (true), F (false), or NI (no information).

  __T__   1.   Ernie thinks people should be involved in their communities.

  ____   2.   He wants people to vote "yes" for a new recreation center.

  ____   3.   He isn't interested in political issues.

  ____   4.   His neighbor volunteers five hours each month.

  ____   5.   If you don't speak English well, you shouldn't volunteer.

  ____   6.   Planting trees is one way to improve your neighborhood.

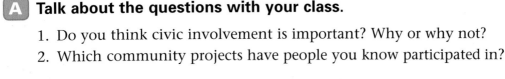

2 Write a letter to a newspaper

A **Talk about the questions with your class.**

1. Do you think civic involvement is important? Why or why not?
2. Which community projects have people you know participated in?

B **Write a letter to a newspaper. Use the model in 1B and the questions below to help you.**

Opening: Begin your letter with "Dear Editor,".

Paragraph 1: What's one thing people can do to be involved in their community?
            Give an example of something you've done in your community.

Paragraph 2: What's another way that people can be involved?
            Give an example of something another person has done.

Paragraph 3: How can people work together to make the community better?
            Give an example.

Closing: Sign your name and write your city and state.

> Dear Editor,
>   It's important for people to be
> involved in their community. One
> thing people can do is...

C **Use the checklist to edit your writing. Check (✔) the true sentences.**

Editing checklist	
1. I wrote "Dear Editor," to begin my letter.	
2. I used an example from my experience.	
3. I used an example from another person's experience.	
4. I signed my name and wrote my city and state.	

D **Exchange letters with a partner. Read and comment on your partner's work.**

1. Point out one sentence that you think is very interesting.
2 Ask your partner a question about his or her letter.

TEST YOURSELF ✔

Write a new opinion letter to a newspaper. Use your own idea or write an answer to this question: Why is it important for citizens to vote?

1 Learn verbs + infinitives

A Read the form. Which job would you like to volunteer for?

FIVE-MILE WALK/RUN IN THE PARK

Dear neighbors,
    Please join us this Saturday for our community walk/run event. All money collected will go to the River City Children's Hospital. We need your help! Please let us know how you can help.

Name: _____

Address: _____

Phone Number: _____

☐ I plan to walk.   ☐ I volunteer to serve food.

☐ I plan to run.   ☐ I volunteer to clean up.

☐ I agree to pledge $ _____ for _____ .
                                    Name of runner/walker

B Study the chart. Underline the 5 examples of infinitives in the form above.

Verb + infinitive	
I plan **to walk**.	I don't plan **to run**.
Judy agreed **to serve** food.	She didn't agree **to clean up**.
I will volunteer **to clean up**.	I won't volunteer **to serve** food.

Notes
• An infinitive is *to* + the base form of the verb.
• These verbs are often followed by an infinitive:
want   agree   volunteer   plan   decide   hope   need   forget

C Complete the sentences with infinitives. Use the verbs in the box.

volunteer   go   mail   ~~serve~~   pledge   run

1. I agreed ___to serve___ food at the event on Saturday.

2. Paul and Ellen decided _____ at the event. They will help clean up.

3. Ellen wants _____ some money. Do you know any runners?

4. Henri hoped _____, but he hurt his knee and can't do it now.

5. David doesn't plan _____ to the event on Saturday because he has to work.

6. Maggie forgot _____ her pledge form, but she will bring it on Saturday.

D Write answers to the questions.

1. What did you volunteer to do last year?

   _____

2. What do you try to do every day?

   _____

3. What do you hope to do this weekend?

   _____

4 What will you volunteer to do this year?

   _____

5. What class(es) have you decided to take when this class ends?

   _____

2 Learn verbs + gerund or infinitive

A Study the charts. Then circle a gerund or infinitive to complete the sentences below. Circle two answers when possible.

Verb + gerund
We enjoy **studying**.
Tom disliked **running**.
I will practice **speaking** English.

Verb + gerund or infinitive	
We like **playing**.	We like **to play**.
He began **working**.	He began **to work**.
I will continue **studying**.	I will continue **to study**.

Note
These verbs are often followed by gerunds:
enjoy   dislike   practice

Note
These verbs can be followed by gerunds or infinitives:
like   begin   continue

1. Regina likes ((meeting) / (to meet)) new neighbors.
2. When do you practice (playing / to play) the piano?
3. Do you enjoy (listening / to listen) to the radio?
4. Do you think we should continue (learning / to learn) English?

B Get the form. Work with your class. Which sentences can be rewritten as verb + infinitive? Rewrite the sentences when possible. Write "no change possible" when not possible.

1. They continued working last night.   They continued to work last night.
2. I like volunteering.   _____
3. Sue enjoys helping people.   _____
4. He began studying at 8:00.   _____

3 Grammar listening

🎧 **Listen and circle *a* or *b* to complete the sentences.**

1. a. to volunteer this summer.
   b. volunteering this summer.

2. a. to clean up after the dance.
   b. cleaning up after the dance.

3. a. to speak Spanish every day.
   b. speaking Spanish every day.

4. a. to serve food.
   b. serving food.

5. a. to be on a jury.
   b. being on a jury.

6. a. to get involved.
   b. getting involved.

4 Practice gerunds and infinitives

A **Complete the chart with your own ideas. Use gerunds or infinitives.**

My Community Involvement		
I like…	I dislike…	I plan…
talking to my neighbors.	going to neighborhood meetings.	to volunteer at a school.

B **Work with a group of 3 students. Ask and answer questions about the chart. Take notes about answers that are the most interesting to you.**

A: *What do you like doing in your community?*
B: *I like volunteering at the senior center.*

C **Tell your classmates about the interesting things you learned.**

Irma likes talking to her neighbors, but she dislikes going to neighborhood meetings.

TEST YOURSELF ✔

Write 6 complete sentences about your classmates' likes, dislikes, and plans. Use the chart in 4A.

1 Learn to protect your rights

A **Read the flyer. Listen to the conversations. Then answer the questions below with your classmates.**

1. What is Mrs. Delgado's problem?
2. What is Mr. Tran's problem?

COMMUNITY LEGAL CLINIC
Providing community-based legal services for all

SERVICES INCLUDE:

○ **Tenant Rights**   ○ **Employment Rights**

○ **Immigration**   ○ **Traffic Accidents**

○ **Credit Problems**

CALL 555-8495

B **Listen and read. Why does the man think he was fired?**

Client:	Hello. I called yesterday. The man on the phone told me to come in.
Law Clerk:	How can I help you today?
Client:	Well, I don't know what to do. I've worked at the same company for 20 years. Two weeks ago my boss told me to go home. He fired me, and now I don't have a job.
Law Clerk:	Do you have any idea why?
Client:	No. I work hard and I'm never late. It might be because I'm over 55. Can they do that?
Law Clerk:	No, they can't. I think I can help you.

> **In other words...**
>
> **Describing possible reasons**
> It might be because…
> I think it's because…
> I suspect it's because…

C **Role-play a conversation at a legal clinic with a partner. Use the example in 1B to make a new conversation.**

Partner A: You're a client. You've lived in the same apartment for eight months. Last week, the landlord told you that you have to move next month. You have a one-year lease and you're a good tenant. You think the owner wants to give the apartment to his sister.

Partner B: You are a law clerk at the legal clinic. Ask about the problem. Offer to help.

☑ Describe a legal problem   **165**

2 Learn to report requests

A Study the pictures. Then circle the correct words in the sentences below.

Notes

• To report an affirmative request, use *told* + person + infinitive.
• To report a negative request, use *told* + person + *not* + infinitive.

She told him to *pick up the kids*.   They *told her not to forget* to write.

1. Frank told me ((to call) / call) him later.
2. She told him (write / to write) what happened.
3. They told us (not to / to don't) worry about it.
4. I told (she / her) to come to the office tomorrow.
5. We told them (to ask / ask) for help.

B Read about Sasha. Then write reported requests.

Yesterday Sasha had jury duty. Here are some things the court clerk told her to do.

1. "Sit down over there." ___The clerk told Sasha to sit down___.
2. "Fill out this form." ___Then he told her to_____.
3. "Don't leave the building." ___Next,_____.
4. "Listen to the judge's instructions." ___Finally,_____.

3 Practice your pronunciation

A Study the chart. Listen to the pronunciation of the homophones in these sentences.

Homophones	
I don't know what **to** do. I was fired **two** weeks ago.	**They're** at school. **There** are five pens. **Their** books are on the table.
We can protect our **rights**. Jim **writes** opinion letters.	

Note

Homophones are words that are spelled differently but that are pronounced the same.

B Listen to the sentences. Underline the homophones.

1. a. I get the <u>mail</u> every day.
   b. Pat is a 10-year old <u>male</u>.
2. a. I need to buy some food.
   b. The market is by the bank.
3. a. Tim is a new citizen.
   b. He knew he could pass the exam.
4. a. I'll go to the market.
   b. Apples are in aisle six.

C Listen again and check. Repeat the sentences.

4 Focus on listening

A **Talk about the questions with your class.**

1. Have you ever attended a town meeting?
2. What issues in your community are people concerned about right now?

B **Listen to the town meeting. Circle the correct words.**

1. The people at the meeting are talking about the location of a new (street / high school).
2. Some people don't want a school on (Green / Central) Street.
3. The people at the meeting (agree / disagree) about the proposal.

C **Listen again. Mark the sentences T (true) or F (false).**

___T___ 1. Many people want to express their opinions.

_____ 2. A lot of people have strong feelings about the high school.

_____ 3. Some people don't want a new school.

_____ 4. The city wants to buy property on Green Street.

_____ 5. One woman told everyone to calm down.

5 Real-life math

Study the voter poll. Answer the questions.

1. How do most people feel about the high school?

_____

2. If half of the undecided people vote "no" for the high school, which side will win?

_____

3. How many undecided people must vote "yes" for the high school to pass?

_____

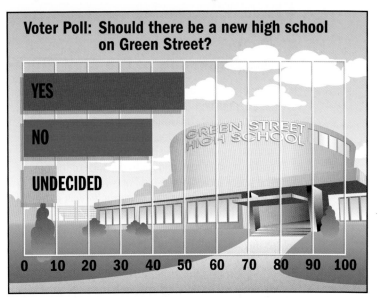

Voter Poll: Should there be a new high school on Green Street?

TEST YOURSELF ✔

Role-play a conversation at a legal clinic. Partner A: You're a landlord. You're having a problem with a tenant. Partner B: You work at the clinic. Ask for more information and offer to help. Then change roles.

1 Get ready to read

A **What are some ways people in the U.S. can protect their rights?**

B **Read the definitions.**

movement: (noun) a large group of people who work for the same goal
boycott: (verb) to refuse to buy or use something to show protest or disagreement
Civil Rights Act: (noun) a set of laws passed in 1964 that promises equal treatment in
  public places to all people in the U.S.

C **Look at the title of the article and the photograph. Complete the sentences.**

1. From the title, I know this article is about _____.

2. From the photograph I know that _____ was an
   important person in the Civil Rights Movement.

2 Read and respond

A **Read the article.**

🛈 Internet Search　　　　　　　　　　　　　　　　　　　　　　　　　 _ □ x

A̲ddress http://www.civilrights.movement　　　　　　　　　　　　　　 ▼ Go

The Beginning of the Civil Rights Movement

In 1955, bus seats for African Americans and whites were segregated[1] in parts of the U.S. On December 1, 1955, in the city of Montgomery, Alabama, a conflict, or disagreement, started when an African American woman named Rosa Parks refused to give her bus seat to a white man and go to the back of the bus. The police took 42-year-old Parks to jail.

The African American community was extremely angry. They had a meeting and decided to work together to protest discrimination. They agreed to boycott the buses on the day that Parks went to court. The day was a success. Empty buses drove through the streets. The city lost money. The community decided to continue the boycott. They elected a man named Martin Luther King, Jr. to be the leader.

The boycott continued for more than one year. It was difficult for African Americans to get to work

Rosa Parks

without buses, but they didn't stop the boycott. The city continued to lose money. Finally, the U.S. Supreme Court decided that Montgomery's bus laws were unfair and gave the African American community equal rights. On December 21, 1956, after 376 days, the bus boycott ended.

The Montgomery Bus Boycott was the beginning of the Civil Rights Movement. The movement eventually led to the Civil Rights Act in 1964, a set of laws that made discrimination a crime. During the Montgomery Bus Boycott, people worked together to change the government. Today, people in the U.S. continue to work together for change. Now hundreds of organizations and community groups work to protect the rights of U.S. citizens and residents.

[1]segregated: separated

B Listen and read the article again.

C Write a summary of the article by answering the questions in your own words.

1. Why did the African-American community boycott the buses in Montgomery?

   _____.

2. Why did the boycott end?

   _____.

3. When was the Civil Rights Act passed?

   _____.

D Study the chart. Underline the word stress in the sentences below.

> **Word Study: Word stress in nouns and verbs**
>
> Change the stress within the word to change a noun to a verb.
> **con**flict (noun) — con**flict** (verb)
>
> **per**mit (noun) — per**mit** (verb)   **ob**ject (noun) — ob**ject** (verb)
> **pro**test (noun) — pro**test** (verb)

1. Did you hear? A construction company got a **permit** to make City Park into a parking lot!
2. Oh, no! The city can't **permit** that! Let's start a **protest**.
3. We want to avoid **conflict** with the company. Let's talk to them first.
4. First, we **object** strongly. Then we listen to what they have to say.
5. We can meet at 9:00. Any other time will **conflict** with my classes.

 E Listen and check your answers.

3 Talk it over

A Think about the questions. Make notes about your answers.

1. Think about a protest you've seen or read about. Describe what you saw or read.
2. Would you ever participate in a boycott? Why or why not?

B Talk about the answers with your classmates.

> **BRING IT TO LIFE**
>
> Tell a friend or family member the story of Rosa Parks and the Civil Rights Movement. Write what they say about the story. Bring their comments to class.

1 Grammar

A Read the first sentence. Complete the second sentence with an infinitive. Use the underlined verbs.

1. Andy will speak about the new taxes.

   Andy wants _to speak about the new taxes_.

2. Emily will volunteer at the senior center.

   She hopes _____.

3. We will report the traffic accident to the police.

   We agreed _____.

4. The police immediately checked the driver's license.

   The police didn't wait _____.

5. Please sign up for the community event.

   Don't forget _____.

B Complete the sentences with gerunds.

1. In class we practice _reading English_ .

2. My best friend enjoys _____.

3. I dislike _____.

4. Next month I will begin _____.

5. We will continue _____.

C Answer the questions with an infinitive or gerund.

1. What do you dislike doing? _____

2. What did you practice last week? _____

3. What do you enjoy doing? _____

4. What class did your friends decide to take? _____

5. What do you plan to do next weekend? _____

D Read the first sentence. Complete the second sentence to make reported requests.

1. "Take a break."   My boss told me _to take a break_ .

2. "Get some milk at the store."   My sister told me _____.

3. "Sign up for another class."   My teacher told me _____.

4. "Come to the town meeting."   My neighbor told me _____.

5. "Call the Legal Aid Office."   Mrs. Peterson told me _____.

6. "Know your rights."   Everyone told me _____.

2 Group work

A Work with 2–3 classmates. Write a paragraph about the picture. Share your paragraph with the class.

People in my community are concerned about education.

B Interview 3 classmates. Write their answers.

1. Do people in your community help each other?
2. What rights are most important to you? Why?
3. Why don't some people become involved in community events?

C Talk about the answers with your class.

PROBLEM SOLVING

A Listen and read about Ruben.

Ruben had a traffic accident this morning. At a stoplight, the driver behind him hit his car. Ruben got out of the car to exchange insurance information, but the other driver had a different idea. He didn't want the insurance companies to get involved. He offered to pay Ruben for the damage to his car. It didn't look like there was much damage to the car, but Ruben isn't sure if he should take the man's money or call his insurance company.

B Work with your classmates. Answer the questions.

1. What is the problem?
2. What can Ruben do? Make a list and discuss your ideas. What is the best thing for Ruben to do?

UNIT 1　Learning Together

Pg. 4　Lesson 1—Exercise 1C

N = Narrator, W = Woman

W: David is a student in an intermediate English class at Central Adult School. He studies hard and learns many things because he has good study skills and habits.

1. W: In class, David always takes notes in his notebook. The teacher asks the class to take notes on the grammar and vocabulary.
   N: take notes
2. W: David spends a lot of time in the library. He can always find a quiet place to study there. It's important to find a quiet place to study.
   N: find a quiet place
3. W: Sometimes David's teacher asks the class to look up information and do research at the library. David likes to do research because he learns many new things.
   N: do research
4. W: David always takes a break every couple of hours. He knows it's important to take a break if he gets tired.
   N: take a break
5. W: When David needs to find information on the Internet, he searches online. He uses the library computers to search online.
   N: search online
6. W: At home, David always organizes his books and papers. He knows it's important to organize materials he uses all the time.
   N: organize materials
7. W: Making a study schedule helps David plan his time. He tries to make a study schedule every week.
   N: make a study schedule
8. W: David memorizes a few new words every day. He likes to memorize words and then use them in conversation.
   N: memorize words
9. W: When David has to write a long story or paper, he makes an outline. He writes the main ideas first and writes the details under each idea to make an outline.
   N: make an outline

Pg. 10　Lesson 3—Exercise 3

1. Shannon isn't studying this afternoon. She's cleaning her apartment.
2. Juan asked his teacher for help and she answered his questions.
3. Mary did research at the library. She didn't do it at home.
4. Franco doesn't organize his study materials very often.
5. We're taking a break before the next chapter.
6. I always take notes in class.

Pg. 11　Lesson 4—Exercise 1A

C = Counselor, T = Tara, Ca = Carlos

C: What kind of career are you thinking about, Tara?
T: I'm just not sure. There are so many choices.
C: What kinds of thing do you like to do?
T: Well, I volunteered at the middle school last year. I enjoyed that. I'm studying many things now. I like my classes and I'm doing well.
C: You should think about a career in education. It's a good field and schools always need good teachers.

C: What kind of career are you thinking about, Carlos?
Ca: I really don't know. There are so many choices.
C: What kinds of thing do you like to do?
Ca: Well, I work part-time in a hotel. I enjoy that. I'm taking a business management class now. I like my class and I'm doing well.
C: You should think about a career in hotel management. It's a good field with plenty of job opportunities.

Pg. 13　Lesson 4—Exercise 4B

N = Narrator, M = Marie, ML = Malik

N: Today we're talking with two students from Freemont High School. Freemont is very different from most high schools. At Freemont, students study the usual subjects like languages, history, math, and science, but they also get real-world experience in the careers of their choice. This is Marie Charles. She's a student at Freemont. Marie, tell us about your high school experience.

M: Well, my family came to this country from Jamaica when I was 12. When it was time for high school, my teachers encouraged me to apply to Freemont. I was so happy when I was accepted. Everyone said I would do well there. I got involved in the school's banking program and I loved it. I knew that a career in banking was right for me. Freemont gave me the chance to practice in the real world and study hard at the same time. Last summer I completed a summer training program at Central Savings Bank. The bank has offered me a full-time job in the Customer Service Department when I graduate next month!

N: Thank you Marie. And good luck with the new job. Our next guest is Malik Emami. Malik graduated from Freemont High School last year. Malik, can you tell us about your time at Freemont and what you're doing these days?

ML: I love making things. My teachers at Freemont encouraged me to do that and they helped me think carefully about what kind of career would make me happy. By my second year at Freemont, I knew I wanted to be a carpenter. So I took all my academic classes and a lot of carpentry classes. In my last year of high school, I worked part-time on a city building project. I helped build an apartment building near the school. It was really exciting to work with real carpenters and learn so much. Now I'm working as a carpenter during the day, and I study drawing and design at nights at the local community college.

N: Thanks Malik. It sounds like you're on your way to a great career.

UNIT 2   Ready for Fun

Pg. 18   Lesson 1—Exercise 1C

N = Narrator, W = Woman

W: Welcome to City Center Recreation Plaza. Thanks for coming to our opening weekend tour. Let me show you around.

1. W: Do you like to buy food straight from the farm? Then come on down to the farmers' market for the freshest fruits and vegetables. The farmers' market is open every weekend.
   N: farmers' market
2. W: This is the theater. You can see wonderful plays performed by the best actors in town every week at our theater.
   N: theater
3. W: For those of you who love excitement, the amusement park is a perfect place to play. There are great rides and games at the amusement park.
   N: amusement park
4. W: If you like dancing to the hottest new sounds, then you'll love the Stardust nightclub. You can dance all night on Fridays and Saturdays at our nightclub.
   N: nightclub
5. W: We are proud to have a state of the art gym at the Plaza. There are low membership rates at our gym.
   N: gym
6. W: Bring the whole family for a whole day of fun at our new zoo. You can see animals from around the world at the zoo.
   N: zoo
7. W: This is our new bowling alley. You can bowl until midnight all weekend at our bowling alley.
   N: bowling alley
8. W: Come visit our playground. The playground is safe, clean, and free! Bring your children to the playground for some great exercise.
   N: playground
9. W: As you can see, the swimming pool is very popular. You can swim from 7 a.m. to 10 p.m., Monday through Saturday at the swimming pool.
   N: swimming pool

Pg. 24   Lesson 3—Exercise 3

1. Sam's going to visit his friends this evening.
2. I'll go to the meeting after work.
3. We're gonna go to the amusement park tomorrow.
4. I think it will rain tomorrow.
5. I'll drive you to class next week.
6. John thinks that he will be a manager at his company in five years.

Pg. 25   Lesson 4—Exercise 1A

M = Man, W = Woman

1. W: Do you want to get together this Wednesday?
   M: Sure. What would you like to do?
   W: Well, on Wednesday night there's a new nightclub that's opening or there's a movie on TV. Take your pick.

M: I think I'd rather watch a movie. Should I pick you up at 7:00?
W: Let's play it by ear. I'll call you on Tuesday night.
M: Sounds good.

2. M: Do you want to get together this Friday?
   W: Sure. What would you like to do?
   M: Well, on Friday night there's a two-for-one special at the bowling alley or there's a sale at the mall. It's up to you.
   W: I think I'd rather go to the mall. Should I pick you up at 6:00?
   M: Let's play it by ear. I'll call you on Thursday night.
   W: Sounds good.

Pg. 27   Lesson 4—Exercise 4B

Happy Independence Day and thank you for calling the Greenville Stadium information line. Here's what's going on this 4th of July holiday weekend.

On Friday, July 4th at 7 p.m., come see Jackie "Funny Man" Nelson live in concert. Jackie's got comedy and laughs for the whole family! Come early for great seats. Great fireworks and music will follow the show.

On Saturday evening, July 5th, come join us for *A Taste of Greenville*. *A Taste of Greenville* is the popular food festival that we hold on the holiday weekend every year. Restaurants from around the city will be here with samples of their finest food. There's great food, good music, and probably even some dancing under the stars. The festival runs from 5 to 10 p.m. Tickets are $9 for adults and $5 for children ages 6 to 12. Children 5 and under are free.

On Sunday, July 6th, let the games begin! Come out and watch, or come out and play in our youth soccer league from 8 a.m. to noon. Kids from 6 to 17 can play. Each team plays eight games during July and August. The cost to join is $30 per child. That's a great price for a summer full of fun.

UNIT 3   A Job to Do

Pg. 32   Lesson 1—Exercise 1C

M = Man, N = Narrator

M: This is the office where we work. Let me show you around.

1. M: That is Luis. He's a graphic designer. Graphic designers design and prepare art. Most graphic designers work on computers.
   N: graphic designer
2. M: Luis uses a keyboard to do his work. The keyboard is delicate. Take my advice. Never spill water on your keyboard.
   N: keyboard
3. M: Janet is the office manager. The office manager makes sure that everything in the office gets completed on time.
   N: office manager
4. M: Joan is putting pictures on her computer from her digital camera. A digital camera is very important for her job.
   N: digital camera
5. M: Joan is a photographer. She takes pictures and uses her computer to make them look better.
   N: photographer

6. W: Raj sometimes wears a headset. He can listen to things on the computer when he wears his headset.
   N: headset
7. M: That monitor is new. It's larger than the old monitor.
   N: monitor
8. M: The CPU isn't working. They might need to buy a new CPU if Raj can't fix it.
   N: CPU
9. M: Raj is our office's computer technician. A computer technician fixes computer problems.
   N: computer technician

Pg. 38 Lesson 3—Exercise 3

My name is Lin. I'm an office manager for a large insurance company. I usually order all of our office supplies from Office Star or Business Max. For everyday items like paper and file folders, Office Star is usually less expensive than Business Max. For special items like printer ink, Office Star is the most expensive. But, I've noticed that the people who work at Business Max are not as helpful as the people who work at Office Star. The sales people at Office Star are more professional than the salespeople at Business Max. Oh, and I almost forgot! When I order from Office Star, my orders arrive faster than my orders from Business Max. They arrive in 48 hours or less, or they're free!

Pg. 39 Lesson 4—Exercise 1A

C = Ms. Clark, B = Bill, S = Sue
1. C: Bill, can I see you for a moment?
   B: Yes, Ms. Clark? What is it?
   C: You're a good worker, Bill. You're the most creative person in the office, and you're great with customers on the phone.
   B: Thanks, Ms. Clark.
   C: But, Bill, you're very disorganized. You have to be more organized.
   B: I'm sorry, Ms. Clark. You won't have to tell me again.
   C: Thank you, Bill.
2. C: Sue, can I see you for a moment?
   S: Yes, Ms. Clark? What is it?
   C: You're a good worker, Sue. You're the friendliest person in the office, and you're always on time.
   S: Thanks, Ms. Clark.
   C: But, you're always calling and talking to other employees. You have to be more professional.
   S: I'm sorry, Ms. Clark. I promise I'll do better.
   C: Thank you, Sue.
3. C: Now, where is Vicki?

Pg. 40 Lesson 4—Exercise 3B

1. Vicki
2. Becky
3. Fran
4. Brandon
5. Farrah
6. Vera

Pg. 41 Lesson 4—Exercise 4B

J = Mr. Jones, E = Elizabeth, B = Ben 3, H = Habib
1. J: Come in, Elizabeth. Let's talk about your work. I know you're working very hard this year. You're more organized than you were last year. You're the most creative worker in your department, but I'm a little concerned about one thing. I notice you come to work late sometimes. Please try to be on time.
   E: Thanks for the feedback, Mr. Jones. You won't have to tell me again.
2. J: Well, Ben, I've been thinking a lot about your work this year. Customers always tell me that you are the most helpful person in the store. You are very reliable. I know I can always count on you, but I'm a little worried about your paperwork. Please try to be more organized. Let's work on that this year.
   B: Sure thing, Mr. Jones. I didn't know it was a problem. I'm sure I can do better.
3. J: Habib, your work has been very good this year. You're careful and you're confident. I'm really happy about that. But it's part of your job to help new employees. Please try to be more helpful with new workers this year.
   H: Sorry Mr. Jones. Don't worry. I promise to do better.

UNIT 4   Good Work

Pg. 46 Lesson 1—Exercise 1C

N = Narrator, W = Woman
   W: When you are at a job interview, there are a few Interview Do's and Do not do's. First let's look at the things you shouldn't do in an interview.
1. W: If you are late for the interview, the interviewer will think you will be late to work. Don't be late for an interview.
   N: don't be late
2. W: Don't look nervous at an interview. If you talk too fast or can't sit still, the employer might think you look nervous.
   N: don't look nervous
3. W: Don't wear inappropriate clothes at an interview. The employer will think you aren't serious about the job if you dress inappropriately.
   N: don't dress inappropriately
4. W: If you carry a cell phone, turn it off before the interview starts. Don't use your cell phone at an interview.
   N: don't use a cell phone
   W: Now, let's talk about the things you should do at a job interview.
5. W: It's good to arrive on time for an interview. You should leave home a little early. Then you can be sure that you will arrive on time.
   N: arrive on time
6. W: It's important to greet the interviewer. Look the interviewer in the eye, shake hands, and use the interviewer's name. This is the best way to greet the interviewer.
   N: greet the interviewer

7. W: Employers like confident workers. If you stand up straight and make eye contact, you will look confident. Try to look confident.
   N: look confident
8. W: Always dress professionally. For an office job, wear a suit or other conservative clothing. Always wear clean neat clothing. You dress for success when you dress professionally.
   N: dress professionally
9. W: A resume tells the employer that you are organized and serious about the job. It's a good idea to bring your resume to an interview.
   N: bring your resume

Pg. 52   Lesson 3—Exercise 3

My name is Sasha. I work for J & J Shipping Company. I haven't worked here for very long, but I've made some great friends. My best friends at work are named Julie and Jenna. Both Julie and Jenna have worked here for 12 years. They've been in the same department since they started. Jenna helped me learn the company's computer programs and Julie has helped me with all kinds of things. I haven't had a chance to transfer to their department, but I hope I will someday.

Pg. 53   Lesson 4—Exercise 1A

N = Narrator, M = Manager, O = Mrs. Ortiz
N: 2005
M: How long have you been a server at Henri's Restaurant, Ms. Ortiz?
O: I've been a server here since 2003.
M: Why do you think you should be the new assistant chef?
O: I'm a fast learner. I want to learn how to help create delicious food for Henri's customers.
M: Have you ever been an assistant chef before?
O: No, but I know I can do it.
M: That's terrific, Ms. Ortiz.

Pg. 54   Lesson 4—Exercise 3B

1. Is Claudia at home today?
2. Are they going to work this week?
3. Hector sat next to me yesterday.
4. I'm a fast learner and a team player.
5. How many other employees did they interview for the promotion?
6. This store is my family's favorite place to shop.

Pg. 55   Lesson 4—Exercise 4B

I = Interviewer, M = Miguel
I: Tell me about your education, Miguel.
M: Well, I studied accounting and computers at City College for four years. I graduated with honors.
I: Have you worked in a hospital before?
M: Yes, I have. I've worked at Center Street Hospital since February, 2005.
I: Are you working there now?
M: Yes, I am. I work in the billing department. I'm an assistant accounts manager.
I: I see. And why are you looking for a new job?
M: Center Street Hospital is a great place to work, but it's an hour drive from my house. I'd like to work here at Springfield General Hospital because it's an excellent hospital and it's closer to home.

UNIT 5   Community Resources

Pg. 60   Lesson 1—Exercise 1C

M = Man, N = Narrator
   M: Thank you for calling the Lakeside City Services hotline. Please listen and select from the following menu.
1. M: City hall is the place where the mayor and city council work. Many other city government offices are also located inside city hall. Press 1 for city hall.
   N: city hall
2. M: Plastic, paper and glass can be recycled at the recycling center seven days a week. Press 2 for the recycling center.
   N: recycling center
3. M: Sign up now at the recreation center for children's and adults' sports classes and teams. Press 3 for the recreation center.
   N: recreation center
4. M: The community clinic offers free and low-cost health services. Clinic hours are Monday through Saturday from 9:00 to 7:00. Press 4 for the community clinic.
   N: community clinic
5. M: The animal shelter is the place to find a lost dog or cat. The animal shelter has a pet adoption day once a week. Press 5 for the animal shelter.
   N: animal shelter
6. M: The Department of Motor Vehicles, or the DMV, is where you go to get a driver's license or to register your car. Press 6 for the DMV.
   N: Department of Motor Vehicles (DMV)
7. M: The senior center offers exercise classes every day. Adults 65 years of age and over can take classes and receive services. Press 7 for the senior center.
   N: senior center
8. M: The employment agency has job listings in the community. Press 8 for the employment agency.
   N: employment agency

Pg. 66   Lesson 3—Exercise 3

M = Man, W = Woman
1. M: Mark hasn't ever been to New York, but he's been to Los Angeles.
2. W: Have you been to the new recreation center yet?
   M: Yes, I've already been three times, but I haven't taken a class there yet.
3. M: Have you gotten a new dog yet?
   W: No, but I'm going to the animal shelter to look this weekend.
4. W: Have Toshi and Roberto started working at the senior center yet?
   M: Toshi hasn't started yet, but Roberto started last weekend.
5. M: Have you ever written a letter to a school board member?
   W: I've never written a letter, but I've gone to three board meetings.
6. W: Have you already gone to the job fair this weekend?
   M: Yes. In fact, I went yesterday afternoon and I went back this morning for more information.

Pg. 67 Lesson 4—Exercise 1A

J = John, S = Ms. Schneider
J: Hi, Ms. Schneider. Did you go to the residents' meeting Wednesday night? I didn't see you there.
S: No, I didn't, John. I'm sorry. I had to work.
J: That's OK. By the way, have you signed the petition for a new onsite recycling center?
S: No, I haven't. What's it about?
J: The nearest recycling center is 15 miles away. We want to have one in the apartment complex. We're asking the building owners to put in a recycling center.
S: A recycling center in the apartment complex? I don't want to sign the petition. There's a recycling center on my way to work.

Pg. 68 Lesson 4—Exercise 3B

1. The woman volunteers at the senior center.
2. Check the website for the next job fair.
3. I haven't signed the petition yet.
4. Alex waited in line for two hours yesterday.
5. We've completed the class project already.

Pg. 69 Lesson 4—Exercise 4B

T = Talk show host, L = Dr. Lopez
T: Hello, and welcome to Earth Talk. We're here today with Dr. Arturo Lopez to talk about recycling in the United States. Dr. Lopez, can you tell us a little about the history of recycling?
L: Recycling paper, glass and metal isn't a new idea. It's been around for a long time. The first paper recycling began just outside of Philadelphia in the year 1690. The first recycling center was built in New York City in 1897.
T: And tell us, Dr. Lopez, why is recycling so important?
L: To say it simply, Sylvia, we produce too much trash! The average person in this country throws away one thousand six hundred pounds of trash every year. Just imagine how much trash that is! And our population is still growing.
T: So, I guess the big question is how are we doing? Are we recycling enough?
L: Well, in 1970 only 6.5 percent of the people in the U.S. were recycling paper, glass, and plastic on a regular basis. In the year 2005, that number went up to 32 percent. So we're making progress. But we need to do much, much more.

UNIT 6   What's Cooking?

Pg. 74 Lesson 1—Exercise 1C

R = Ramon, A = Assistant, J = Josh, N = Narrator
R: Welcome to Ramon's restaurant. I'm Ramon. I'm too busy cooking to talk right now, but my assistant will tell you what we're doing.
1. A: Welcome to the kitchen. I'm chopping vegetables right now. I have to chop the onions into very small pieces.
   N: chop
2. A: Ramon, the chef, is pouring broth into his famous soup. He must pour only a little bit in at a time.
   N: pour

3. A: He is also stirring his famous soup. He must stir this soup every five minutes.
   N: stir
4. A: The chef always uses a large pan for his vegetables. He put some oil in the pan first and then he added the vegetables to the pan.
   N: pan
5. A: I think that the large pot on the stove is for spaghetti. You need just the right pot for pasta.
   N: pot
6. A: It looks like the water for the pasta is boiling. Excuse me, Ramon? Do you want the water to boil so fast?
   N: boil
7. A: Pardon me. I need to talk to our dishwasher, Josh, for a moment… Josh! I need a bowl for these onions. Do you have a clean bowl?
   J: Just a minute. I'll bring you a bowl.
   N: bowl
8. A: Oh, Josh…can you bring me a plate too?
   J: The plates are in the sink. I'll clean a plate right away.
   N: plate
9. A: Josh works hard. He has to. Ramon makes sure that every glass in his restaurant is very clean. Josh spends almost 2 minutes washing each glass.
   N: glass
10. A: In the kitchen or in the dish room, you have to watch out for knives. Josh usually washes each knife separately and lets it dry on the counter.
    J: That way I never cut myself on a knife.
    N: knife
11. J: But forks can be dangerous too! I wash each fork carefully.
    N: fork
12. R: Josh! I need some spoons to let everyone taste my delicious soup.
    J: OK, Ramon. There's a clean spoon on the counter and I'll wash some more spoons right away.
    N: spoon
    R: Here, let me give you each a small bowl of soup and a spoon. It's delicious, isn't it?…I thought so.

Pg. 80 Lesson 3—Exercise 3

1. I just can't get over this cold.
2. I'd like a salad, but could you leave out the onions?
3. I need to take out the trash. Tomorrow is trash day.
4. I wrote down the phone number. I'm looking for it now.
5. They'll come over later this afternoon.
6. I got off the bus in front of my house.

Pg. 81 Lesson 4—Exercise 1A

C1 = Customer 1, C2 = Customer 2, S1 = Server 1, S2 = Server 2
C1: Excuse me. I have a question about the menu. I've never heard of a sloppy joe before. What is it?
S1: It's a spicy meat sandwich with tomato sauce.
C1: Sounds good. OK. I'll try it.
S1: Excellent. Ours is the best in town.
C1: Oh, one more thing. Is a sloppy joe salty?
S1: No, it isn't. Our cook doesn't use much salt.
C1: Good. I'm trying to cut down on salt.

C2: Excuse me. I have a question about the menu. I've never heard of a chicken pot pie before. What is it?

S2: It's a pie made with chicken, vegetables, and potatoes.
C2: Sounds good. OK. I'll try it.
S2: Excellent. Ours is the best in town.
C2: I'd also like a baked apple. Are yours sweet?
S2: No, they aren't. Our cook doesn't use much sugar.
C2: Good. I'm trying to cut down on sugar.

Pg. 82   Lesson 4—Exercise 3B

M = Man, W = Woman
1. M: Can you help me look for my keys?
   W: I'll help you look for them in a minute.
2. W: Don't forget to turn off the oven.
   M: I'll turn off the oven as soon as the chicken is done.
3. M: Where do you get off the train?
   W: We get off at Grant Street Station.
4. W: Did you turn on the oven before you put the cake in?
   M: Yes, I did. I always remember to turn on the oven.
5. M: I went over to Jimmy's house yesterday afternoon.
   W: You always go over to Jimmy's house before you go over to Larry's house.
6. W: I couldn't get on that elevator because it was too crowded.
   M: That's OK. We'll get on the next one.

Pg. 83   Lesson 4—Exercise 4B

M = Man, W = Woman
M: Well, that was a good lunch.
W: Yes, it was. The kids enjoyed their meals, too. Are you going to pay the bill?
M: First let me check the math. OK, let's see…we had three hamburgers at six dollars each. That's eighteen dollars. And we had 2 turkey burgers at five-fifty each. That's eleven dollars.
W: The service was great. Let's leave a good tip.
M: Just a minute. I'm still doing the math. Then we had three lemonades for the kids, one coffee and a water.
W: How much were the lemonades?
M: Two dollars each. OK. So that's six dollars. This looks right. And coffee is a dollar-fifty. OK.
W: What about the tip. Is the tip included?
M: No, it's not included. OK. Everything looks correct.
W: Leave a good tip.
M: I will.

UNIT 7   Money Wise

Pg. 88   Lesson 1—Exercise 1C

N = Narrator, M = Male customer, T = Female teller,
F1 = Female customer 1, S = Security guard,
F2 = Female customer 2, L = Loan officer,
F3 = Female customer 3, A = Accounts manager
1. M: I need to get a cashier's check because I'm buying a car. Could I please get a cashier's check for seven thousand five hundred dollars?
   N: get a cashier's check
2. T: I'm a teller. Tellers work in banks and help customers with deposits and withdrawals.
   N: teller
3. F1: I started to go to the first teller window near the door but it's closed. It's strange to close a teller window at such a busy time of day.
   N: teller window

4. S: I'm a security guard. I keep the bank safe. I've been a security guard at this bank for 12 years.
   N: security guard
5. F2: I'm Mrs. Ramirez. My husband and I are applying for a loan. We're a little nervous, but it's pretty easy to apply for a loan at State Bank.
   N: apply for a loan
6. L: A loan officer helps people get bank loans or money from the bank so they can buy houses or cars. I'm a loan officer
   N: loan officer
7. A: Welcome to the account services desk. You can open or close your bank accounts at the account services desk.
   N: account services desk
8. F3: I need to open a checking account. How do I open an account with your bank?
   N: open an account
9. A: I'm Mr. Sanchez, the accounts manager. An accounts manager helps new customers with questions about their checking or savings accounts.
   N: accounts manager

Pg. 94   Lesson 3—Exercise 3

1. If you have to get a new car, how will you pay for it?
2. If you have the time to go to the bank, what will you do there?
3. What will you do if the bank is closed?
4. Where will you go if you need new clothes?
5. If I have questions, will the accounts manager help me?
6. If you start saving now, when will you reach your goal?

Pg. 95   Lesson 4—Exercise 1A

M = Min, C = Customer service
M: I'm calling to report a problem on my credit card bill.
C: What seems to be the problem?
M: It says that I spent fifteen hundred dollars in Pacific City, but that's impossible! I've never been to Pacific City.
C: OK. I'll talk to my supervisor and ask him to review it before we send your next bill.
M: So, do I have to pay the fifteen hundred dollar charge this month?
C: Let's wait and see. When you receive your next bill, you'll see your new balance.

Pg. 96   Lesson 4—Exercise 3B

1. Your sister brought her friend. What's her friend's name?
2. Tim will brush his teeth before he goes to bed.
3. He'll go to the bank before he comes home.
4. When he gets his paycheck, Jack will buy a new TV.

Pg. 97   Lesson 4—Exercise 4B

Welcome to State Bank's automated account information system. For savings account information, press one now. For checking account information, press two now. To speak to a customer service representative, press zero now.

Your checking account balance as of 3/15/08 is $625.10. To hear your last five transactions, press one now.

March 7th, 2008: check number 266 in the amount of $44.73.

March 7th, 2008: check number 268 in the amount of $106.50.

March 9th, 2008: check number 267 in the amount of $56.00.

March 9th, 2008: check number 270 in the amount of $27.61.

March 12th, 2008: check number 271 in the amount of $175.90.

UNIT 8   Living Well

Pg. 102   Lesson 1—Exercise 1C

M = Man, W = Woman, N = Narrator
- M: The human body is an amazing machine. It's important to keep the parts of this machine healthy and strong. Let's look at what aerobic exercise can do for your body.
1. W: Believe it or not, aerobic exercise is great for your skin. Doing aerobics improves circulation so your skin looks healthy.
   N: skin
2. W: Aerobic exercise is also good for your lungs. Healthy lungs help you breathe more easily.
   N: lungs
3. W: Aerobic exercise, like running or bicycling, makes your heart beat faster, and that makes your heart strong.
   N: heart
4. W: When you do aerobics, you use the major muscle groups in your body. This makes your muscles stronger and healthier.
   N: muscles
5. W: Cycling and other exercise move the blood through the body. This improves your circulation, or blood flow.
   N: blood
   M: Another way to take care of yourself is with good nutrition. Remember, you are what you eat!
6. W: Scientists are learning more about what foods are good for the brain. Fish, eggs and plenty of water all help your brain process or learn new information and stay sharp. These foods are good for your brain.
   N: brain
7. W: Take care of your bones and teeth by getting plenty of calcium in your diet. Cheese, milk and dark green vegetables help make strong bones.
   N: bones
8. W: Pasta and rice, in small amounts, are good for your stomach. This food helps protect your stomach from acid.
   N: stomach

9. W: The intestines are an important part of your digestive system. Whole grain bread, fruit, and dark green vegetables are excellent for your intestines. This food has fiber that helps your intestines work well.
   N: intestines

Pg. 108   Lesson 3—Exercise 3A

1. Livia used to eat white bread, but she doesn't anymore. Now she eats brown bread.
2. Her youngest son, Carlos, didn't used to go to the park, but now he does. He plays in the park every evening.
3. Her oldest son, Tomas, used to spend a lot of money on fast food. Now he cooks healthy dinners at home every night. He saves a lot of money.
4. Her husband, Paulo didn't used to exercise during the week. He used to only exercise on the weekend. Now he exercises four days a week.
5. Elena, their daughter, doesn't play basketball anymore. She used to play all the time, but she hurt her knee. Now she walks for exercise.

Pg. 108   Lesson 3—Exercise 3B

1. When did the kids use to go to bed?
2. Patrick didn't use to stay up all night.
3. John and Gina use to go to bed at nine.
4. Did Gina use to complain about going to bed? I don't remember.
5. They all complain now. We didn't use to have so much stress at bedtime.

Pg. 109   Lesson 4—Exercise 1A

D = Doctor, M = Man, W = Woman
Patient 1
- D: I'm a little concerned about your weight, Mr. Ruiz.
- M: I've been under a lot of stress recently.
- D: Have you been getting enough exercise?
- M: Well, I used to jog every day, but it's too cold outside now.
- D: Heart problems run in your family, so you need to exercise. Why don't you walk inside the mall to exercise?
- M: Good idea. I'll try it.
Patient 2
- D: I'm a little concerned about your blood pressure, Mrs. Thompson.
- W: I've been under a lot of stress recently.
- D: Have you been getting enough exercise?
- W: Well, I used to go to the gym, but I moved far away from the gym.
- D: High blood pressure runs in your family, so you need to exercise. Why don't you walk in your neighborhood?
- W: OK. I can do that. I'll give it a try.

Pg. 111   Lesson 4—Exercise 3B

1. What do most people use to cook vegetables?
2. These days, they use steamers and microwaves.
3. There was a time when people didn't use to eat a lot of vegetables.
4. They didn't use microwaves, because there weren't any!

Pg. 111 Lesson 4—Exercise 4B

D = Donna, K = Katie

D: Welcome to fat-free radio, the radio program that answers your questions about diet and exercise. I'm Donna, your host. Let's take a call. Katie, are you there?

K: Hi Donna. Thanks for taking my call. I'd really like to lose ten pounds. What's the best exercise for me? I'm in good health, but I don't have a lot of time.

D: Great question, Katie. To lose weight, you want to use more calories than you eat. Everything you do uses calories. For example, watching TV uses calories, but only about 60 calories an hour. Cleaning your house uses calories, too! It's great exercise for busy people. You can burn about 225 calories per hour by cleaning the house. So remember, a cleaner house means a leaner you! Another great way to use calories is walking. Experts say that walking is the best way to lose weight. Depending on how fast you walk, you can use about 300 calories per hour. Try walking instead of driving or taking the bus if you want to lose weight. If you have time, swimming burns an average of 425 calories per hour. It's a great way to lose weight and it's easy on the body. If you are in good shape, running might be a good exercise for you. You can burn about 550 calories per hour. Thanks for the call, Katie. Hope you find the exercise that's right for you. Good luck.

UNIT 9   Hit the Road

Pg. 116 Lesson 1—Exercise 1C

R = Ramiro, N = Narrator

R: Hello there. I'm Ramiro. I work at Quick Change and I know a lot about cars. Here are some of the basics you should know.

1. R: Always keep the windshield clean. You can't see the road if the windshield is dirty.
   N: windshield
2. R: The headlights are on the front of the car. They help you see and be seen. Both headlights must work. It's illegal to drive with only one headlight.
   N: headlight
3. R: Check your tires once a month. A low tire or a flat tire can be very dangerous, so check your tires often.
   N: tire
4. R: Many important car parts are under the hood. To check the engine's oil level, open the hood.
   N: hood
5. R: Use the turn signal when you turn left or right. Let other drivers know what you're planning to do and use your turn signal.
   N: turn signal
6. R: Many people forget to keep their gas tanks full. Then they run out of gas. Remember to fill your gas tank. Oh! Don't forget to close the gas tank when you're done.
   N: gas tank
7. R: It's good to have a first aid kit in the trunk. And don't forget a blanket. Put it in the trunk too.
   N: trunk

8. R: You have to have a license plate on your car; it's your car's identification number. It's a good idea to memorize your license plate number.
   N: license plate
9. R: The bumper protects you and your car if you have an accident. There is a bumper on the front and a bumper on the back.
   N: bumper
   R: Well, it's time for me to get back to work. Drive safely.

Pg. 122 Lesson 3—Exercise 3

1. After we called the mechanic, we took the car to the garage.
2. Anna stopped at the gas station before she picked me up.
3. When I stopped the car, I saw my friend on the corner.
4. Before he took his driving test, Mr. Chen was nervous.
5. Before she buys a new car, Susan will sell her old car.
6. When Anthony moves to Los Angeles, he'll learn to drive.
7. After I got an oil change, I went on a trip.
8. After Karla starts the car, she adjusts the rearview mirror.

Pg. 123 Lesson 4—Exercise 1A

D = Car dealer, C = Customer

D: This is a really nice car. It only has 30,000 miles on it, and it has a two-year warranty too.

C: 30,000 miles? That sure is nice. How much is it?

D: It also has a new stereo, and new paint too.

C: Uh-huh. And how much is it?

D: I can sell it to you today for twelve thousand five hundred dollars. It's a great deal.

C: Twelve thousand-five hundred!?!? But the bumper is dented and the windshield has a crack!

D: Uhhh....Let me talk to my manager about the price. We're flexible at Mid-City cars.

Pg. 125 Lesson 4—Exercise 4B

La = Larry, Lo = Lorraine, M = Matt

La: Welcome to Car Time, the radio show that answers all your car questions. I'm Larry.

Lo: And I'm Loraine. Let's take a call now from Matt in Dallas. Hi, Matt.

La: Hello, Matt.

M: Hi, Larry and Lorraine. I'm getting ready to buy my first car.

Lo: Congratulations, Matt!

M: Thanks. Um, my question is, how much money will I need every month for gas, insurance, and other expenses?

La: Great question, Matt. Now is the right time to be planning for expenses.

Lo: The biggest expense will be car insurance. For most people, that's a monthly expense. You have to get insurance. It's the law! Insurance can be expensive. How much you pay depends on the kind of car you have, your age, your driving record, and where you live.

La: That's right Lorraine. And you should think about gas money. How much will you drive every week? The average person drives about 15,000 miles per year. Look for a car that gets good gas mileage. Anything above 30 miles per gallon is considered good. Some of today's cars can get over 60 miles per gallon.

Lo: In many states, you'll also have to pay taxes on your car every year. How much depends on the price, or value of the car.

La: The last major expense is car maintenance and repairs. This cost will be different for new cars and used cars. With any car, you need to think about how many miles you drive per year, so you can plan for maintenance like oil changes and new tires. You should get an oil change every 5,000 miles. If you have an older car, add money for other problems that might come up.

M: OK. Thanks a lot guys.

Lo: Good luck with that car!

La and Lo: Bye, Matt.

UNIT 10 Crime Doesn't Pay

Pg. 130   Lesson 1—Exercise 1C

K = Kevin, S = Su-Ling, N = Narrator

K: Hi. I'm Kevin, and this is my wife Su-Ling. We had a strange evening recently. We were glad that we knew a lot of neighborhood safety.

S: Here's what happened.

1. S: We went out for a walk. I locked the door. Locking the doors is one of the best ways to keep your home safe. We always lock the doors when we leave home.

N: lock the doors

2. K: I put my wallet in my jacket pocket. That's a good way to protect your wallet. You should always protect your wallet or purse when you are out in public.

N: protect your wallet or purse

3. K: We don't walk alone at night. It's not a good idea to walk alone when it's dark out.

N: don't walk alone at night

4. S: We always walk together in well-lit areas. We walk down streets that have many lights. It's much safer to walk in well-lit areas.

N: walk in well-lit areas

5. K: So, the other night when we were walking, we saw a young man commit a crime. He was spray-painting the hood of a car! We couldn't believe that someone would commit a crime like that in front of us.

N: commit a crime

6. S: We were witnessing a crime! At first we weren't sure what to do. Then we remembered that we should call 911. Kevin called 911 on his cell phone and told them that we were witnessing a crime.

N: witness a crime

7. K: When the police arrived, we reported the crime. It's every person's responsibility to report crimes they see or hear. Be prepared to answer a police officer's questions when you report a crime.

N: report a crime

8. S: The police found the young man a few blocks away and arrested the suspect. Remember that arresting a suspect is a job for the police. Don't try to stop or arrest a suspect yourself.

N: arrest a suspect

Pg. 136   Lesson 3—Exercise 3

1. Everyone in the courtroom is listening to the witness.
2. Telling the truth is very important in court.
3. Explaining the rules is the judge's job.
4. The attorneys are asking the witness a lot of questions.
5. The defendant is wearing a suit and tie.
6. Deciding what to do won't be easy for the jury.

Pg. 137   Lesson 4—Exercise 1A

P = Male police officer, W = Witness

P: Police department. How can I direct your call?

W: I'd like to report a crime I witnessed.

P: OK. Please tell me what happened.

W: While I was entering my apartment building, I saw a man in the hallway. First he broke into an apartment. Then he took a TV.

P: What happened after that?

W: I think he saw me because, all of a sudden, he ran away.

P: OK. Hold on. An officer will fill out a complete report. Reporting this was the right thing to do.

W: Thank you.

Pg. 138   Lesson 4—Exercise 3B

1. I called the police. Nobody else had a cell phone.
2. I saw the whole thing, officer. They came out of the bank. I saw them. They ran that way.
3. We walk every evening. We never walk in the morning. We're too busy.

Pg. 139   Lesson 4—Exercise 4B

P = Male police officer, A = Ms. Aziz

P: Thank you for holding. This is Officer Wong. What's your name, please?

A: My name is Roya Aziz.

P: Okay, Ms. Aziz. I need to get some information about what you saw. Can you tell me where you were when you witnessed the mugging?

A: Yes. I was sitting on a park bench.

P: Okay. What happened first?

A: I saw a man run by. He was moving fast, but I saw that he was carrying a lady's purse.

P: What did he look like?

W: I didn't get a good look at his face, but he was tall and thin.

P: Okay. What happened next?

A: Next, a woman ran by. She was yelling for the man to stop. She kept saying, "He has my purse! He has my purse!"

P: And what happened after that, Ms. Aziz?

A: Well, I stood up to see what was happening. The man fell and dropped the purse. Then he got up and ran away. The woman picked up her purse and asked me to call the police.

P: Okay, Ms. Aziz. Is the woman there with you now?

A: Yes, she's right here. She says she's fine.

P: A police car should be there in a few minutes. Both of you please wait there until the officers arrive.

UNIT 11 That's Life

Pg. 144 Lesson 1—Exercise 1C

C = Carlos Ortega, N = Narrator

   C: My name is Carlos Ortega, and this is the story of my life.

1. C: I was born on August 22nd. I guess I couldn't wait to get started because I was born 3 weeks early. My mother couldn't wait for me to be born either!
   N: be born

2. C: I graduated from high school at the top of my class when I was 18. My parents were very proud. I'm the first person in my family to graduate from high school.
   N: graduate

3. C: On my first job with ACME Glass, I was promoted from assembly worker to plant manager in only a few years. I remember how excited I was to get a promotion.
   N: get a promotion

4. C: I met Nora, the love of my life, at the factory. We got engaged after only six months. I asked her to marry me at our favorite restaurant. I was so nervous to get engaged.
   N: get engaged

5. C: When we got married, we were both 30 years old. In those days, you didn't get married at that age, but we did.
   N: get married

6. C: We had our first child a year later. We were nervous and excited to have a baby.
   N: have a baby

7. C: Everything was going well at the factory, but I wanted to run my own business—so I started Ortega's Fine Foods. It's a lot of hard work to start a business, but it's worth every minute.
   N: start a business

8. C: Five years ago, I decided it was time to retire. I wanted to travel and spend more time with Nora, so I retired.
   N: retire

9. C: Two years ago, I became a grandfather. That's right, Nora and I have a grandson. You feel like a kid again when you become a grandparent!
   N: become a grandparent

Pg. 150 Lesson 3—Exercise 3

1. Smoking is not permitted in the restaurant.
2. A reception is planned immediately after the wedding.
3. Babies born at Glenview Hospital are taken care of by our excellent team of nurses.
4. The party is given by my friends, Tina and Lim.
5. All guests are welcomed by the bride.
6. Birth announcements and death notices are found in Section C of the local paper.

Pg. 151 Lesson 4—Exercise 1A

M = Min, P = Peter

M: Hello, Peter? It's Min. I've got some good news and some bad news.

P: Oh, no. What's the bad news?

M: Well, I had car trouble and I was almost late for my final exam.

P: Oh, no. That's too bad.

M: Yes, but the good news is that I got an A on the test. I'll be able to graduate next month!

P: Terrific! That's the best news I've heard all day. Let's celebrate this weekend.

M: That sounds great. I'll call you Friday.

Pg. 152 Lesson 4—Exercise 3B

1. That's right!
2. That's right.
3. Wait. I can't find my ticket.
4. Wait! I see my friend over there.
5. I got the job! I can start on Wednesday.
6. I got the job....if I want it.

Pg. 153 Lesson 4—Exercise 4B

N = Narrator, W1 = Woman 1, W2 = Woman 2

N: Around the World in 60 Seconds

W1: Do you like to attend weddings? Are you curious about wedding traditions around the world? Maybe you're getting married in the near future? If marriage is on your mind, you'll love today's topic on *Around the World in 60 Seconds*.

W2: That's right. Today we're talking about wedding traditions from around the world. For example, did you know that in Venezuela the bride and groom don't say goodbye to anyone at their wedding reception? It's good luck for them to leave without saying goodbye to their guests.

W1: Yes. And in Greece, dishes are broken for good luck at wedding receptions.

W2: It seems that every culture has their own unique and interesting wedding traditions. Did you know that in Mexico and Panama brides are given 13 gold coins at the wedding ceremony? In China and India, brides often wear red wedding gowns.

W1: And have you ever wondered why rice is often thrown at the bride and groom by wedding guests in the U.S.?

W2: That's right. It's all for good luck.

W1: These are just a few of many traditions from around the world. And the most popular tradition around the world? You guessed it. Almost anywhere you go, the wedding ends with a kiss.

UNIT 12 Doing the Right Thing

Pg. 158 Lesson 1—Exercise 1C

N = Narrator, W = Woman

1. W: The right to vote is a constitutional right of U.S. citizens. Most people think the right to vote is their most important right.
   N: the right to vote

2. W: Everyone in the U.S. has freedom of speech. This first amendment right gives people the right to express their opinions and thoughts. Freedom of speech has played an important role in U.S. history.
   N: freedom of speech

3. W: Freedom of the press means that newspapers and other news sources are free to report the news. The government cannot tell news sources what to say because of freedom of the press.
   N: freedom of the press

4. W: The right to a fair trial guarantees that a judge or a jury will hear both sides of the story. In the United States, anyone accused of a crime has the right to a fair trial.
   N: the right to a fair trial
5. W: In the U.S., people have freedom of peaceful assembly. That means a group of people can get together and protest or voice their opinions in public. Freedom of peaceful assembly is another basic first amendment right.
   N: freedom of peaceful assembly
   W: Carrying a U.S. passport makes traveling in and out of the United States easier. All U.S. citizens have the right to carry a U.S. passport.
   N: the right to carry a U.S. passport

Pg. 164 Lesson 3—Exercise 3

1. The hospital has a great volunteer program. George plans…
2. Lee wanted to help, so he volunteered…
3. Marta likes to speak Spanish with the residents at the senior center. She practices…
4. Jill usually volunteers to clean up after events. She dislikes…
5. Raul is studying to be an attorney. He enjoyed…
6. We were all worried about the future of our city. We decided…

Pg. 165 Lesson 4—Exercise 1A

D = Mrs. Delgado, L1 = Law clerk 1, T = Mr, Tran, L2 = Law clerk 2
D: Hi. I called yesterday. My name is Marta Delgado. The woman on the phone told me to come in.
L1: How can we help you today?
D: Well, I'm not sure what I should do. I've lived in my apartment for eight months. I have a one-year lease. Last week, my landlord told me I have to move.
L1: Do you have any idea why?
D: No. I pay my rent on time and I'm a good tenant. I suspect it's because her brother needs an apartment and the building is full. Can she do that?
L1: No, she can't. I think we can help you keep your apartment.
T: Hello. I called yesterday. I'm Tommy Tran. I'm having a problem with a car I bought last month. The man on the phone told me to come in.
L2: How can we help you today?
T: Well, I don't know what to do. I bought a new car last month. There's a problem with the electrical system. It's been broken three times since I bought it. Now the dealer won't fix it or replace it.
L2: Do you have any idea why?
T: The dealer said there is no lemon law because the car was fine when I bought it. I'm pretty sure they aren't telling the truth. I think it's because they don't want to replace the car. Can they do that?
L2: No, they can't. I think I can help you.

Pg. 166 Lesson 4—Exercise 3B

M = Man, W = Woman
1. W: I get the mail every day.
   M: Pat is a 10-year old male.
2. W: I need to buy some food.
   M: The market is by the bank.
3. W: Tim is a new citizen.
   M: He knew he could pass the exam.
4. W: I'll go to the market.
   M: Apples are in aisle six.

Pg. 167 Lesson 4—Exercise 4B

M1 = Man 1, W1 = Woman 1, M2 = Man 2, W2 = Woman 2, M3 = Man 3, W3 = Woman 3, W4 = Woman 4, M4 = Man 4
M1: The first issue on tonight's agenda is the proposal for the new high school. Let's hear voter comments on that now. Would anyone like to comment?
W1: Yes. I think the new high school is a great idea, but it can't be built on Green Street. The street's too small. Traffic would be terrible.
M2: I agree. There isn't enough parking there for the neighborhood now.
W2: I disagree. Green Street is a great place for a high school. The real problem is the cost of a new high school. The property on Green Street is already owned by the city. It's the best place at the best price.
W3: We don't need a new high school! We should just make Central High School bigger. That would be cheaper.
W4: Cheaper, but not better!
M3: Our taxes are already too high! We don't need a new school!
M4: Order, everyone! Please calm down! Everybody has a right to his or her opinion. Let's give everyone a chance to talk.
M1: Thank you Mr. Kovak. Okay, let me repeat the comments so far. Mrs. Bailey thinks that Green Street is too small for a new high school and the neighborhood is too crowded. Ms. Martinez wants us to build the high school on Green Street because the cost will be less. Ms. Neal prefers making our old high school bigger. Mr. Kovak called for order to give everyone a chance to speak. Who else would like to comment? Yes. First Mrs. Rodriguez, then Mr. Cho.

GRAMMAR CHARTS

THE SIMPLE PRESENT

Statements

I You	work	
He She It	works	every day.
We You They	work	

Negative statements

I You	don't	work	
He She It	doesn't	work	every day.
We You They	don't	work	

Contractions

do not	= don't
does not	= doesn't

Yes/No questions

Do	I you	
Does	he she it	work?
Do	we you they	

Answers

Yes,	I you	do.		No,	I you	don't.
	he she it	does.			he she it	doesn't.
	we you they	do.			we you they	don't.

THE PRESENT CONTINUOUS

Statements

I'm You're He's She's It's We're You're They're	working	now.

Negative statements

I'm You're He's She's It's We're You're They're	not working	now.

Contractions

I am	= I'm	I am not	= I'm not
you are	= you're	you are not	= you aren't
he is	= he's	he is not	= he isn't
she is	= she's	she is not	= she isn't
it is	= it's	it is not	= it isn't
we are	= we're	we are not	= we aren't
they are	= they're	they are not	= they aren't

THE SIMPLE PAST

Statements		
I You He She It We You They	worked	last Friday.

Negative statements		
I You He She It We You They	didn't work	last Saturday.

Contractions
did not = didn't

Yes/No questions			
Did	I you he she it we you they	work	last Friday?

Answers					
Yes,	I you he she it we you they	did.	No,	I you he she it we you they	didn't.

PRESENT AND PAST VERB FORMS

	Simple present	Present continuous	Simple past
If verb ends in *–y*	study, studies	studying	studied
If verb ends in *-e*	use, uses	using	used
If verb ends in a consonant	walk, walks search, searches	walking searching	walked searched

ADJECTIVES AND ADVERBS

Adjectives without *–ly* that describe nouns	
close	My car is close.
loud	The music is loud.
quiet	It is a quiet place.

Adverbs with *–ly* that describe verbs	
closely	He watched closely.
loudly	The band played loudly.
quietly	He spoke quietly.

PREFIXES AND SUFFIXES

Prefix	Meaning	Examples
dis-	not	disorganized, disagree, disobey, dishonest, dislike
un-	not	unclean, unhealthy, unsafe, unhappy, unimportant
re-	do again	refill, reprint, reread, reuse, rewrite

Suffix	What the suffix does	Examples
-ful	Changes some nouns or verbs to an adjective	stressful, careful, beautiful, colorful, helpful, thankful
-tion	Changes some verbs to a noun	description, addition, education, invitation, dictation, production
-al	Changes some nouns to an adjective	personal, accidental, national, musical, professional

THE FUTURE WITH *BE GOING TO* AND *WILL*

Statements

I'm You're He's She's It's We're You're They're	going to	work next Tuesday.

Negative statements

I'm You're He's She's It's We're You're They're	not going to	work next Tuesday.

Statements

I'll You'll He'll She'll It'll We'll You'll They'll	probably work next week.

Negative statements

I You He She It We You They	probably won't work next week.

Contractions

I will	= I'll
you will	= you'll
he will	= he'll
she will	= she'll
it will	= it'll
we will	= we'll
they will	= they'll

COMPARATIVE AND SUPERLATIVE ADJECTIVES

	Comparative form		**Superlative form**
Add *-er than* to most adjectives with one syllable.	faster than, cheaper than, newer than, smaller than, kinder than, greater than	Add *-est* to most adjectives with one syllable.	fastest, cheapest, newest, smallest, kindest, greatest
In adjectives ending in *-y*, add *-er than* and change the *-y* to *-i*.	heavier than, happier than, angrier than, friendlier than	Add *-est* and change the *-y* to *-i* in adjectives ending in *-y*.	heaviest, happiest, angriest, friendliest
Add *-r than* to adjectives that end in *-e*.	safer than	Add *-st* to adjectives ending in *-e*.	safest
Double the final consonant and add *-er than* in some adjectives.	bigger than, hotter than	Double the final consonant and add *-est* in some adjectives.	biggest, hottest

THE PRESENT PERFECT

Statements

I've You've He's She's It's We've You've They've	worked in a store.

Negative Statements

I You	haven't	worked in a store.
He She It	hasn't	
We You They	haven't	

Contractions

I have	= I've
you have	= you've
he has	= he's
she has	= she's
it has	= it's
we have	= we've
they have	= they've
have not	= haven't
has not	= hasn't

Yes/No questions

Have	I you	worked in a store?
Has	he she it	
Have	we you they	

Answers

Yes,	I you	have.
	he she it	has.
	we you they	have.

No,	I you	haven't.
	he she it	hasn't.
	we you they	haven't.

Forms of irregular verbs

Base form of verb	Simple past	Past participle
be	was/were	been
do	did	done
drink	drank	drunk
eat	ate	eaten
get	got	gotten
go	went	gone/been
have	had	had

Forms of irregular verbs

Base form of verb	Simple past	Past participle
hear	heard	heard
make	made	made
read	read	read
see	saw	seen
take	took	taken
write	wrote	written

Ever, already, and yet

ever = at any time; never = not at any time
A: Have you ever worked in a store?
B: No, I haven't. I've never worked in a store.

already = some time before now; Use only with affirmative statements.
A: Have you already eaten lunch?
B: Yes, I have.

yet = any time until now; Use only with negative statements.
A: Have you bought a car yet?
B: No, I haven't.

PHRASAL VERBS

Separable phrasal verbs

bring in	Please **bring** the chair **in** the room.	take out	Now **take** the cake **out**.
chop up	Please **chop** the onion **up**.	turn off	**Turn** the oven **off**.
figure out	I can **figure** the recipe **out**.	turn on	**Turn** the light **on**.
leave out	**Leave** the salt **out** of the soup.	use by	**Use** the milk **by** next week.
pick up	Please **pick** the trash **up**.	write down	**Write** the recipe **down**.
put in	Put the cake **in** the oven		

Inseparable phrasal verbs

go over	Will you **go over** to the apartment?	get over	I hope you **get over** your headache.
get off	**Get off** the chair.	look after	Please **look after** the baby.
get on	Don't **get on** the bus.	look for	**Look for** the bus.

POSSESSIVE ADJECTIVES AND PRONOUNS

Possessive adjectives

That is **my** book.
How are **your** french fries?
Is **his** chicken soup good?
Her sandwich looks delicious.
The dog is looking for **its** food.
Do you like **our** hamburgers?
Is **your** soup too salty?
Is **their** apple pie too sweet?

Possessive pronouns

That is **mine**.
How are **yours**?
Is **his** good?
Hers looks delicious.
Its food is in the bowl.
Do you like **ours**?
Is **yours** too salty?
Is **theirs** too sweet?

Note

Its shows possession (*its taste*). *It's* is a contraction for *it is* (*it's spicy*).

REAL CONDITIONAL STATEMENTS

──If clause──	──Main clause──
If I go to the bank,	I'll apply for a loan.
If you save money,	you'll buy a TV.
If he buys it,	he'll pay $100.
If she wants the car,	she'll buy it.
If it is on sale,	it'll be cheaper.
If we find a house,	we'll get a loan.
If you wait,	you'll save money.
If they get jobs,	they'll buy the house.

──Main clause──	──If clause──
I can apply for a loan	if I go to the bank.
You'll buy a TV	if you save money.
He can pay $100	if he buys it.
She'll buy it	if she wants the car.
It'll be cheaper	if it is on sale.
We'll get a loan	if we find a house.
You'll save money	if you wait.
They'll buy the house	if they get jobs.

USED TO

Statements

I You He She It We You They	**used to**	eat junk food.

Negative Statements

I You He She It We You They	**didn't use to**	eat junk food.

Questions

Did	I you he she it we you they	**use to**	eat junk food?

Answers

Yes,	I you he she it we you they	did.	No,	I you he she it we you they	didn't.

THE PRESENT PERFECT CONTINUOUS

Statements

I You	have	
He She It	has	been working for a year.
We You They	have	

Negative Statements

I You	haven't	
He She It	hasn't	been working for a year.
We You They	haven't	

Questions

Have	I	
	you	
Has	he	
	she	been feeling well this week?
	it	
Have	we	
	you	
	they	

Answers

Yes,	I	have.	No,	I	haven't.
	you			you	
	he	has.		he	hasn't.
	she			she	
	it			it	
	we	have.		we	haven't.
	you			you	
	they			they	

DESCRIBING PRESENT, PAST, AND FUTURE EVENTS WITH TIME CLAUSES

Present	When I see a red light, I stop the car.
	I stop the car when I see a red light.
Past	Before I turned left, I used my turn signal.
	I used my turn signal before I turned left.
Future	After I wash the car, I'll drive to the bank.
	I'll drive to the bank after I wash the car.

AND...TOO, AND...NOT EITHER, BUT

and...too	I like to travel. My friend likes to travel.
	I like to travel, **and** my friend does, **too**.
and...not either	The car doesn't need gas. The car doesn't need oil.
	The car doesn't need gas, **and** it does**n't** need oil **either**.
but	I live in an apartment. My friend lives in a house.
	I live in an apartment, **but** my friend lives in a house.

GERUNDS AND INFINITIVES

Gerund
Driving at night is dangerous.
Locking the car doors is a good idea.
Going out alone at night is not safe.

Infinitive
It is dangerous **to drive** at night.
It is a good idea **to lock** the car doors.
It is not safe **to go** out alone at night.

Notes
• A gerund is a form of a verb that ends in *-ing*.
• An infinitive is *to* + the base form of a verb.

USING GERUNDS AND INFINITIVES WITH VERBS

Verb + Gerund
I enjoy **cleaning** the house.
Ted practiced **playing** the piano.
They continued **studying**.

Verb + Infinitive
Tom volunteered **to clean** the house.
We like **to play** the piano.
Did you continue **to study**?

Notes
• These verbs are often followed by a gerund: *dislike, enjoy, practice*
• These verbs are often followed by an infinitive: *like, begin, continue, want, agree, volunteer, plan, decide, hope, need*
• These verbs are often followed by a gerund or infinitive: *like, begin, continue*

THE PRESENT PASSIVE

The present passive		
I	am	
You	are	
He She It	is	invited to the party.
We You They	are	

Notes

- The present passive uses a form of the verb *be* + the past participle.
  Lunch **is served**.
- Use *by* + person/thing to say who/what performs the action in a passive sentence.
  Lunch is served **by Sara**.
- We usually use the active voice in English.
  Sara serves lunch.

BE ABLE + INFINITIVE (*TO* + VERB) FOR ABILITY

Future	
I you he she it we you they	will be able to go to the party.

Note

In the present, it is more common to use *can* for ability.
  I can go to the party.

In the past, it is more common to use *could* for ability.
  I could go to the party.

TOLD + PERSON + *TO*

Told + person + infinitive
I **told her to ask** for help.
They **told us to sit**.

Told + person + *not* + infinitive
I **told her not to ask** for help.
They **told us not to sit**.

Notes

- To report an affirmative request, use *told* + person + infinitive.
- To report a negative request, use *told* + person + *not* + infinitive.

VOCABULARY LIST

A

abuse	140
accidental	99
account services desk	88
accounts manager	88
addition	43
adult school	5
after-school programs	28
air-conditioning	64
already	65
amusement park	18
angry	40
animal shelter	60
apply for a loan	88
arrest a suspect	130
arrive on time	46
assignment	7
assistant manager	53
attorney	131

B

bacteria	84
be able to	152
be born	144
be going to	22
be informed	159
beat	75
beautiful	29
become a grandparent	144
benefits	45
big	40
bill	95
birth announcement	145
blood	102
boil	74
bones	102
boring	19
bounced check	89
bowl	74
bowling alley	18
boycott	168
brain	102
bride	149
bring your resume	46
bumper	116
bush	70

C

calories	111
car accidents	125
car fees	125
car insurance	125

car maintenance	125
car owner's manual	125
cardiology	103
career	11
careful	12
carefully	12
celebrate	151
check out	14
checking account	89
chop	74
chop up	80
city hall	60
civic	160
Civil Rights Act	168
clear	12
clearly	12
colorful	29
come over	79
commit a crime	130
common	98
community	60
community clinic	60
community college	5
company	34
computer technician	32
congratulate	151
conservative	57
consumers	126
courtroom	131
CPU	32
crash	33
creative	44
creative thinker	47
crime	28
criminal	98
crowded	19
customer	81
customer services	95

D

death notice	145
deep	84
defect	126
defendant	131
Department of Motor Vehicles (DMV)	60
description	43
desktop	33
dictation	43
digital camera	32
direct deposit	89
disability	154
disagree	15

discrimination	154
dishonest	15
disobey	15
disorganized	15
do research	4
do something	20
doctor	109
don't be late	46
don't dress inappropriately	46
don't look nervous	46
don't use your cell phone	46
don't walk alone at night	130
dosage	112
dress professionally	46
dumpster diving	98

E

easily	12
easy	12
eating habits	104
editor	160
education	13
efficient	40
elementary school	5
email	20
emergency	103
employees	34
employment agency	60
engine	120
entertaining	19
environment	70
evaluation	41
event	27
ever	65
exciting	19

F

fair	154
familial status	154
farmers' market	18
fast	40
feedback	39
figure out	78
financial plan	90
find a quiet place	4
flexible	42
food poisoning	84
fork	74
freedom of peaceful assembly	158

freedom of speech 158
freedom of the press 158
friendly 40
funeral 145

G

gas mileage 125
gas tank 116
generic drug 112
get a cashier's check 88
get a promotion 144
get engaged 144
get married 144
get off 79
get on 79
get over 79
get together 20
give a presentation 7
glass 74
glove compartment 117
go out 20
goal 90
go-getter 47
good 12
good leader 47
graduate 144
graphic designer 32
grate 75
great 40
greet the interviewer 46
groom 149
gross pay 55
gym 18

H

hang out 20
happy 40
hard (adj.) 12
hard (adv.) 12
have a baby 144
headlight 116
headset 32
healthy 104
heart 102
helpful 29
her 82
hers 82
high school 5
his 82
hit the road 118
home security 132
honest 56
hood 116

horn 117
hot 40
housewarming 146

I

identity theft 98
ignition 117
immune system 28
interpersonal skills 56
intestines 102
introduce ourselves 7
invitation 43

J

job application 50
job fair 61
job interview 59
joint account 89
journal entry 6
judge 131
jury 131

K

keyboard 32
kind 40
knife 74

L

landlord 132
law enforcement 140
lease 155
laptop 36
leave out 78
leftovers 84
lemon 126
librarian 14
license 212
license plate 116
learn 8
litter 70
loan officer 88
lock the doors 130
look after 79
look confident 46
look for 79
loud 19
lungs 102

M

make a study
    schedule 4
make an outline 4
manage stress 104

manager 34
market 56
maternity 103
mechanic 120
medication 112
meet our classmates 7
meetings 58
memo 34
memorize words 4
middle school 5
mine 82
mix 75
monitor 32
mouse 33
movement 168
muscles 102
musical 99
my 82

N

national 99
natural resources 70
neighbors 23
neighborhood 23
network 56
nightclub 18
nurse's station 103

O

obey the law 159
object 169
occasion 147
office manager 32
online banking 89
open an account 88
open house 61
options 140
order a meal 81
organize materials 4
organized 40
OTC (over-the-counter)
    medication 112
our 82
ours 82
outdoors 28
outline 104
over my head 14

P

pan 74
park 28
parking lot 62
patient 40

pay taxes	159
pediatrics	103
peel	75
permit	169
pet adoption	61
petition	67
phishing	98
photographer	32
physical exam	104
pick up	78
plan	22
plate	74
play it by ear	25
playground	18
pledge	162
policies	34
pollution	70
pot	74
pour	74
prediction	24
prepare	76
principal	39
problem-solver	47
production	42
professional	99
promise	22
promotion	53
protect your wallet or purse	130
protest	169
put in	78

Q

quantity	112
quick	12
quickly	12

R

radiology	103
rearview mirror	117
reception	150
recipe	76
recreation	18
recreation center	60
recycle	69
recycling center	60
relaxing	19
repair	64
report a crime	130
reprint	113
reread	113
research	169
resident	67

respect the rights of others	159
respond	146
retire	144
reuse	113
rewarding	140
rewrite	113
rights	154
road trip	118

S

safe	132
safety	133
salespeople	37
salty	81
savings account	89
school board	62
school counselor	11
search online	4
security features	133
security guard	88
segregated	168
self-starter	47
senior center	60
serve	148
serve on a jury	159
shoulder surfing	98
side effect	112
skills	48
skin	102
slice	75
sour	81
speedometer	117
spicy	81
spoon	74
stand up for	160
start a business	144
statement	95
steam	75
steering wheel	117
stir	74
stomach	102
strengthen	28
stress	28
stressful	29
study	9
supervisor	95
sweet	81
swimming pool	18

T

take a break	4
take notes	4

take out	78
talk about our goals	7
team player	47
technician	36
technology	42
teller window	88
thankful	29
thank-you letter	48
the right to a fair trial	158
the right to carry a U.S. passport	158
the right to vote	158
theater	18
their	82
theirs	82
thin	40
throw out	84
tip	83
tire	116
tradition	153
train	42
transfer money	89
trash	71
trunk	116
trying to cut down on	81
turn off	78
turn on	78
turn signal	116

U

under warranty	126
unhappy	71
unhealthy	71
unimportant	71
university	5
unsafe	71
used to	106

V

vacation	118
virus	33
volunteer	11
volunteer program	61

W

walk in well-lit areas	130
warranty	123
wedding announcement	145
well	12
wellness checkup	61
went over	79

will	22
window	33
windshield	116
witness (noun)	131
witness a crime	130
work	50
would rather	25
write about ourselves	7
write down	78

X,Y,Z

yet	65
your	82
yours	82
zoo	18

INDEX

ACADEMIC SKILLS

Grammar

Adjectives, 12, 36, 38, 82
    Comparisons with, 36, 38
    Possessive, 82
Adverbs, 12
Be able to + verb, 152
Conjunctions
    And...not, 124
    And...not either, 124
    But, 124
Ever, already, and *yet,* 65
Future Conditional, 92, 93, 94
    Questions and Answers, 93
Future (with *be going to* and *will*), 22, 23, 24
    Future plans, 22, 24
    Predictions, 23, 24
    Promises, 22, 24
Gerunds, 134, 135, 136, 138, 163, 164
    as Subject, 134, 136, 138
    Verb + gerund, 163, 164
Infinitives, 138, 162-164
    Verb + infinitive, 162, 163, 164
Parts of Speech, 3
    Adjectives, 3
    Adverbs, 3
    Nouns, 3
    Prepositions, 3
    Verbs, 3
Past Participles, 50 58
    of irregular verbs, 50, 58
Phrasal verbs
    Inseparable phrasal verbs, 79-80
    Separable phrasal verbs, 78, 80
Possessive Adjectives, 82
Possessive Pronouns, 82
Prefixes
    dis-, 15
    re-, 113
    un-, 71
Prepositions
    of location, 3
Present continuous, 8-10, 135
    Yes/No questions, 9
Present Passive, 148-150
    with *by,* 149
Present perfect, 50, 51, 52, 54, 64, 65, 66, 68
    Contractions, 54
    Ever, already, and *yet,* 65
    Negative statements, 50
    Statements, 50
    Yes/No questions, 64
Present perfect continuous, 110
Pronouns
    Possessive, 82
Simple Past, 8-10, 68
    Yes/No questions, 9

Simple present, 8-10
    Negative statements, 8
    Statements, 8
    Yes/No questions, 9
Suffixes
    -al, 99
    -ful, 29
    -tion, 43
Superlatives
    -est, least, most, 37, 40
Time Clauses
    Past, 120-122
    Present, 120-122
    Future, 96, 120-122
Used to
    Negative statements, 106-108
    Statements, 106-108
    Questions and Answers, 107, 108
would rather + verb, 26
Yes/No questions, 9, 64

Graphs, Charts, Maps

13, 69, 97, 111, 127, 139, 141, 167

Listening

Account information, 97
Advice columns, 15
Automobiles, 116, 125
Banking, 88
Be going to, will, 24
Careers, 11
Choosing a job field, 141
Civics, 158, 160
Community resources, 60
Comparisons, 10, 13, 38, 52, 66, 80, 94, 108, 122, 150, 164
Comparisons with adjectives, 38
Computers and offices, 32
Crime, 139
Earth Day, 71
Email invitations, 20
Events and holidays, 27
Following doctor's advice, 109
Gerunds vs. present continuous, 136
Gerunds vs. infinitives, 164
Future conditional, 94
Getting a promotion, 57
Giving and responding to feedback, 39
Home security, 132
Improving your community, 67
Identity theft, 99
Interview thank you letters, 48
Interviewing for a promotion, 53
Job applications, 55
Job interviews, 46
Journal entries, 6, 60
Kitchens, 74
Lemon laws, 127

Letters to the school board, 62
Life events, 144, 151
Memos, 34
Moving, 155
Negotiating a price, 123
Neighborhood parks, 29
Ordering a meal, 81
Parts of body, 102
Phrasal verbs, 80
Present and past verb forms, 10
Present perfect, 52, 66
Protecting your rights, 165
Protecting yourself from food poisoning, 85
Qualities of employees, 41
Recreation, 18
Recycling, 69
Reporting a billing or banking error, 95
Reporting a crime 137
Restaurant bills, 83
Road trips, 118
Safety vocabulary, 130
Separable and inseparable phrasal verbs, 80
Simple present passive, 150
Statistics, 71, 155
Staying healthy, 104
Story about a family recipe, 76
Study skills and habits, 4
Talking about preferences, 25
The Civil Rights Movement, 169
Time clauses, 122
Town meetings, 167
Used to, 108
Using medication safely, 113
Workplace training, 43

Math

Addition, 111, 153
Averages, 41
Calculating amounts of change, 27
Calculating gross pay, 55
Calculating interest, 97
Calculating tip, 83
Division, 111
Handling injuries, 115
Interpreting statistics, 69
Multiplication, 55, 125, 153
Percentages, 13
Reading a poll, 167
Reading a survey, 139

Problem Solving

Choosing a credit card, 101
Comparing jobs, 45
Dealing with auto problems while driving, 129
Determining what to do after an auto accident, 171
Getting involved in the community, 73
Handling injuries, 115
Handling suspicious behavior, 143

Handling tipping after a bad meal, 87
Making friends, 17
Preparing for a job interview, 59
Resolving disagreements in preferences, 31
Responding to an invitation, 157

Pronunciation

Homophones, 166
Intonation patterns, 152
Linked words, 96
Phrasal verbs, 82
S or *z* sounds, 111
Schwa sound, 124
Sh, ch, or *j* sounds 12
J and *ch* sounds in linked words, 26
Stressed words in sentences, 138
Th, 54
V, b, and *f,* 40
Y, w, and *j,* 68

Reading

Articles, 14, 28, 42
Car problems, 120
Civic involvement, 160
Classes, 8
Clothes, buying, 92
Community action, 62
Community, improving your, 67
Computer ads, 36
Crimes, 134
Describing events, 120
Doctor's advice, following, 109
Email invitations, 20
Family recipes, 76
Financial planning and goals, 90
Food poisoning, protecting yourself from, 84
Earth Day, 70
Home security, 132
Identity theft, 98
Interview thank you letters, 48
Interviewing for a promotion, 53
Invitations to events, 146, 147
Job applications, 50
Job field, choosing, 140
Journal entries, 6
Lemon laws, 126, 127
Life events, 151
Lifestyle changes, 106
Memos, 34
Mistakes, 78
Mortgage agreements, 155
Moving, 154
Negotiating a price, 123
Ordering a meal, 81
Personal strengths, 47
Plans, 22
Project reports, 64
Promotion, getting a, 56, 57

Protecting your rights, 169
Reporting a billing or banking error, 95
Reporting a crime, 137
Retirement communities vs. apartments, 148
Road trips, 118,
Staying healthy, 104
The Civil Rights Movement, 168
Using medication safely, 112
Volunteering, 162

Speaking

Automobiles, 116
Banking services, 89
Banking, 88
Cars, 117
Choosing a job field, 11, 141
Civic involvement, 161, 167
Civic responsibility, 159
Civics, 158
Community resources, 60
Community services, 61
Computers, 32
Crime, 134
Criminal justice system, 131
Daily activities, 54
Describing places and events, 19, 20, 27
Earth Day, 71
Educational system, 5
Email invitations, 21
Family recipes, 77
Feedback, giving and responding to, 39
Financial planning and goals, 90, 91
Food, 87
Food poisoning, protecting yourself from, 85
Freedom and rights, 159
Home security, 133
Identity theft, 99
Interior of car, 117
Interview thank you letters, 48, 49
Invitations to events, 146, 147
Job application information, 55
Job interviews, 46, 47
Job training, 43
Journal entries, 7
Kitchens, 74
Lemon laws, 127
Life events, 144
Medical departments, 103
Moving, 155
Neighborhood meetings, 67
Neighborhood parks, 29
Ordering a meal, 81
Parts of the body, 102
Personal strengths, 57
Preparing foods, 75
Protecting your rights, 169
Reading, 15
Recreation, 18, 25

Recycling, 69, 71
Road trips, 118, 119
Safety, 130
School problems, 35, 63
Staying healthy, 105
Study skills and habits, 4, 7, 17
The Civil Rights Movement, 169
Using medication safely, 113
Wedding traditions, 153
Workplace training, 43

Writing

Automobile, 116
Banking, 88
Civics, 158, 159
Community resources, 60
Community services, 61
Computers, 33
Criminal justice system, 131
Educational system, 5
Email invitations, 21
Family recipes, 77
Financial planning, 91
Future planning, 94
Future predictions, 24
Home security, 133
Interior of car, 117
Interview thank you letters, 49
Journal writing, 7
Kitchens, 74, 75
Letter to city hall, 63
Letter to newspaper, 161
Letter to school board, 63
Life events, 144
Likes and dislikes, 164
Medical departments, 103
Memos, 35
Moving, 122
Parties, 150
Places and events, 19
Invitations to events, 147
Road Trips, 119
Safe and dangerous situations, 136
Safety vocabulary, 130
Staying healthy, 105
Summaries, 169
Vacations, 122

CIVICS

Advocacy, 60, 61, 70, 71, 73
Banking, 88, 89, 90, 91, 95, 97
Consumer complaint, 126, 127, 129
Directory (locate maps and services), 103
Diversity, 64, 67, 73
Employment resources, 32, 33, 34, 35, 39, 42, 43, 46, 47, 48, 49, 53, 55, 56, 57, 60, 61
Environment, 60, 61, 69, 70, 71, 73

Government and Law—Citizenship Prep, 130, 131, 137, 139, 158, 159, 165, 168, 169
Health care, 102, 103, 104, 105, 108, 109, 111, 115
History and government, 158, 159, 168, 169
Identify educational opportunities/training, 4, 5, 7, 11, 13
Law—legal rights, 137, 138, 139, 158, 159, 161, 165, 168, 169
Locate community resources, 14, 20, 27, 28, 29, 60, 61, 62, 63, 67, 148, 160, 164, 167, 171
Pharmacy, 112, 113
Recreation, 18, 19, 20, 27, 28, 29, 31
Safety measures, 62, 63, 130, 131, 132, 133, 136, 140, 141, 143
Services for seniors, 60, 61, 62, 63
Volunteers, 60, 61, 62, 63, 73
Voting process, 158, 159, 161

LIFE SKILLS

Consumer Education

ATM and banking, 88, 89, 90, 91, 95, 97
Financial planning, 90, 91
Negotiating a price, 123

Environment and the World

Environmental improvement, 70, 71, 73
Recycling, 69, 70, 73

Family and Parenting

Life events, 144, 151
Traditions, 153

Government and Community Resources

Community resources, 60, 61
Community services, 60, 61
Library, 14, 15

Health and Nutrition

Body parts, 102, 104, 105, 109
Directions and warnings on medical labels, 112, 113

Interpersonal Communication

Leisure activities, 18, 19, 20
Invitations to events, 146, 147
Study Skills, 4, 5, 7

Safety and Security

Identity theft, 98, 99

Transportation and Safety

Automobiles, 116, 117, 125, 126, 127, 129
Road Trips, 118
Travel, 118, 119

TOPICS

A Job To Do, 32–45
Community Resources, 60–73
Crime Doesn't Pay, 130–143
Doing the Right Thing, 158–171
Good Work, 46–59
Hit the Road, 116–129
Learning Together, 4–17
Living Well, 102–115
Money Wise, 88–101
Ready for Fun, 18–31
That's Life, 144–157
The First Step, 2–3
What's Cooking, 74–87

WORKFORCE SKILLS

Applied Technology

Computers, 32, 33

Maintaining Employment

Computers and offices, 32, 33
Getting a promotion, 56, 57
Interviewing for a promotion, 53
Memos, 34, 35
Responding to feedback, 39

Obtaining Employment

Career options, 140, 141
Interview thank you letters, 48, 49
Job interviews, 46, 47, 48, 49
Personal strengths, 47, 57